Cloning Internet Applications with Ruby

Make your own TinyURL, Twitter, Flickr, or Facebook using Ruby

Chang Sau Sheong

BIRMINGHAM - MUMBAI

Cloning Internet Applications with Ruby

Copyright © 2010 Packt Publishing

First published: August 2010

Production Reference: 1110810

Published by Packt Publishing Ltd.
32 Lincoln Road
Olton
Birmingham, B27 6PA, UK.

ISBN 978-1-849511-06-3

www.packtpub.com

Cover Image by Asher Wishkerman (a.wishkerman@mpic.de)

Credits

Author
Chang Sau Sheong

Reviewer
Warren Brian Noronha
Francisco

Acquisition Editor
Douglas Paterson

Development Editor
Chaitanya Apte

Technical Editors
Alfred John
Kartikey Pandey

Indexer
Hemangini Bari

Editorial Team Leader
Aanchal Kumar

Project Team Leader
Lata Basantani

Project Coordinator
Jovita Pinto

Proofreader
Aaron Nash

Graphics
Geetanjali Sawant

Production Coordinator
Arvindkumar Gupta

Cover Work
Arvindkumar Gupta

About the Author

Chang Sau Sheong has more than 15 years experience in software application development and has spent much of his career working on Web and Internet-based applications. He started up elipva, an e-business software company, and was the Vice President of Product Engineering as well as Chief Architect. Subsequently he was Director of Software Development for Welcome Real-time, a bank loyalty software company, Engineering Director for Yahoo! Southeast Asia and Chief Technology Officer for Garena Online, an online game publishing company. He is currently the Director of the Applied Cloud Computing Lab in HP Labs Singapore, the research arm of Hewlett Packard, leading a team of engineers to implement cloud computing solutions.

Sau Sheong frequently writes for technical magazines and journals, including Java Report, Java World, and Dr. Dobb's Journal. He is a passionate programmer who contributes to open source projects in various technologies including Ruby and Java. He has a wide range of experience in web application development on the Internet and mobile devices. His first book was 'Ruby on Rails Mashup Projects' in 2008, also published by Packt Publishing.

Sau Sheong hails from tropical Malaysia but spent most of his adult and working life in sunny Singapore, where he shares his spare time between enthusiastically writing software and equally enthusiastically playing Nintendo Wii with his wife and son. He has a Bachelors degree in Computer Engineering, a Masters degree in Commercial Law, and is a certified international arbitrator.

Acknowledgement

Firstly, many thanks to Douglas Paterson who agreed to this second book project, the book reviewers who have helped me improve my sprawling book and Jovita, the patient project coordinator who would wait patiently and gently prompt me as my chapter deadline approaches. I would also like to thank my Twitter and Hackerspace friends who on many occasions had to endure my relentless requests to test my 'clones' and provide feedback on them. A big thank you to Philippe Monnet who helped to review the first few chapters and even offered to re-draw a diagram for me. Final thanks to the love of my life, Wooi Ying, who suffered my erratic 'nightlife' in huddling in front of my laptop, creating software and writing yet another book (with her eyes rolling), and then there is Kai Wen who understands Daddy is finally an author.

About the Reviewers

Warren Noronha is an entrepreneur and a geek. Computers have been part of Warren's life since he was four years old. He began his career as a system administrator, but ended up doing everything from security, design, to product development. He enjoys managing people as much as he does managing code or machines. Having worked with small startups as well as Fortune 500 companies, Warren is also a staunch supporter of free software and free speech. He has been a frequent speaker at various colleges and events, discussing subjects ranging from technology and media to launching a startup.

Warren loves working with new technologies, a trait which lead him to become one of the first users of GNU/Linux, Drupal, and Ruby on Rails, much before they grew exponentially and became mainstream technologies. He spends his time working on databases, distributed computing, and social computing, and enjoys using the Internet and communication technology to bridge the digital divide.

Francisco started out as a software architect and a project manager for various desktop and web applications. Then after falling out of love with outdated technologies and processes switched over to system admin and server infrastructure expert. Ruby was the catalyst to bring him back to the software development with agile processes. Currently a Mac lover and Ruby all in one backend expert. His experience in the server provisioning world and background as software developer resulted in quick rollout of fast, secure, and reliable backend Ruby on Rails applications for the enterprise.

Table of Contents

Preface

We stand on the shoulders of giants. This has been true since the time of Newton (and even before) and it is certainly true now. Much of what we know and learn of programming, we learnt from the pioneering programmers before us and what we leave behind to future generations of programmers is our hard-earned experience and precious knowledge. This book is all about being the scaffolding upon which the next generation of programmers stands when they build the next Sistine Chapel of software.

There are many ways that we can build this scaffolding but one of the best ways is simply to copy from what works. Many programming books attempt to teach with code samples that the readers can reproduce and try it out themselves. This book goes beyond code samples. The reader doesn't only copy snippets of code or build simple applications but have a chance to take a peek at how a few of the most popular Internet applications today can possibly be built. We explore how these applications are coded and also the rationale behind the way they are designed. The aim is to guide the programmer through the steps of building clones of the various popular Internet applications.

What this book covers

Chapter 1, Cloning Internet Applications gives a brief description of the purpose of the book, the target readers of the book, and a list of the four popular Internet applications we will be cloning in the subsequent chapters. The bulk of this chapter gives a brief run-down on the various technologies we will be using to build those clones.

Chapter 2, URL Shorteners – Cloning TinyURL explains about the first popular Internet application that we investigate and clone in the book, which is TinyURL. This chapter describes how to create a TinyURL clone, its basic principles, and algorithms used.

Chapter 3, Microblogs – Cloning Twitter. The clone in this chapter emulates one of the hottest and most popular Internet web applications now – Twitter. It describes the basic principles of a microblogging application and explains how to recreate a feature-complete Twitter clone.

Chapter 4, Photo -sharing – Cloning Flickr. Flickr is one of the most popular and enduring photo-sharing applications on the Internet. This chapter describes how the reader can re-create a feature complete photo-sharing application the simplest way possible, following the interface and style in Flickr.

Chapter 5, Social Networking Services – Cloning Facebook 1. The final two chapters describe the various aspects of Internet social networking services, focusing on one of the most popular out there now – Facebook. These two chapters also describe the minimal features of a social networking service and show the reader how to implement these features in a complete step-by-step guide. The first part is described in this chapter, which sets the groundwork for the clone and proceeds to describe the data model used in the clone.

Chapter 6, Social Networking Services – Cloning Facebook 2. The final chapter is part two in describing how to create a Facebook clone. This chapter follows on the previous chapter and describes the application flow of the Facebook clone we started earlier.

What you need for this book

Basic Ruby programming skills and basic level operational knowledge of Sinatra, DataMapper, Haml, Blueprint CSS, and MySQL.

Who this book is for

This book is written for web application programmers with an intermediate knowledge of Ruby. The reader should also know how web applications work and have used at least some of the cloned Internet services before.

A typical reader would be a programmer looking to write their own customized TinyURL, Twitter, Flickr, or Facebook. Programmers who want to include features of these Internet services into their own web applications will also find this book interesting.

Conventions

In this book, you will find a number of styles of text that distinguish between different kinds of information. Here are some examples of these styles, and an explanation of their meaning.

Code words in text are shown as follows: "The many-to-many association can be defined with the `has n` and `belongs_to` methods."

A block of code is set as follows:

```
after :create, :create_wall
def create_wall
self.wall = Wall.create
self.save
end
```

Any command-line input or output is written as follows:

```
$ sudo gem install Haml
```

New terms and **important words** are shown in bold. Words that you see on the screen, in menus or dialog boxes for example, appear in the text like this: "The one big difference is of course, the list of statuses belongs to only that user, and there is a big **follow** button for the viewing user to follow him."

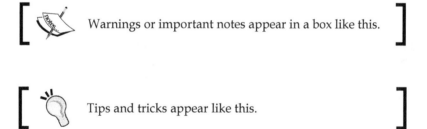

Warnings or important notes appear in a box like this.

Tips and tricks appear like this.

Reader feedback

Feedback from our readers is always welcome. Let us know what you think about this book—what you liked or may have disliked. Reader feedback is important for us to develop titles that you really get the most out of.

To send us general feedback, simply send an e-mail to feedback@packtpub.com, and mention the book title via the subject of your message.

If there is a book that you need and would like to see us publish, please send us a note in the **SUGGEST A TITLE** form on www.packtpub.com or e-mail suggest@ packtpub.com.

If there is a topic that you have expertise in and you are interested in either writing or contributing to a book on, see our author guide on www.packtpub.com/authors.

Customer support

Now that you are the proud owner of a Packt book, we have a number of things to help you to get the most from your purchase.

> **Downloading the example code for this book**
>
> You can download the example code files for all Packt books you have purchased from your account at http://www.PacktPub.com. If you purchased this book elsewhere, you can visit http://www.PacktPub.com/support and register to have the files e-mailed directly to you.

Errata

Although we have taken every care to ensure the accuracy of our content, mistakes do happen. If you find a mistake in one of our books — maybe a mistake in the text or the code — we would be grateful if you would report this to us. By doing so, you can save other readers from frustration and help us improve subsequent versions of this book. If you find any errata, please report them by visiting http://www.packtpub.com/support, selecting your book, clicking on the **errata submission form** link, and entering the details of your errata. Once your errata are verified, your submission will be accepted and the errata will be uploaded on our website, or added to any list of existing errata, under the Errata section of that title. Any existing errata can be viewed by selecting your title from http://www.packtpub.com/support.

Piracy

Piracy of copyright material on the Internet is an ongoing problem across all media. At Packt, we take the protection of our copyright and licenses very seriously. If you come across any illegal copies of our works, in any form, on the Internet, please provide us with the location address or website name immediately so that we can pursue a remedy.

Please contact us at copyright@packtpub.com with a link to the suspected pirated material.

We appreciate your help in protecting our authors, and our ability to bring you valuable content.

Questions

You can contact us at questions@packtpub.com if you are having a problem with any aspect of the book, and we will do our best to address it.

1
Cloning Internet Applications

This book is about copying. Copying has an unpleasant reputation in these copyright and intellectual property sensitive times, but it's probably unknown to many, that it has an illustrious past. When we were babies, the main way we learnt was through copying what our parents did. If you have young children you soon learn to your regret the first time you utter any insalubrious words and how quickly your child copies your exclamation and mannerisms. Our number system was copied from the Arabs (that's why they are called Arabic numerals) but it was first used by the Indians from the Indian subcontinent, and subsequently copied by the Arabs in the Middle-East. The English language regularly copies words from other languages. In fact the word 'copy' comes from the Old French word *copie* which comes from the Medieval Latin word *copia*.

That is not to say infringing copyright is the right thing to do when someone else has spent tremendous effort in coming up with the original. However, it should be recognized that not all things are copyrightable, patentable, or can be trademarked, and that is for a good reason. Ideas for example are generally not considered as intellectual property. Copyright is the protection of expressions of ideas, not the protection of the ideas themselves. Patent law is used for the protection of inventions for a limited time in return for the disclosure of the invention. Again it is not a protection of ideas; the concept of patent law is to promote the liberation of the idea in exchange for limited monopoly. Google is well known to have dominance in the search engine market but it doesn't mean it has monopoly on search engines. Anyone else is free to write his/her own search engine (though taking part of Google's search engine code to write your own search engine is copyright infringement).

This idea of copying is the basis of the book you are holding. In short, the premise of this book is to learn how each of the popular Internet applications we clone work through copying the ideas behind them.

In this chapter we will cover:

- A brief description of the type of people who would like to read this book
- The popular Internet applications described in this book and why we chose them
- The various technologies used in this book, including Sinatra, DataMapper, and Haml

Who would find this book useful

The primary audience for this book are Ruby programmers with an intermediate level of experience in Ruby as well as web application programming. This sounds quite limiting but in reality if you have any intermediate level of programming in any object-oriented language you should be able to follow the implementations with relative ease. Of course, if you know something about the Ruby programming language it helps a lot too.

The technology stack that we will be using for these clones is slightly off the usual track for the Ruby on Rails crowd. The main reason is because it's a simpler stack to use. Ruby on Rails, while extremely easy to use and very powerful, has a lot of added frills to the framework, which adds on unnecessary complexity for a book that focuses on clones and features of the clones only. The chosen stack however does not different too greatly for programmers who are familiar with Rails. In this chapter we will go through all that is needed to follow the rest of the chapters in this book.

So why are we interested in cloning these applications at all, since we can't possibly build a clone that is better than the original? There are plenty of reasons for doing so but let me just give four common ones:

1. To learn how these applications work. We use them all the time and while we would know how these applications functionally work, cloning them will teach us how these features can be implemented. Although the implementation is not definitive, at least learning how difficult or easy it is to clone them gives us a better appreciation of how things work behind the scenes to provide us with the features.

2. To incorporate features of the clones into your own application. As you will see in this book, each chapter shows how key features in those applications are implemented. If you want to build these key features into your own application, learning how these features are implemented will give you an insight into building them for your own use.

3. To build a customized clone. While each popular Internet application has plenty of features to go with, there will be special niche needs that can only be fulfilled by a customized version of that application.

4. Learning the technology stack. The best way to learn any new technology stack is to build something with it. Going through the chapters in this book will give you ample exercise in this stack.

If you find yourself having any of the above needs then this book is for you.

Popular Internet applications

Why did we choose the Internet applications in this book and not others? Firstly and most obviously, the applications must be popular and have a large number of users. Secondly the application should be a mainstream one for consumers and not for businesses. We want applications that have a more direct interface to the final consumers of the application. Thirdly, we don't want to deal with payment related issues in this book so any e-commerce applications are left alone. The reason is simple — e-commerce is no longer rocket science but implementing payment well is still not a trivial undertaking, and we did not want to mislead users into believing it is easy to clone payment features. Finally (and most importantly for me) the applications we chose to clone must also be easy to implement and would fit in nicely into a single chapter.

With these criteria, we have picked the following small number of applications to cover in this book:

- A URL shortener — TinyURL
- A microblogging application — Twitter
- A photo sharing application — Flickr
- A social networking service — Facebook

It's interesting that none of the crop of popular Internet applications we are cloning in this book is the true original implementation of the main idea in that application. There have been URL shorteners before TinyURL, there were micro-blogging sites before Twitter, photo-sharing before Flickr, and definitely social networking services before Facebook. However, each of these is, as of writing, the most popular service of its kind.

Technologies used

The technology stack used in this book consists of mainly Ruby-only libraries and tools:

- Sinatra — a Ruby domain-specific language (DSL) with a minimalist approach in building web applications

- DataMapper — a Ruby object-relational mapping library

- Haml — a Ruby-friendly markup language that allows us to manipulate XHTML of any web document programmatically

We will be going in depth in each of these technologies. While this seems a bit too much to cover within a single chapter, each technology is essentially not complex. Once you have grasped the basics of each technology, a quick reference back to the documentation will allow you do to anything you want.

Sinatra

Sinatra is a domain-specific language built with Ruby, used to build web applications. Sinatra was created with a minimalist approach in mind and focuses on the fastest way to get a web application up and running. For example, you can create a simple web application with just the following in a file named `hello.rb`:

```
require 'rubygems'
require 'sinatra'

get '/' do
"Hello world, it's #{Time.now} at the server!"
end
```

After that just run the following command:

ruby hello.rb

Then go to `http://localhost:4567/` and you will see the hello statement with the current time. Writing a web application becomes almost trivial up to this stage. Of course as web applications become more complex, unlike other full-fledged web frameworks such as Ruby on Rails or Merbs, you will need to write more code.

As mentioned earlier, one of the reasons why we chose Sinatra is because of its simplicity and minimalist approach. In a book that teaches how application features can be implemented, more complex frameworks can often add to the clutter because of 'the way it works' rather than clarifying the implementation of the feature. As a result, a DSL such as Sinatra, where nothing is taken for granted, is very useful as a teaching tool.

Installing

Sinatra can be easily installed through Rubygems:

```
$ sudo gem install sinatra
```

That's all there is to it. You will be able to use Sinatra immediately after that.

Routes

In Sinatra, a route is HTTP method and a URL matching pattern. For example, this is a route:

```
get '/' do
  . . .
end
```

And so are these:

```
post '/some_url' do
  . . .
end

put '/another_url' do
  . . .
end



delete '/any_url' do
  . . .
end
```

Whenever a HTTP request comes in, the request will be matched in the order they are defined. For example, if a POST request is made to http://localhost:4567/some_url, the some_url route will be invoked. The route pattern matching includes named parameters, for example:

```
get '/hello/:name' do
  puts "Hello #{params[:name]}!"
end
```

Patterns may also include other matching conditions such as user agents. This is useful if we want to determine the type of device that is accessible by the application, for example if we create an iPhone web application we can indicate that the user agent is the following:

```
Mozilla/5.0 (iPhone; U; CPU iPhone OS 2_0 like Mac OS X; en-us)
AppleWebKit/525.18.1 (KHTML, like Gecko) Version/3.1.1 Mobile/1A543
Safari/525.20
```

```
get '/hello', :agent => /iPhone/ do
  puts "You are using an iPhone!"
end
```

GET and POST methods are quite simply implemented above, but how about PUT and DELETE? These two methods are normally not natively supported by most browsers but can be worked around using a POST. If you set up a HTML form that sends a POST with a hidden element with the name '_method' and the value 'put' or 'delete' accordingly, Sinatra will interpret it accordingly and invoke the correct route.

For example:

```
<form method="post" action="/destroy">
  <input name="_method" value="delete" />
  <button type="submit">Destroy</button>
</form>
```

The above code will invoke this route:

```
delete '/destroy' do
  ...
end
```

Splitting a route into multiple files

Sinatra looks very good and simple if we're writing simple web applications with only a few routes but what if the application is much larger? Managing all those routes in a single file becomes a hassle and is rather unwieldy. Remember Sinatra is also all-Ruby, so you use `load` to load in other files that contain routes. This way you can make your application more modular by placing related routes in the same file.

```
%w(photos user helpers).each {|feature| load "#{feature}.rb"}
```

In the example code snippet above, we have three files named `photos.rb`, `users.rb`, and `helpers.rb` in which we place related routes. This helps us to include features that we want and potentially to remove features we do not want by changing the list. The code snippet above would then be placed in the main file such as `myapp.rb`.

Redirection

Sometimes within a route you want to redirect the user somewhere else. This can be some other route or to an external site. This can be done using the redirect helper, for example:

```
redirect '/'
redirect 'http://www.google.com'
```

The redirect actually sends back a `302 Found` HTTP status code to the browser and tells the browser where to go next. To force Sinatra to send a different status code, just add the status code to the redirection helper.

```
redirect '/', 303
redirect '/', 307
```

Note that this sends the browser to another route or site and not to a view.

Filters

Sinatra has a simple filtering mechanism. If you define a `before` filter, it will be invoked every time before a route is invoked.

```
before do
  ...
end
```

This becomes especially useful in securing routes because we can check if the user has access to that route before it is invoked. Any instance variables defined in the `before` filter will be available to the route and the views subsequently.

Similarly, if you define an `after` filter, it will be invoked every time after a route is invoked.

```
after do
  ...
end
```

Just as the `before` filter, you can modify the instance variables that go to the view. You can also modify the response.

Static pages

By default, all pages in a folder named `public` are served out as static pages. For example, if you have a `page.html` file in the `public` folder, you will be able to access it from `http://localhost:4567/page.html`. This means that you can also serve out Javascript libraries, CSS stylesheets, and image files through the same folder.

If you want to change default public folder, just change the settings:

```
set :public, File.dirname(__FILE__) + '/static'
```

Views

Similarly, by default Sinatra looks for view templates in a folder named `views`. You can also change the default directory by changing the settings as follows:

```
set :views, File.dirname(__FILE__) + '/templates'
```

View templates are files that are used to display data that is processed by a route. For example, this route will redirect to a Haml view template, which is a file called `view_page.haml` in the `views` folder:

```
get '/page/view' do
  . . .
  haml :view_page
end
```

Besides Haml, Sinatra also supports a variety of view template types such as Erb, Erubis, Sass, Builder, and so on. We will discuss Haml in a later section in this chapter.

Note that the templates always need to be referenced as symbols, even in subdirectories. For example, if the Haml view template is in a file called `view.haml` in the `views/page` subfolder, then you should reference it as: `'page/view'`.

Layouts

While you are not required to use any layouts, if you have a file named `layout.haml` (or `layout.erb` and so on) in your `views` folder, it will be used as a layout template. A layout template is a view template that is re-used for multiple views. For example, this is a Haml layout:

```
html
  %head
    %title Cloning Internet Applications with Ruby
  %body
    #container
      =yield
```

Any view rendered for Haml will now use this layout and the page will include the layout with the view replaced in the `yield`.

Helpers

If you have some functions you need repeatedly, you can create helpers. Helpers in Sinatra are methods that can be reused in routes and templates.

```
helpers do
  def encrypt(data)
    . . .
  end
end

get '/secret/:policy' do
  encrypt(params[:policy])
end
```

One use of helpers we employ repeatedly in this book is to create partials. Sinatra does not support partials on its own, which can be a bit annoying, but the implementation of partials is easily done.

```
helpers do
    def snippet(page, options={})
    haml page, options.merge!(:layout => false)
    end
end
```

Essentially we just render a given page template, and declaring that we do not use the layout.

Error handling

Sinatra handles error in a minimalist way. There are two basic handlers. If any resource or route is not found, and if `not_found` is defined, it will be invoked.

```
not_found do
  'This is nowhere to be found'
end
```

Any other errors will be caught by `error`. By default `error` will catch `Sinatra::ServerError` and Sinatra will pass you the error through `sinatra.error` in `request.env`.

```
error do
  'Sorry there was a nasty error - ' + request.env['sinatra.error'].
name
end
```

You can also customize the errors such as the following:

```
error MyCustomError do
  'So what happened was...' + request.env['sinatra.error'].message
end
```

This could happen:

```
get '/' do
  raise MyCustomError, 'something bad'
end
```

In which case, the error helper will be called and the message displayed.

That was a whirlwind tour of Sinatra but it has covered everything you need to know about Sinatra to start writing Sinatra applications. For more information on Sinatra please head on to http://www.sinatrarb.com.

DataMapper

DataMapper is a Ruby object-relational mapping library, one of the three main libraries as of writing. Object-relational mapping libraries exist to resolve impedance mismatch between Ruby, the object-oriented programming language, and a relational database. Essentially it maps database tables as classes, rows as objects, and columns as properties and values of an object while mapping relationships as one-to-one, one-to-many, or many-to-many.

Object-oriented programming languages and relational databases are a common match and a large number of applications have been developed with such pairing of technologies. However, the underlying principles of object-oriented programming and relational databases do not match and can potentially cause problems. For example, the basic principles of classes of objects, inheritance, and polymorphism don't exist in relational databases and the expectations of the data types often differ. This mismatch is commonly known as the object-relational impedance mismatch.

One way to overcome this mismatch is to use object-relational mapping or ORM tools such as DataMapper. Such tools map a relational database to a layer of objects that can be manipulated by the application. As a result the application does not interact with the relational database directly. Instead, it manipulates data through the ORM, which in turn controls how the data is finally persisted into the database.

DataMapper and ActiveRecord (the default ORM library in Ruby on Rails) are quite similar. If you have prior experience in ActiveRecord, most of what you read here will be very familiar.

A note on the DataMapper version used in this book. As of writing, the latest version of DataMapper is 0.10.2. However, in this book we will be using version 0.9.11. This is because a feature we need in the projects in this book (self-referential many-to-many) is not supported in 0.10.2. In fairness the feature has been removed to prepare a better implementation in a future version. Unfortunately, for this book we will be using a slightly older version.

Installing

DataMapper is broken up into the core library, `dm-core`, various database adapters and a number of optional libraries collectively known as `dm-more`. While you can install `dm-more` as an umbrella library, it is generally more advisable to just install those that you need. For a basic installation, you need to install the core library as well as at least one database adapter:

```
gem install dm-more
```

The most popular adapters are probably ones that relate to the DataObjects library. The DataObjects library is an attempt to rewrite existing database drivers to conform to a standard interface and has some of the more popular databases supported. For example to install support for MySQL:

```
gem install do_mysql
```

Connecting to the database

The first thing you need to do before you start using DataMapper is to specify the connection to the database. This is easily done by specifying the database connection string:

```
DataMapper.setup(:default, 'mysql://localhost/ database_name')
```

Creating models

Once you have the connection, you can define your DataMapper models. Unlike ActiveRecord (or Sequel, the other popular ORM library), DataMapper does not need a separate migration step or file to create the database tables. The database tables are created from the definition of the model itself.

An example of a DataMapper model is as follows:

```
class User
  include DataMapper::Resource
  property :id,          Serial
  property :email,       String, :length => 255
  property :nickname,    String, :length => 255
  property :birth_date, DateTime
  property :education,   Text
  property :work_history, Text
  property :description, TExt
end
```

Let's go through several key elements of this definition. Firstly all DataMapper models are classes that include the `Datamapper::Resource` module. This provides them with the necessary methods used in defining the model. Each property of the model is defined with the method property, with a given name and a type. The types used are atypical. The `Serial` type however is a shortcut for defining an auto-incrementing integer that is a primary key. Otherwise you'll need to define it yourself like this:

```
property :some_id, :key => true
```

Note that DataMapper supports composite keys, meaning we can make more than one property in the model a primary key.

While `dm-core` supports the standard set of properties you'll find in any database, DataMapper actually supports a lot more other types if you include `dm-types`, including CSV (comma-separated values), IP addresses, JSON, URIs and so on.

Properties can be configured to be lazy loaded, which means that the value of the property is not requested from the data store by default but only loaded when its accessor is called for the first time. Some properties, such as the `Text`, are lazily loaded by default to improve performance.

Lazy loading can also be done together. For example, if one property is loaded, we can force related properties to be loaded. For example, the three properties for the User model above, `education`, `work_history`, and `description` are `Text` and are lazily loaded by default. If we define them this way:

```
property :education,   Text,  :lazy => [:show]
property :work_history, Text  :lazy => [:show]
property :description, Text
```

If the `education` property is called, the `work_history` property will also be loaded from the datastore, since both of them are members of the `:show` group. However, the description property will only be fetched when it's asked.

Defining associations between models

A major use of ORM libraries such as DataMapper is that it provides object-oriented convenience for relationships between rows in different tables. The three main types of relationships or associations between tables are:

- One-to-one
- One-to-many
- Many-to-many

One-to-one

DataMapper's one-to-one association uses the `has 1` and `belongs_to` methods.

```
class User
  include DataMapper::Resource
  property :id, Serial
  has 1, :account
end


class Account
  include DataMapper::Resource
  property :id, Serial
  belongs_to, :user
end
```

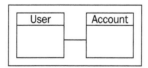

Very simply put, the `has 1` method shows the user owning one account while `belongs_to` defines the two-way relationship back to the user.

The database tables generated from these models looks like the following:

```
Terminal — mysql
mysql> describe accounts;
+---------+---------+------+-----+---------+----------------+
| Field   | Type    | Null | Key | Default | Extra          |
+---------+---------+------+-----+---------+----------------+
| id      | int(11) | NO   | PRI | NULL    | auto_increment |
| user_id | int(11) | YES  |     | NULL    |                |
+---------+---------+------+-----+---------+----------------+
2 rows in set (0.01 sec)

mysql> describe users;
+-------+---------+------+-----+---------+----------------+
| Field | Type    | Null | Key | Default | Extra          |
+-------+---------+------+-----+---------+----------------+
| id    | int(11) | NO   | PRI | NULL    | auto_increment |
+-------+---------+------+-----+---------+----------------+
1 row in set (0.06 sec)

mysql> []
```

To use these models, fire up `irb`.

```
$ irb -r models.rb
>> user = User.create
=> #<User id=1>
>> account = Account.create
=> #<Account id=1 user_id=nil>
```

We create a user and an account. Note that when the account is created it's not attached to any users yet.

```
>> user.account = account
=> #<Account id=1 user_id=nil>
>> user.save
=> true
>> user.account
=> #<Account id=1 user_id=1>
```

By specifying that user only has 1 account, we added in the `User#account` and `User#account=` methods to the `User` class. This allows us to set our new account to the user object. Notice that even after having set the account to the user, the `Accounts` table `user_id` column is still unpopulated. This is because we are still manipulating in memory. We need to persist it by saving the object.

One-to-many

The one-to-many association can be defined with the `has n` and `belongs_to` methods, shown as follows:

```
class User
  include DataMapper::Resource
  property :id, Serial
  has n, :comments
end



class Comment
  include DataMapper::Resource
  property :id, Serial
  belongs_to, :user
end
```

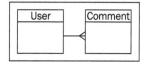

The database tables created from these models look like the following:

```
Terminal — mysql
mysql> describe comments;
+---------+---------+------+-----+---------+----------------+
| Field   | Type    | Null | Key | Default | Extra          |
+---------+---------+------+-----+---------+----------------+
| id      | int(11) | NO   | PRI | NULL    | auto_increment |
| user_id | int(11) | YES  |     | NULL    |                |
+---------+---------+------+-----+---------+----------------+
2 rows in set (0.00 sec)

mysql> describe users;
+-------+---------+------+-----+---------+----------------+
| Field | Type    | Null | Key | Default | Extra          |
+-------+---------+------+-----+---------+----------------+
| id    | int(11) | NO   | PRI | NULL    | auto_increment |
+-------+---------+------+-----+---------+----------------+
1 row in set (0.00 sec)

mysql>
```

The database tables look exactly the same as in the one-to-one. This is because the controls and logic are actually set by the `has n` method we used in the `User` class. Let's look at how we use the one-to-many relationship. As before let's start with creating the user and some comments:

```
>> user = User.create
=> #<User id=1>
>> comment1 = Comment.create
=> #<Comment id=1 user_id=nil>
>> comment2 = Comment.create
=> #<Comment id=2 user_id=nil>
```

To add the comments to the user, we treat `user.comments` as an array and simply stuff the comments in using the `<<` operator:

```
>> user.comments << comment1 << comment2
```

Note that `user.comments` can be treated as an array, and even be converted to one if necessary:

```
>> user.comments.class
=> DataMapper::Associations::OneToMany::Proxy
>> user.comments.to_a
=> [#<Comment id=1 user_id=1>, #<Comment id=2 user_id=1>]
```

Many-to-many

The many-to-many association can be defined with the `has n` and `belongs_to` methods. There are two ways of defining many-to-many associations. The first is to use a concrete model to represent the relationship between the two models. In this example, we have a user who can borrow many books and books that can be borrowed by many users. To represent the relationship between users and books, we will create a concrete model called `Loan`.

```
class User
  include DataMapper::Resource
  property :id, Serial
  has n, :loans
  has n, :books, :through => :loans
end
```

```
class Loan
  include DataMapper::Resource
  property :id,  Serial
  property :created_at, DateTime

  belongs_to :user
  belongs_to :book
end


class Book
  include DataMapper::Resource
  property :id, Serial
  has n, :loans
  has n, :users, :through => :loans
end
```

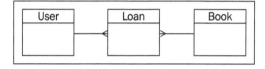

This creates the database tables as follows:

```
mysql> describe users;
+-------+---------+------+-----+---------+----------------+
| Field | Type    | Null | Key | Default | Extra          |
+-------+---------+------+-----+---------+----------------+
| id    | int(11) | NO   | PRI | NULL    | auto_increment |
+-------+---------+------+-----+---------+----------------+
1 row in set (0.00 sec)

mysql> describe loans;
+------------+----------+------+-----+---------+----------------+
| Field      | Type     | Null | Key | Default | Extra          |
+------------+----------+------+-----+---------+----------------+
| id         | int(11)  | NO   | PRI | NULL    | auto_increment |
| created_at | datetime | YES  |     | NULL    |                |
| user_id    | int(11)  | YES  |     | NULL    |                |
| book_id    | int(11)  | YES  |     | NULL    |                |
+------------+----------+------+-----+---------+----------------+
4 rows in set (0.01 sec)

mysql> describe books;
+-------+---------+------+-----+---------+----------------+
| Field | Type    | Null | Key | Default | Extra          |
+-------+---------+------+-----+---------+----------------+
| id    | int(11) | NO   | PRI | NULL    | auto_increment |
+-------+---------+------+-----+---------+----------------+
1 row in set (0.01 sec)

mysql>
```

To use these models:

```
>> user1 = User.create
=> #<User id=1>
>> book1 = Book.create
=> #<Book id=1>
>> Loan.create(:book => book1, :user => user1)
=> #<Loan id=1 created_at=nil user_id=1 book_id=1>
>> user1.books.to_a
=> [#<Book id=1>]
```

Why can't we add the books to the user right away like that we did in the one-to-many? Unfortunately, DataMapper in version 0.9.11 has a bug that does not allow this. It has been fixed in version 0.10.2 but as mentioned earlier it is not the version used in this book.

The second way of defining many-to-many associations is through an anonymous resource:

```
class User
  include DataMapper::Resource
  property :id, Serial
  has n, :books, :through => Resource
end


class Book
  include DataMapper::Resource
  property :id, Serial
  has n, :users, :through => Resource
end
```

These are the tables generated by the models:

```
Terminal — mysql
mysql> describe users;
+-------+---------+------+-----+---------+----------------+
| Field | Type    | Null | Key | Default | Extra          |
+-------+---------+------+-----+---------+----------------+
| id    | int(11) | NO   | PRI | NULL    | auto_increment |
+-------+---------+------+-----+---------+----------------+
1 row in set (0.00 sec)

mysql> describe books;
+-------+---------+------+-----+---------+----------------+
| Field | Type    | Null | Key | Default | Extra          |
+-------+---------+------+-----+---------+----------------+
| id    | int(11) | NO   | PRI | NULL    | auto_increment |
+-------+---------+------+-----+---------+----------------+
1 row in set (0.00 sec)

mysql> describe books_users;
+---------+---------+------+-----+---------+-------+
| Field   | Type    | Null | Key | Default | Extra |
+---------+---------+------+-----+---------+-------+
| user_id | int(11) | NO   | PRI | NULL    |       |
| book_id | int(11) | NO   | PRI | NULL    |       |
+---------+---------+------+-----+---------+-------+
2 rows in set (0.00 sec)

mysql>
```

Notice that a table named `books_users` has been created for you with the `user_id` and `book_id` primary keys.

The shorter way of adding books to users works here as in one-to-many:

```
>> user1 = User.create
=> #<User id=1>
>> book1 = Book.create
=> #<Book id=1>
>> user1.books << book1
=> . . .
>> user1.save
=> true
>> user1.books.to_a
=> [#<Book id=1>]
```

There are some reasons why you would use one way or the other. You can have additional attributes for the concrete models so if you need to add additional attributes you cannot run away from them. In the preceding example we can include the date and time when the loan was made. We can't do this with the anonymous resource. However, the anonymous resource way is much shorter and simpler to maintain and at least at this point in time works better than the awkward creation of the many-to-many concrete model.

Creating the database tables

Creating the database tables is relatively simple. We just need to log into `irb` with the necessary models loaded and run `auto_migrate`. Assuming that the database setup and model definitions are in a file named `models.rb`:

```
$ irb -r models.rb

>> DataMapper.auto_migrate!
```

This will create the necessary tables.

Finding records

One of the most important and frequent actions with DataMapper would be to find and retrieve data from the database. DataMapper provides a few methods of retrieving data. The simplest is to retrieve a record by its key:

```
>> User.get(1)
```

We can also find a record by any of the columns using the `first` method:

```
>> User.first(:nickname => 'sausheong')
```

We can get all the records in the table:

```
>> User.all
```

Records can also be filtered and the filters can be chained:

```
>> active_users = User.all(:active => true)
>> male_active_users = active_users.all(:sex => 'male')
```

The `all` and `first` methods can both have more than one filter and these filters can use certain symbols to specify how the filters work. For example, the filters below indicate that we want to find all users who are born after 1980, who are not married and the sex as male:

```
>> User.all(:birth_date.gt => '1980-01-01', :marital_status.not =>
'married', :sex => 'male')
```

However, note that these filters are AND filters, meaning that the records retrieved must pass all the filters before they are retrieved. In the later 0.10.2 release, you can combine these queries using OR or more complex filtering conditions.

DataMapper is very powerful and we have only scratched the surface on its capabilities. DataMapper supports an aspect-oriented approach in doing callbacks or hooks, chained association calls, single table inheritance, multiple data stores, and many other features that are provided by various optional packages in dm-more. To find out more about DataMapper you should visit `http://www.datamapper.org` and go through the existing documentation.

Haml

Haml (which stands for XHTML Abstraction Markup Language) is a markup language that cleanly describes XHTML without the use of inline code. Haml was originally written for Ruby but has since been used in many other languages including Python, PHP, Perl, ASP.NET and even Scala.

Installing

Installing Haml is very easy and done through the usual Haml gem:

```
$ sudo gem install Haml
```

Using Haml

The easiest way to explain Haml is to do a quick comparison between Haml and HTML. This is a simple HTML snippet:

```
<div id='content'>
  <div class='left column'>
    <h2>Welcome to our site!</h2>
    <p>Some basic information</p>
  </div>
  <div class="right column">
    Some more information
  </div>
  <div>
    <a href="/some_url">here</a>
  </div>
</div>
```

And this is the Haml equivalent:

```
#content
  .left.column
    %h2 Welcome to our site!
    %p Some basic information
  .right.column
    Some more information
  %a{:href => "/some_url"}
```

Note that the Haml template is smaller and easier to read without the opening and closing tags. We can do away with the tags because Haml is whitespace active, meaning whitespaces are important in Haml. The indentation defines how the tags are grouped. While this can be restrictive at times, it actually helps us to write code that is more easily debugged and maintained. Ultimately the Haml template is compiled into the same HTML.

Here are some simple rules to start using Haml:

- All tags are replaced with %. For example, instead of writing `<h2>` you just need to do `%h2`. The exception to this is the DIV tag, which is used so often that it is simply omitted if there are attributes.

- As mentioned earlier, indentation is important and defines the nesting in the tags. For example, in the snippet above the H2 tag is at the same indentation level as the P tag. This means they are not nested but are sibling tags. If instead of being on the same level, the P tag is indented another level to the H2 tag, the P tag will be nested within the H2 tag.

- Brackets represent a Ruby hash that is used for specifying the attributes of a tag. For example `%a{:href => '/some_url'}` here is compiled to `<a href='/some_url'>here</a>`.

- Borrowing from CSS, we can use the . shortcut to indicate a `class` attribute and the # shortcut to indicate an `id` attribute. For example, `.left.column` is compiled to `<div class='left column'>` since DIV is assumed if no tag is used.

Haml and Ruby

While Haml is interesting and useful as a means to simplify HTML, it is only really powerful as a templating engine when combined with Ruby. Here is the same snippet above, re-written to include some Ruby code:

```
#content
  .left.column
    %h2 Welcome to our site #{@user.name}!
```

```
%p Some basic information
%ol
   - @some_array.each do |item|
     %li= item.name

.right.column
  Some more information
  %a{:href => "/some_url"}
```

There are a few ways Ruby code can be integrated within Haml:

- To evaluate some Ruby code and insert the output into the compiled document, we use the equals(=) sign. This can be placed after the tag to place the output within the tag.

- To evaluate some Ruby code but not insert any output into the compiled document, we the dash(-) sign. We can place the dash sign anywhere. If the evaluated code is a block, we don't need to explicitly close the block, Haml will take care of it.

- To evaluate some Ruby code and insert the output within some text, you can use #{} and place it within any text just as you would do with a Ruby string.

For more information on Haml please go to `http://www.haml-lang.com`.

Now that we have wrapped up the quick tour of the technology stack, let's get back to the book and describe how to approach reading it.

How this book works

Before we start with the first clone chapter, let's review how each of the subsequent chapters are structured. Each chapter after this book has the same structure:

- We start off with a description of the kind of application we will be cloning in the chapter. For example, in the second chapter we will clone TinyURL, so we will start off by discussing URL shorteners in general. This will include the history of URL shorteners and how they came about.

- After that we follow with a description of the specific application that we will be cloning, for example TinyURL. This might include discussion of its market share and why it is the most popular application of its kind.

- Next we list the specific major features of the application we want to clone and briefly explain what the feature is all about.

- After the list of features we jump into a discussion on how we design the clone of each feature.

- Before jumping into the actual code, we run through various technologies and third party providers we will be using for the clone.

- The actual code and description of the implementation will cover both the data model as well as the application flow. This will be the bulk of the chapter.

- After the description of the implementation we describe how the clone can be deployed.

- Finally we wrap up with a summary of what we have done for the chapter.

Caveat

A word of warning for the reader. The code in this book is by no means production quality and is meant for educational and illustrative purposes only. There is little to no security consideration and not much exception handling built into the code either. Do not attempt to use the code directly in your application without thinking through some of these considerations.

Summary

This first chapter started off with a discussion on the objectives of the book as well as the target readers for the book. The reasons behind choosing each chapter were also briefly mentioned. The bulk of this chapter however dealt with the technology stack we will use in the rest of the book. We started off the technology discussion with Sinatra, the domain specific language used for developing web applications, followed by DataMapper, a popular Ruby object-relational mapping (ORM) library and finally rounding off with Haml, a Ruby-specific templating engine. We rounded off this chapter with a description of the structure of the rest of the chapters. With this, let's start with the first clone chapter.

2
URL Shorteners – Cloning TinyURL

We start off with an easy application, a simple yet very useful Internet application, URL shorteners. We will take a quick tour of URL shorteners before jumping into the design of a simple URL shortener, followed by an in-depth discussion of how we clone our own URL shortener, Tinyclone.

All about URL shorteners

Internet applications dont always need to be full of features or cover all aspects of your Internet life to be successful. Sometimes it's ok to be simple and just focus on providing a single feature. It doesn't even need to be earth-shatteringly important—it should be just useful enough for its target users. The archetypical and probably most extreme example of this is the URL shortening application or URL shortener.

This service offers a very simple but surprisingly useful feature. It provides a shorter URL that represents a normally longer URL. When a user goes to the short URL, he will be redirected to the original URL. For this simple feature, top three most popular URL shortening services (TinyURL, bit.ly, and is.gd) collectively had about 11 million unique visitors, 110 million page views and a reach of about 1% of the Internet in June 2009. In 2008, the most popular URL shortener at that time, TinyURL, was made one of Time Magazine's Top 50 Best Websites.

The idea to shorten long and unwieldy URLs into shorter, more manageable ones has been around for some time. One of the earlier attempts to make it a public service is **Make A Shorter Link (MASL)**, which appeared around July 2001. MASL did just that, though the usefulness was debatable as the domain name was long and the shortened URL could potentially be longer than the original.

However, the pioneering site that popularized this concept (and subsequently bought over MASL and a few other similar sites) is TinyURL. TinyURL was launched in January 2002 by Kevin Gilbertson to help him to link directly to newsgroup postings which frequently had long URLs. It rapidly became one of the most popular URL shorteners around. In 2008, an estimated 100 similar services came to existence in various forms.

> URLs or Uniform Resource Locators are resource identifiers that specify where identified resources are available and how they can be retrieved. A popular term for URL is a eeb address. Every URL is made up of the following:
>
> ```
> <resource type>://<username>:<password>@<domain>:<port
> >/<file path name>?<query string>#<anchor>
> ```
>
> Not all parts of the URL are required by a browser, if the resource type is missing, it is normally assumed to be `http`, if the port is missing, it is normally assumed to be `80` (for http). The username, password, query string, and anchor components are optional.

Initially, TinyURL and similar types of URL shorteners focused on simply providing a short representative URL to their users. Naturally the competitive breadth for shortening URLs was rather well, short. Many chose TinyURL over MASL because TinyURL had a shorter and easier to remember domain name (`http://tinyurl.com` over `http://makeashorterlink.com`).

Subsequent competition over this space intensified and extended to providing various other features, including custom short URLs (TinyURL, bit.ly), analysis of click-through statistics (bit.ly), advertisements (Adjix, Linkbee), preview pages (TinyURL, is.gd) and so on.

The explosive growth of Twitter (from June 2008 to June 2009, Twitter grew 1,164%) opened a new chapter for URL shorteners. Twitter chose a limit of 140 characters for each tweet to accommodate the 160 characters in an SMS message (Twitter was invented as a service for people to use SMS to tell small groups what they are doing). With Twitter's popularity skyrocketing, the need arose for users to shorten URLs to fit into the 140 characters limit. Originally Twitter used TinyURL as its default URL shortener and this triggered a steep climb in the usage of TinyURL during the early days of Twitter.

However, in May 2009, bit.ly replaced TinyURL as Twitter's default URL shortener and the impact was immediate. For the first time in that period, TinyURL recorded a drop in the number of users in May 2009, dropping from 6.1 million to 5.3 million unique users, while bit.ly jumped from 1.8 million to 2.9 million almost overnight. That's not the end of the story though. In April 2010 during Twitter's Chirp conference, Twitter announced its own URL shortener (twt.tl). As of writing it is still unclear the market share will pan out but it's clear that URL shorteners have good value and everyone is jumping into this market. In December 2009, Google came up with its own two URL shorteners, goo.gl and youtu.be. Amazon.com (amzn.to), Facebook (fb.me), and Wordpress (wp.me) all have their own URL shorteners as well.

Next, let's do a quick review of why URLs shorteners are so popular and why they attract criticism as well.

Here's a quick summary of the benefits:

- Create short and easy to remember URLs
- Allow passing of links in character-limited services such as Twitter
- Create vanity URLs for marketing purposes
- Can verbally pass URLs

The most obvious benefit of having a shortened URL is that it's, well, short. A typical example of an URL gone bad is a link to a location in Google Maps:

```
http://maps.google.com/maps?f=q&source=s_q&hl=en&geocode=&q=singapore
+flyer&vps=1&jsv=169c&sll=1.352083,103.819836&sspn=0.68645,1.382904&g
=singapore&ie=UTF8&latlng=8354962237652576151&ei=Shh3SsSRDpb4vAPsxLS3
BQ&cd=1&usq=Singapore+Flyer
```

Such URLs are meant to be clicked on as it is virtually impossible to pass it around verbally. It might be justifiable if the URL is cut and pasted on documents, but sometimes certain applications will truncate parts of the URL while processing. This makes a long URL difficult to click on and even produces erroneous links. In fact, this was the main motivation in creating most of the earlier URL shorteners—older e-mail clients tend to truncate URLs when they are more than 80 characters.

Short links are of course crucial in character-limited message passing systems like Twitter, Plurk, and SMS. Passing long URLs is impossible without URL shorteners.

Short URLs are very useful in cases of vanity URLs where for example, the Google Maps link above could be shortened to `http://tinyurl.com/singapore-flyer`. Such vanity URLs are useful when passing from one person to another, or even when being used in a mass marketing way. Sticking to the maps theme in our examples, if you want to give a Google Maps link to your restaurant and put it up in catalogs and brochures, you will not want to give the long URL. Instead you would want a nice, descriptive, and short URL.

Short URLs are also useful in cases of accessibility. For example, reading out the Google Maps link above is almost impossible, but reading out the TinyURL link (vanity or otherwise) is much easier in comparison.

Many popular URL shorteners also provide some form of statistics and analytics on the usage of the links. This feature allows you to track your short URLs to see how many clicks it received and what kind of patterns can be derived from the clicks. Although the metrics are usually not advanced, they do provide basic usefulness.

On the other hand, URL shorteners have their fair share of criticisms as well. Here is a summary of the bad side of URL shorteners:

- Provide the opportunity to spammers because they hide original URLs
- Could be unreliable if dependent on them for redirection
- Possible undesirable or vulgar short URLs

URL shorteners have security issues. When a URL shortener creates a short URL, it effectively hides the original link and this provides the opportunity for spammers or other abusers to redirect users to their sites. One relatively mild form of such an attack is 'rickrolling'. Rickrolling uses a classic bait-and-switch trick to redirect users to a Rick Astley music video of *Never Gonna Give You Up*. For example, you might feel that the URL `http://tinyurl.com/singapore-flyer` goes to Google Map, but when you click on it, you might be rickrolled and redirected to that Rick Astley music video instead.

Also, because most short URLs are not customized, it is quite difficult to see if the link is genuine or not just from the URL. Many prominent websites and applications have such concerns, including MySpace, Flickr, and even Microsoft Live Messenger, and have one time or another banned or restricted usage of TinyURL because of this problem. To combat spammers and fraud, URL shortening services have come up with the idea of link previews, which allows users to preview a short URL before it redirects the user to the long URL. For example, TinyURL will show the user the long URL on a preview page and requires the user to explicitly go to the long URL.

Another problem is performance and reliability. When you access a website, your browser goes to a few DNS servers to resolve the address, but the URL shortener adds another layer of indirection. While DNS servers have redundancy and failsafe measures, there is no such assurance from URL shorteners. If the traffic to a particular link becomes too high, will the shortening service provider be able to add more servers to improve performance or even prevent a meltdown altogether? The problem of course lies in over-dependency on the shortening service.

Finally, a negative side effect of random or even customized short URLs is that undesirable, vulgar, or embarrassing short URLs can be created. Earlier on, TinyURL short URLs were predictable and it was exploited, such as embarrassing short URLs that were made to redirect to the White House websites of then U.S. Vice President Dick Cheney and Second Lady Lynne Cheney.

We have just covered significant ground on URL shorteners. If you are a programmer you might be wondering, "Why do I need to know such information? I am really interested in the programming bits, the others are just fluff to me."

Background information on the application we want to clone is very important. It tells us why that application exists in the first place and gives us an idea of what the main features are (what makes it popular). It also tells us what problems it faces, such that we are aware of the problem while programming it, or even avoid it altogether. This is important when we come to the design of the application. Finally, it gives us better appreciation of the application and the motivations and issues faced by the product and technical people behind the application we wish to clone.

Main features

Next, let's list down the features of a URL shortener. In subsequent chapters we will go down similar paths with each popular Internet application. The intention in this section is to distill the basic features of the application, features that define the service. Features listed here will be features that make the application what it is.

However, as much as possible we want to also explore some additional features that extend the application and are provided by many of its competitors. Most importantly, the features here are mostly features of the most popular and definitive web application in the category. In this chapter, this will be TinyURL.

These are the main features of a URL shortener:

- Users can create a short URL that represents a long URL
- Users who visit the short URL will be redirected to the long URL

- Users can preview a short URL to enable them to see what the long URL is

- Users can provide a custom URL to represent the long URL

- Undesirable words are not allowed in the short URL

- Users are able to view various statistics involving the short URL, including the number of clicks and where the clicks come from (optional, not in TinyURL)

URL shorteners are simple web applications and the one that we will design and build will also be simple.

Designing the clone

Cloning TinyURL is relatively simple but there is some thought behind the design of the application. We will be building a clone of TinyURL called Tinyclone, which will be hosted at the domain `http://tinyclone.saush.com`.

Creating a short URL for each long URL

The domain of the short URL is fixed. What's left is the file pathname. We need to represent the long URL with a unique file pathname (a key), one for each long URL. This means we need to persist the relationship between the key and the URL.

One of the ways we can associate the long URL with a unique key is to hash the long URL and use the resulting hash as the unique key. However, the resulting hash might be long and hashing functions could be slow.

The faster and easier way is to use a relational database's auto-incremented row ID as the unique key. The database will help ensure the uniqueness of the ID. However, the running row ID number is base 10. To represent a million URLs would already require seven characters, to represent 1 billion would take up nine characters. In order to keep the number of characters smaller, we will need a larger base numbering system.

In this clone we will use base 36, which is 26 characters of the alphabet (case insensitive) and 10 numbers. Using this system, we will only need five characters to represent 1 million URLs:

```
1,000,000 base 36 = lfls
```

And 1 billion URLs can be represented in just six characters:

```
1,000,000,000 base 36 = gjdgxs
```

Automatically redirecting from a short URL to a long URL

HTTP has a built-in mechanism for redirection. In fact it has a whole class of HTTP status codes to do this. HTTP status codes that start with 3 (such as 301, 302) tell the browser to go look for that resource in another location. This is used in the case where a web page has moved to another location or is no longer at the original location. The two most commonly used redirection status codes are *301 Move Permanently* and *302 Found*.

301 tells the browser that the resource has moved away permanently and that it should look at that location as the permanent location of the resource. 302 on the other hand (despite its name) tells the browser that the resource it is looking for has moved away temporarily.

While the difference seems trivial, search engines (as user agents) treat the status codes differently. 301 tells the search engines that the short URL's location has moved permanently away to the long URL, so credit for the long URL goes to the long URL. However, because 302 only tells the search engine that the location has moved temporarily, the credit goes to the short URL. This can cause issues with search engine marketing accounting.

Obviously in our design we will need to use the *301 Moved Permanently* HTTP status code to do the redirection. When the short URL `http://tinyclone.saush.com/singapore-flyer` is requested, we need to send a HTTP response:

```
HTTP/1.1 301 Moved Permanently
Location: http://maps.google.com/maps?f=q&source=s_q&hl=en&geocode=&q=
singapore+flyer&vps=1&jsv=169c&sll=1.352083,103.819836&sspn=0.68645,1.
382904&g=singapore&ie=UTF8&latlng=8354962237652576151&ei=Shh3SsSRDpb4v
APsxLS3BQ&cd=1&usq=Singapore+Flyer
Content-Type: text/html
Content-Length: 235

<html>
  <head>
   <title>Moved</title>
  </head>
  <body>
   <h1>Moved</h1>
   <p>This page has moved to <a href="http://maps.google.com/maps?f=q
&source=s_q&hl=en&geocode=&q=singapore+flyer&vps=1&jsv=169c&sll=1.35
2083,103.819836&sspn=0.68645,1.382904&g=singapore&ie=UTF8&latlng=8354-
962237652576151&ei=Shh3SsSRDpb4vAPsxLS3BQ&cd=1&usq=Singapore+Flyer">Si
ngapore Flyer</a>.</p>
  </body>
</html>
```

Providing a customized short URL

Providing a customized short URL with the above design we had in mind before makes things less straightforward. Remember that our design uses the database row ID in base 36 as the unique key. To customize the short URL we cannot use this database row ID, so the customized short URL needs to be stored separately.

In Tinyclone we store the customized short URL in a separate secondary table called Links, which in turn points to the actual data in a table called Url. When a short URL is created and the user doesn't request a customized URL, we store the database record ID from the Url table as a base-36 string into the Links table. If the user requests a customized URL, we store the customized URL instead of the record ID.

A record in the Links table therefore maps a string to the actual record ID in the URL table. When a short URL is requested, we first look into the secondary table, which in turn points us to the actual record in the primary table.

Filtering undesirable words out

While we could use more complex filtering mechanisms, URL shorteners are simple web applications, so we stick to a simpler filtering mechanism. When we create the secondary table record, we compare the key with a list of banned words loaded in memory on startup.

If it is a customized short URL and the word is in the list, we prevent the user from using it. If the key was the actual record ID in the primary table, we create another record (therefore using another record ID) to store the URL.

What happens if the new record ID is also coincidentally in the banned words list? We'll just have to create another one recursively until we find one that is not in the list. There is a probability that two or more consequent record IDs are in the banned words list, but the frequency of it happening is low enough that we don't need to worry about it.

Previewing the long URL

This feature is simple to implement. When the short URL preview function is called, we will show a page that displays the long URL instead of redirecting to that page. In Tinyclone we lump the preview long URL page together with the statistics information page.

Providing statistics

To provide statistics for the usage of the short URL, we need to store the number of times the short URL has been clicked and where the user is coming from. To do this, we create a `Visits` table to store the number of times the short URL has been visited. Each record in the `Visits` table stores the information about a particular visit, including its date and where the visitor comes from.

We use the environment variable from the server called REMOTE_ADDR to find out where the visitor comes. REMOTE_ADDR provides the remote IP address of the client that is accessing the short URL. We use this IP address with an IP geocoding provider to find the country that the visitor comes from then store the country code as well as the IP address.

Collecting the data is only the first step though. We will need to display it properly. There are plenty of visualization APIs and tools in the market; many of them are freely available. For the purpose of this chapter, we have chosen to use the Google Charts API to generate the following charts:

- A bar chart showing the daily number of visits

- A bar chart showing the total number of visits from individual countries

- A map of the world visualizing the number of visits from individual countries

> You might notice that in our design the user does not need to log into this application to use it. Tinyclone is the only clone in the book that does not have any access control on its pages. Most URL shorteners have a public and main feature that redirects short URLs to their original, long URLs. In addition to that some URL shorteners have user-specific access controlled pages that provide information to the users such as the statistics and reporting feature shown above. However, in this clone we will not be implementing any access controlled pages.

Technologies and platforms used

We will use a number of technologies in this chapter, mainly revolving around the Ruby programming language and its various libraries. The main Ruby technologies have been discussed in detail in *Chapter 1, Cloning Internet Applications*, and this section is a refresher before we jump into the code discussion.

Sinatra

Sinatra is a Domain Specific Language (DSL) for quickly creating web applications in Ruby. It keeps a minimal feature set for developers and is an excellent tool for creating small to mid-sized web applications using Ruby.

We discussed Sinatra in depth in Chapter 1.

Haml

Haml (HTML Abstraction Markup Language) is a simple markup language that is used to cleanly describe HTML in a web page. Haml was originally built for Ruby but has also been ported to other languages and platforms. We discussed Haml in depth in Chapter 1.

DataMapper

DataMapper is an object-relational mapping library for Ruby. While there are a number of Ruby object-relational mapping libraries, DataMapper has a number of good features. It is independent and doesn't tie in with any particular frameworks. It is also built to be fast and efficient, often delaying interacting with the data store until it is needed. It is also very Ruby centric and fits in well with the rest of the technologies that we use in the book.

We discussed DataMapper in depth in Chapter 1.

Blueprint CSS

Blueprint CSS is a simple and effective CSS framework. It provides a basic set of CSS styles that makes developing web applications much easier. One of its most useful features is a set of grid layout styles that allows simple to complex layouts to be created easily and effectively. Used together with HAML, it allows us to create great looking front-ends for our web applications.

Mashups

While the main features in the applications are all implemented within the chapters itself, sometimes we still depend on other services provided by generally well-known providers. In this chapter we use two services—Google Chart API for visualizing the statistics we gather on the short URLs and HostIP to geocode IP addresses we get.

Google Chart API

The Google Chart API provides its users a means of dynamically generating various types of charts. In this chapter, we use the Google Chart API to generate statistics visualizations, specifically bar charts and maps.

The Google Chart API returns a PNG-format image in response to a URL. Several types of image can be generated, and for each image type, you can specify attributes such as size, colors, and labels. The Google Chart API is not rate-limited but Google advises users to let them know if they use more than 250,000 API calls per day.

HostIP

HostIP is a free service that provides geocoding services based on IP addresses. Its usage is very simple—we just need to call a HostIP URL with an IP address and it will return geocoded information on the IP address. HostIP is a community-based project that gets its data from its users so accuracy is not perfect. However, for our purpose it is good enough.

Heroku

Heroku is a Ruby-specific cloud-computing platform that provides specialized Ruby hosting services for developers. It allows Ruby developers to easily and almost instantly deploy web applications to the Internet. Heroku supports Rack-based web applications so deploying our Sinatra applications to Heroku is a breeze. While Heroku charges for hosting, it also provides a free basic tier account. More information on how Heroku is used at the end of this chapter when we talk about deployment.

Building the clone

Finally we get to the meat of the chapter. Here we roll up our sleeves and get to the business of coding Tinyclone. The overall web application is around 200 lines of code, so we will put everything into a single file called `tinyclone.rb`. With a bit of Sinatra magic this becomes our entire web application.

We will be looking at Tinyclone from two simple perspectives. The first is the data model. The data model is an abstract view of the objects that are used to represent the application problem space. The second is the application flow, which describes how the application uses the data model to provide the functions needed. As the application isn't very large, we can inspect its code in detail, something we will not be able to do in later chapters when we deal with larger applications.

Data model

Let's look at the data model first. The model we use has three classes. The `Link` is the main class for the application, one that has an identifier (short URL) that represents an actual URL. A Link object (that is, an instance of the Link class) has a Url object. Url represents the original URL that has been shortened. The reason why we separate the short URL and the original URL is to allow custom short URLs, as described above when we discussed the design.

A Link object has many Visit objects. Each Visit object represents a visit to the short URL and contains information about the visit, namely the date of the visit and where the visitor came from. The diagram below describes the three classes we will be using in Tinyclone:

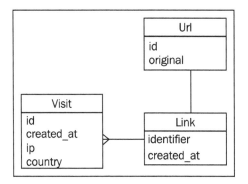

Now that we have the properties of the objects, let's look at the logic that is required for each object.

Url

The `Url` class has no additional built-in logic as it's just a container to store the original URL. Here's the code for the `Url` class:

```
class Url
  include DataMapper::Resource
  property  :id,          Serial
  property  :original,    String, :length => 255
  belongs_to  :link
end
```

Link

The main logic in the `Link` class is based on shortening URLs, that is, turning a given URL into a short URL. Naturally, we create a class method called `shorten` for this, shown as follows:

```
def self.shorten(original, custom=nil)
  url = Url.first(:original => original)
  return url.link if url
  link = nil
  if custom
    raise 'Someone has already taken this custom URL, sorry' unless
Link.first(:identifier => custom).nil?
    raise 'This custom URL is not allowed because of profanity' if
DIRTY_WORDS.include? custom
    transaction do |txn|
      link = Link.new(:identifier => custom)
      link.url = Url.create(:original => original)
      link.save
    end
  else
    transaction do |txn|
      link = create_link(original)
    end
  end
  return link
end
```

We pass in an original URL and optionally a custom label we want for the short URL. First, we check if the original URL is already shortened. If it is, we just return the link. Otherwise, we have split choices, where we will react differently to each situation. If a custom label is provided, we check if the label is already in use. If it is, we throw an exception and ask the user to use another label. We also check the custom label with a list of banned words that we don't want as custom labels. If these two checks are cleared, we proceed to create the Link object and the Url object then save them.

If a custom label is not provided, we will use a recursive method to create the link. We use a recursive method because without a custom label, we will use the record ID as the identifier for the Link object. If coincidentally the custom label is in the list of banned words or if the record ID created is the same as an existing custom label, we want to create another Url object to represent the new Link object. Of course, if even more coincidentally the new Url object ID is also in the banned words list or is a custom label that already exists, we want to create yet another Url object and so on, hence the recursion. The danger that it becomes a never-ending recursion is quite low as it is highly unlikely recursion will happen more than twice.

The list of banned words is loaded up in a separate Ruby file named `dirty_words.rb`. For obvious reasons, this file is not re-printed here.

```
def self.create_link(original)
    url = Url.create(:original => original)
    if Link.first(:identifier => url.id.to_s(36)).nil? or !DIRTY_
WORDS.include? url.id.to_s(36)
        link = Link.new(:identifier => url.id.to_s(36))
        link.url = url
        link.save
        return link
    else
        create_link(original)
    end
end
```

Note that we convert from the Url's ID to a base 36 numbering system before storing it, as explained above.

Visit

The Visit object has the most built-in logic. While storing the data for the visits to the short URL is trivial, we want to also use the Visit object for retrieving the usage charts and statistics.

Remember one of the things we want to do is find and store the country where each visitor comes from. Whenever a visitor visits a short URL in the application, we will create a Visit object and associate it with the correct Link object. Using information from the environment variables, we get the IP address where the visitor comes from. However, getting the IP address is not good enough, as we also want to find out which country the visitor came from. To do this, we use the HostIP IP geocoding API. By sending it the IP address, we will get an XML document that contains information on the country where the client comes from. We parse this XML document and store the country into the Visit object.

To implement this, we use the `after` callback mechanism in the Visit object, where we call a method after the object is created.

```
after :create, :set_country
```

This results in the `set_country` method being called after an object is created. The `set_country` method in turn calls HostIP with the IP and is returned geocoded information in an XML document. Using XmlSimple, we parse that document and set the country code. The country information is in the form of ISO 3166-1 country codes, which are two letter abbreviations of the country name. For example, Singapore would be SG, France would be FR, and the United States would be US.

```
def set_country
    xml = RestClient.get "http://api.hostip.info/get_xml.php?ip=#{ip}"
    self.country = XmlSimple.xml_in(xml.to_s, { 'ForceArray' => false
}) ['featureMember']['Hostip']['countryAbbrev']
    self.save
end
```

Next, we want to get the visit statistics after storing the visit information. We use two methods to do this – one that get the statistics by date, and another by country of origin.

```
def self.count_by_date_with(identifier,num_of_days)
    visits = repository(:default).adapter.query("SELECT date(created_
at) as date, count(*) as count FROM visits where link_identifier =
'#{identifier}' and created_at between CURRENT_DATE-#{num_of_days} and
CURRENT_DATE+1 group by date(created_at)")
    dates = (Date.today-num_of_days..Date.today)
    results = {}
    dates.each { |date|
      visits.each { |visit| results[date] = visit.count if visit.date
== date }
      results[date] = 0 unless results[date]
    }
    results.sort.reverse
end
```

In the `count_by_date_with` method, we use SQL directly on the table to get the data for the range of dates that we want. This results in an array of Ruby Struct objects that contains the information we want. However, we can't use this directly, because there would be some dates without visits, and the SQL doesn't return empty dates. To do this, we create a contiguous list of dates and for each date, we put in the visit count if it is not 0, and 0 if there are no visits. The result we return from this method is a hash table of data with the date as the key and the count as the value.

```
def self.count_by_country_with(identifier)
    repository(:default).adapter.query("SELECT country, count(*) as
count FROM visits where link_identifier = '#{identifier}' group by
country")
end
```

The `count_by_country_with` method is simpler — we just get the count per country.

Getting the numbers is useful but visualizing it in charts and maps is probably more appealing to most users. Tinyclone uses only charts and maps to visualize the statistics and uses the statistics methods described above to get the numbers. Again, we use two methods to return the charts we need.

```
def self.count_days_bar(identifier,num_of_days)
    visits = count_by_date_with(identifier,num_of_days)
    data, labels = [], []
    visits.each {|visit| data << visit[1]; labels << "#{visit[0].
day}/#{visit[0].month}" }
    "http://chart.apis.google.com/chart?chs=820x180&cht=bvs&chxt=x&chco=a
4b3f4&chm=N,000000,0,-1,11&chxl=0:|#{labels.join('|')}&chds=0,#{data.
sort.last+10}&chd=t:#{data.join(',')}"
    end
```

The `count_days_bar` method takes in the identifier and the number of days we want to display the information on and returns a Google Chart API URL that shows image chart that we want. In this case, it is a vertical bar chart that shows the visit count by date.

```
def self.count_country_chart(identifier,map)
    countries, count = [], []
    count_by_country_with(identifier).each {|visit| countries <<
visit.country; count << visit.count }
    chart = {}
    chart[:map] = "http://chart.apis.google.com/chart?chs=440x22
0&cht=t&chtm=#{map}&chco=FFFFFF,a4b3f4,0000FF&chld=#{countries.
join('')}&chd=t:#{count.join(',')}"
    chart[:bar] = "http://chart.apis.google.com/chart?chs=320x240&cht=
bhs&chco=a4b3f4&chm=N,000000,0,-1,11&chbh=a&chd=t:#{count.join(',')}&c
hxt=x,y&chxl=1:|#{countries.reverse.join('|')}"
    return chart
    end
```

The `count_country_chart` method takes in the identifier and the geographical zoom-in of the map we want and returns two charts. The first chart is a horizontal chart showing the number of visits by country and the second chart is a map visualizing the countries where the visits come from. The countries with the larger number of visits are in a darker shade of blue, compared to the countries with the smaller number of visits.

Next, we look at the application flow.

Application flow

Like many web applications, most of the logic for the application lies in the model. The logic in the application flow (as the name suggests) mainly deals with routing or display formatting, besides actually calling the various classes and objects to do their jobs. As a result, this part of Tinyclone is relatively simple. As the routing flow becomes more complex in later chapters, this might not be necessarily true.

The application has six different routes, but only three of them do any significant work. The *main* route (/) does nothing except to display the main page.

```
get '/' do haml :index end
```

The *create shortened URL* route is a HTTP POST request to (/). It is used to create the short URL. First, it makes sure that the input is a valid HTTP or HTTPS URL. If it is, it will use the shorten method in the Link class to create a Link object, which is then passed on to the view.

```
post '/' do
  uri = URI::parse(params[:original])
  custom = params[:custom].empty? ? nil : params[:custom]
  raise "Invalid URL" unless uri.kind_of? URI::HTTP or uri.kind_of?
URI::HTTPS
  @link = Link.shorten(params[:original], custom)
  haml :index
end
```

The *short URL* route is the one that is most frequently used. Given the short URL, it redirects the user to the original URL. At the same time it records the call as a visit.

```
get '/:short_url' do
  link = Link.first(:identifier => params[:short_url])
  link.visits << Visit.create(:ip => get_remote_ip(env))
  link.save
  redirect link.url.original, 301
end
```

The redirect command in Sinatra normally issues a HTTP 302 response code. However, we need to send a 301, as mentioned in the design section. Fortunately, Sinatra is flexible enough to let us send a 301 instead.

To get the IP address of the calling client, we use a method called `get_remote_ip` and pass it the current environment.

```
def get_remote_ip(env)
  if addr = env['HTTP_X_FORWARDED_FOR']
    addr.split(',').first.strip
  else
    env['REMOTE_ADDR']
  end
end
```

Astute readers who already know Sinatra or Rack would know that the Request object inherent in the block has an `ip` method that returns the IP address already and looking at the source it seems to be the same. However, there is a small difference and this has to do with how web applications get the client's IP address.

Most web servers send a set of information when it interacts with the web applications. These environment variables (which are specified in the CGI specification) contain information about the resource that was requested from the web server, and the information in turn can be used by the web application. An example of the information is SERVER_NAME, which gives the web application the host name of the server. Amongst the other information is the REMOTE_ADDR, which tells the web application the IP address of the calling client.

This is all well and good in an ideal world where the clients and servers are connected to and interact directly with the Internet. However, in many production situations, clients and servers are often proxied (by one or more layers) for caching or other reasons. As a result the REMOTE_ADDR variable only gives you the IP address of the last proxy.

Many proxies try to be helpful and add HTTP headers to let the web applications know the real IP address of the calling client. The most popular of these HTTP headers, pioneered by the Squid proxy, is known as *X-Forwarded-For*. X-Forwarded-For provides a list of IP addresses, from the calling client to the last proxy:

```
X-Forwarded-For: client1, proxy1, proxy2
```

Sinatra gets both the REMOTE_ADDR HTTP environment variable and X-Forwarded-For HTTP header through its `env` variable in the Request object provided by Rack. However, the current implementation of Rack (1.0.0) has the `ip` method in the Request class taking the last IP address while what we need is really the first IP address. Therefore we need to modify the implementation slightly in order to get the IP address.

X-Forwarded-For is not very secure though, and any machines along the way can always change the HTTP header to something else altogether. However, as the information is statistical anyway, this is not a big concern for us.

Next is a group of routes that show the information on the short URL:

```
['/info/:short_url', '/info/:short_url/:num_of_days', '/info/:short_
url/:num_of_days/:map'].each do |path|
  get path do
    @link = Link.first(:identifier => params[:short_url])
    raise 'This link is not defined yet' unless @link
    @num_of_days = (params[:num_of_days] || 15).to_i
    @count_days_bar = Visit.count_days_bar(params[:short_url], @num_
of_days)
    chart = Visit.count_country_chart(params[:short_url], params[:map]
|| 'world')
    @count_country_map = chart[:map]
    @count_country_bar = chart[:bar]
    haml :info
  end
end
```

You might notice that we are grouping three different routes under a single block. This is possible under Sinatra because each route is a method that is being called and not being defined in the code. We grouped the routes by placing them in an array and iterating them with a get call.

To show the information in the short URL, firstly we need to establish that the short URL is an existing link in the system. The rest of the code just calls the logic in the models and retrieves the necessary data and charts from the models.

 In this chapter we are discussing the views separately from the routes because the application is very small. In subsequent chapters the routes are discussed alongside the views.

The view in the application is implemented using Haml. The Haml templates are also in the same file. To do this takes a little Sinatra magic. Ruby has a __END__ directive that indicates that anything that comes after it will not be parsed. Instead, we can use the DATA constant to get the rest of the data after the __END__ directive.

Using the command use_in_file_templates! we can tell Sinatra to use whatever after the __END__ directive as the template files. As a result, the Haml templates at the end of the file are the templates for the Sinatra application. This is not the norm for the rest of the chapters though, and is not suitable if there are a large number of views.

Just as in the routes, the view pages are relatively simple. We have a *layout* page, an *index* page and an *info* page. Each inline template page starts with @@ followed by the name of the page. In the Sinatra route, we use this to call a page:

```
haml :index
```

In Sinatra, if we define a template called `layout`, Sinatra will use it as the layout for all pages, unless we tell it specifically not to.

```
@@ layout
!!! 1.1
%html
  %head
    %title Tinyclone
    %link{:rel => 'stylesheet', :href => 'http://www.blueprintcss.org/
blueprint/screen.css', :type => 'text/css'}
  %body
    .container
      = yield
```

We use Blueprint, a CSS framework that provides us with a ready made set of CSS for various styling and layout purposes. Blueprint goes well with Haml.

Let's look at the index page, which is the front page of the application. The index page also acts as a catchall that includes error handling and providing feedback to the user.

```
@@ index
%h1.title Tinyclone
- unless @link.nil?
  .success
    %code= @link.url.original
    has been shortened to
    %a{:href => "/#{@link.identifier}"}
      = "http://tinyclone.saush.com/#{@link.identifier}"
    %br
    Go to
    %a{:href => "/info/#{@link.identifier}"}
      = "http://tinyclone.saush.com/info/#{@link.identifier}"
    to get more information about this link.
- if env['sinatra.error']
  .error= env['sinatra.error']
%form{:method => 'post', :action => '/'}
  Shorten this:
  %input{:type => 'text', :name => 'original', :size => '70'}
  %input{:type => 'submit', :value => 'now!'}
```

```
    %br
    to http://tinyclone.saush.com/
    %input{:type => 'text', :name => 'custom', :size => '20'}
    (optional)
%p
%small copyright &copy;
%a{:href => 'http://blog.saush.com'}
  Chang Sau Sheong
%p
  %a{:href => 'http://github.com/sausheong/tinyclone'}
    Full source code
```

Reading Haml code takes some getting used to but after a while it becomes a breeze. If you feel confused at this point in time please refresh your Haml knowledge in Chapter 1!

The other page is the information page, which provides information of the short URL to the user. To access the information page, the visitor needs to add *info* to the URL path, just before the short URL key, as shown in the following code:

```
@@info
%h1.title Information
.span-3 Original
.span-21.last= @link.url.original
.span-3 Shortened
.span-21.last
  %a{:href => "/#{@link.identifier}"}
    = "http://tinyclone.saush.com/#{@link.identifier}"
.span-3 Date created
.span-21.last= @link.created_at
.span-3 Number of visits
.span-21.last= "#{@link.visits.size.to_s} visits"

%h2= "Number of visits in the past #{@num_of_days} days"
- %w(7 14 21 30).each do |num_days|
  %a{:href => "/info/#{@link.identifier}/#{num_days}"}
    ="#{num_days} days "
  |
%p
.span-24.last
  %img{:src => @count_days_bar}

%h2 Number of visits by country
- %w(world usa asia europe africa middle_east south_america).each do
|loc|
```

```
    %a{:href => "/info/#{@link.identifier}/#{@num_of_days.to_s}/#{loc}"}
      =loc
    |
%p
.span-12
  %img{:src => @count_country_map}
.span-12.last
  %img{:src => @count_country_bar}
%p
```

The information template is mostly laid out using Blueprint CSS. The rules for using Blueprint grid layout are rather simple. Blueprint defines a grid on a page to be 950px, with 24 columns of width 30px, and a 10px margin between columns. By adding a CSS class `selector` that starts with *span* to a tag, we indicate the width of that tag. For example, span-2 means the tag is set a width of two columns. The last tag in the list needs another tag that is *last* to complete the row.

Now that we have gone through the application in detail, let's look at how we can deploy it.

Deploying the clone

There are a few ways to run the Sinatra web application. The simplest is probably to run it off the command line. To do this, we need to set up the database. We assume that for this application you would have installed MySQL. At the command line go into the MySQL interactive command console:

```
$ mysql -u <username> -p <password>
```

Then just execute the following command:

```
mysql> create database tinyclone;
```

This will just create the database. Next, go into IRB and run this command:

```
> require 'tinyclone'
```

This will require the necessary classes for creating the database tables. Next, just run this command:

```
> DataMapper.auto_migrate!
```

This will create the tables for the application. To run the application, we just need to run this at the command line:

```
$ ruby tinyclone.rb
```

Then, go to `http://localhost:4567/` and you will see the running application:

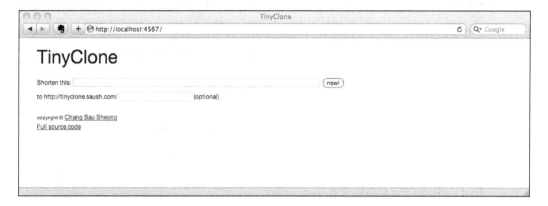

This is how the info page looks:

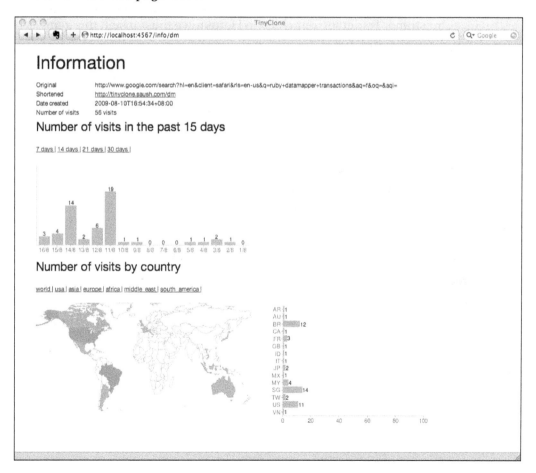

Alternatively we can also deploy to Heroku, the Ruby cloud-computing platform. Deploying Sinatra applications to Heroku is dead simple as well. These are the steps:

1. First, create a `config.ru` file.

    This is the Rack configuration file, which is actually just another Ruby script. All you need to have in this file is the following:

    ```
    %w(sinatra tinyclone).each  { |lib| require lib}
    run Sinatra::Application
    ```

    This tells Rack to include Sinatra and Tinyclone, and then run the Sinatra application.

2. Install the Heroku gem.

    Just execute the following command:

    ```
    $ sudo gem install heroku
    ```

    Heroku provides us with a set of useful tools packaged in a gem, very much like Capistrano. To deploy our clone to Heroku we must install this gem.

3. Initialize an empty git repository in the `tinyclone` folder:

    ```
    $ cd tinyclone

    tinyclone $ git init

    Initialized empty Git repository in .git/

    tinyclone $ git add .

    tinyclone $ git commit -m 'initial import'

    Created initial commit 5581d23: initial import

    2 files changed, 52 insertions(+), 0 deletions(-)

    create mode 100644 config.ru

    create mode 100644 tinyclone.rb
    ```

    This just creates and initializes an empty git repository on your computer.

4. Create the Heroku application:

    ```
    tinyclone $ heroku create tinyclone

    Created http:// tinyclone.heroku.com/ | git@heroku.com: tinyclone.git

    Git remote heroku added
    ```

You will be prompted for your username and password the first time you run a Heroku command. Subsequently this will be saved in ~/.heroku/credentials and you won't be prompted anymore. It will also upload your public key to allow you to push and pull code.

5. Push your code to Heroku:

```
tinyclone $ git push heroku master
Counting objects: 4, done.
Compressing objects: 100% (4/4), done.
Writing objects: 100% (4/4), 999 bytes, done.
Total 4 (delta 0), reused 0 (delta 0)
-----> Heroku receiving push
-----> Rack app detected
Compiled slug size is 004K
-----> Launching....... done
App deployed to Heroku
To git@heroku.com: tinyclone.git
* [new branch]      master -> master
```

Notice that this pushes your code and loads your application into deployment. The application is now deployed, but you'll need to create the database.

6. Log in to the Heroku console and create the database:

```
tinyclone $ heroku console
Ruby console for tinyclone.heroku.com
>> DataMapper.auto_migrate!
=> [Url]
```

Heroku allows you access to a console similar to IRB but with the environment of your deployment loaded up, just like script/console in Ruby on Rails. To create the database, we just need to run DataMapper.auto_migrate! and it will create the database accordingly.

Now go to your application on Heroku (here it is http://tinyclone.heroku.com).

Summary

This is just a warm-up. In this chapter, we cloned one of the simplest popular Internet applications around, TinyURL. Later applications will gradually get more complicated. We started off the chapter with a general introduction to URL shorteners and a list of pros and cons of using URL shorteners. Then we listed the main features and discussed the design of our URL shortener, called Tinyclone. This set the foundation for the discussion on actual construction of the application. After designing our clone, we went briefly into a short refresher on the technologies used before going into detail on how the application was built.

The chapter broke up the application into a data model and an application flow discussion. Both parts were discussed and explained in detail. Finally, we ended the chapter with a description of how Tinyclone can be deployed. We discussed two options for deployment—one to a normal server (simulated locally) by running it off the command line and the other to Heroku, a Ruby cloud-computing platform.

In the next chapter, we will move on to one of the hottest topics today—microblogging, and in particular Twitter.

Microblogs – Cloning Twitter

3

One of the most successful new Internet services of recent times is Twitter. Since its launch it has exploded from niche usage to usage by the general populace, with celebrities such as Oprah Winfrey, Britney Spears, and Shaquille O'Neal, and politicians such as Barack Obama and Al Gore jumping into it.

With so much Twitter coverage sometimes it's difficult to remember that Twitter itself is not unique but is one service in a group of up and coming Internet services generally called microblogs. In this chapter we look at this Internet phenomenon, dissect it and as before, clone its main features.

All about microblogs

Microblogs are nominally condensed blogs where users send brief text updates instead of the usual paragraphs to page-sized updates. One of the first microblogs (also known as tumblelogs) was *Anarchaia*, whose owner Christian Neukirchen described it as *'more than a linkblog but contains less than a usual blog'*. *Anarchaia* was started in March 2005 and various similar services were rolled out over the same period of time. However, it is only when Twitter broke into the scene in 2006 when microblogs gained the most attention.

Microblogs are heavily influenced by numerous technological developments including obviously blogs, Instant Messaging (IM), Internet Relay Chat (IRC), and in more recent times, the mobile phone.

Blogging (a contraction of the word *weblog*) started as an activity on the Internet for people to keep personal online diaries or journals. These diaries, basically running commentaries of the writer's daily lives, appeared on the Internet starting from 1994. Jorn Barger coined the term 'weblog' in 1997 in his blog *Robot Wisdom weblog*, which was a record (or log) of books and articles he read as well as subjects he found interesting. The short form, 'blog', was coined by Peter Merholz, who jokingly broke the word weblog into the phrase 'we blog' in the sidebar of his blog `http://www.peterme.com` in April or May 1999. Shortly thereafter, Evan Williams at Pyra Labs used 'blog' as both a noun and verb ('to blog' meaning 'to post to one's weblog') and used the term 'blogger' to mean a person who blogs. Blogging subsequently became an Internet cultural phenomenon that had wide-reaching influence online as well as offline.

IRC came into existence in 1988. IRC is a form of synchronous text chatting or conferencing. Anything typed on the IRC becomes instantly available, almost like having a bunch of people on IRC chatting with each other. Invented by Jarkko Oikarinen, it was the forerunner to instant messaging tools such as Yahoo! Messenger and Google Talk. The IRC community created specific protocols using special characters that provided instructions to IRC users. Two examples of such protocols are the namespace channel (#namespace) and the directed message (@username), both of which eventually made their way into Twitter.

Instant messaging or IM for short started on a similar but slightly different communications track. Modern, Internet-wide instant messaging clients, as they are known today, began to take off in the mid 1990s with PowWow, then ICQ, followed by AOL Instant Messenger. Soon after, AOL bought Mirabilis, the company who ran ICQ, and other companies started developing their own applications based on proprietary protocols.

While IM and IRC sound and feel pretty similar, there are slight but significant differences in architecture and usage of IRC and IM. Firstly, IRC's chat is real-time and the recipients see what the users were typing. Secondly, while IRC always connects to a server for all communications, IM clients normally only connect to the server to get the contacts list of friends. The actual messages that are communicated are between the users. Finally, while IRC is normally a public forum where people come together to chat about something, IM is more personal and one-to-one (although most IM clients have conference or group chat features).

IM eventually evolved a feature where users are able to leave custom status messages instead of the 'not at my desk' message. After a while it became the norm to express yourself in these status messages and for your friends to catch up with you by reading those messages and even sharing things like songs that you were listening to at the moment or URLs to interesting sites on the Internet.

The final and probably the triggering point is the mobile phone and text messaging. Text messaging is a form of message exchange involving the mobile phone that started with and is predominantly using the GSM network's Short Message Service (SMS) protocol. Most text messages are just text, though other forms of content including sounds, pictures, and videos have been shared through other protocols such as MMS. Text messaging is primarily one-to-one and private though its usage included text marketing (marketing to consumers through sending text messages) and sending text commands (think text voting for American Idol).

SMS technology has been included in GSM as early as 1985 during a GSM meeting in Oslo but the first SMS was sent in the UK in 1992 by Neil Papworth of Sema Group (now Airwide Solutions), who used a personal computer to send "Merry Christmas" to Richard Jarvis of Vodafone, who was using an Orbitel 901 handset. The initial take up for text messaging was quite slow because users were only allowed to send messages to someone using the same operator. It was only in 1999 when messaging was allowed between networks that SMS really started to take off.

As you can probably notice now, all these technologies show their influence in the creation of microblogs. Microblogging evolved from these 'ancestors' to be a new form of blogging that allows people to share their thoughts and also share links, images, and videos, much like their lengthier cousins. The conventions in microblogs such as hash-tagging topics and using @ replies have been adopted from IRC. Instant messaging prepared users for the norm of leaving asynchronous messages (such as status messages) for their friends and sending one-to-one private messages. Finally texting enabled microblogging on a much larger scale by tying text messaging to microblogs, and also prepared users for the norm of composing short and succinct messages. The mobility of texting enabled users to communicate any time they wanted and also showed in the influence of Twitter with their 140-character limitation (SMS limits messages to 160 characters – Twitter limited it to 140 and left 20 for the username).

It is only right that Evan Williams, who helped define the word 'blog' and was also the co-founder of Blogger (one of the earliest blog publishing tools that helped to popularize blogging) eventually co-founded Twitter.

Twitter

Twitter is a phenomenon that broke onto the Internet scene in 2006. The first Twitter prototype was used as an internal service for Odeo employees in March 2006 and was later launched publicly into a full-scale version in July 2006. The tipping point for Twitter happened in March 2007 during the South by Southwest (SXSW) music festival in Austin, Texas. During the event, the number of tweets grew from 20,000 per day to 60,000 per day. The Twitter people placed plasma screens in the conference hallways to stream Twitter, panelists and speakers mentioned the service, and the bloggers in attendance touted it. Reaction at the festival was overwhelmingly positive and that was the event generally known to have sparked the Twitter uptake. Twitter won the festival's Web Award and Twitter staff accepted their prize with the remark "We'd like to thank you in 140 characters or less. And we just did!"

Twitter is obviously the top dog amongst the microblogs. Amongst its more prominent direct competitors are Plurk, Tumblr, Brightkite, Jaiku, Pownce, and Identi.ca, but in recent times the big boys are moving into this area as well. Google bought Jaiku in 2007. Pownce was bought by SixApart in December 2008 and was shutdown in the same month. In 2009, Yahoo! launched a microblogging service called Meme. Even Facebook and LinkedIn got into the act by adding new features that competed with the standalone microblogs.

Nonetheless, Twitter is way ahead of its competitors. According to Compete (`http://www.compete.com`) in September 2009, Twitter had 23.5 million unique users per month, while the nearest competitor Tumblr had about 3.3 million unique users, about eight times less than Twitter. In addition, according to statistics gathered by TwitStat, the 23 million users on Twitter's website represent only 18% of their user base; the rest access Twitter through client applications that connect to Twitter through their API(s).

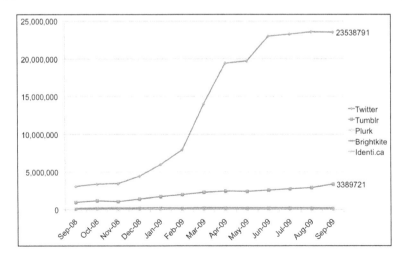

Microblog	Unique users in September 2009
Twitter	23,538,791
Tumblr	3,389,721
Brightkite	246,684
Plurk	214,551
Identi.ca	91,046

To be fair, Facebook, LinkedIn, and other popular social network's microblogging features are not included in this comparison as it is difficult to get accurate numbers that are separate from the rest of their services. It is likely that these services will be the serious challenger to Twitter and not the standalone microblogging sites. On the other hand, Twitter itself is changing and moving ahead to be more of a discovery engine, since buying out the popular Twitter search engine Summize in July 2008.

While there are statistics and more statistics on Twitter, a very quick gauge of Twitter's influence on the Internet and popular culture can be made with a simple search on Google. A quick search on Google in October 2009 on the keyword 'Twitter' returned close to a billion results, as compared with the keyword 'Google', which returned about 2 billion, Facebook about 1.8 billion, and Yahoo! about 2.2 billion. However, the contrasts could not have been bigger—Google has about 20,000 employees, Yahoo! has about 13,000 employees, Facebook has about 1,000 employees, while Twitter has only 74 employees. As a comparison, a similar keyword search for 'Tumblr' only shows 16.4 million results.

Why Twitter?

So how did Twitter succeeded so dramatically? By all accounts, with its sparse features (it mostly just allows users to post and read tweets) and competition there isn't much to argue for its success. The need for such a service was practically nil. Many people in fact couldn't understand why anyone except a narcissist would want to post mundane tweets about themselves.

Although there is no clear-cut reason why Twitter became so wildly successful, the following are some possible reasons.

Simple

Twitter's premise is simple—just type in what you are currently doing in 140 characters and share it with the world. It doesn't care what you share, as long as it's less than 140 characters. Using it isn't rocket science and it's simple enough to pick up and go with it. This philosophy can be seen in its APIs and user interface. Twitter's user interface is uncomplicated and its APIs are easy to use. The proof of the API's simplicity is in its wide adoption. In fact writing Twitter clients are so easy that it's been called the new 'Hello World' application (a 'Hello World' is an application that prints out 'Hello World' on a display device and is widely used as the introductory tutorial application for many programming language text books and tutorials).

A means to have public conversation

An interesting though not unique feature with Twitter and microblogs is to allow users to have public conversations amongst themselves. This is a feature that is inherited from blogs. However, while blogs are all about posting and allowing anyone to comment on that blog post, Twitter allows a user to tweet and have users respond using '@' reply, comment, or re-tweet. Responding with replies emulates a real-world conversation in both its brevity and directedness while comment and re-tweeting emulates spreading of news through the grapevine. This is one of the key strengths of Twitter and microblogs in general.

Let's compare a blog with Twitter. A full blog does not compare directly with Twitter but with an account in Twitter, since a user does not post into Twitter but into his/her own account. In this sense we can consider each user account in Twitter as a *nanoblog* in which the user writes his/her blog posts and Twitter as the *blogosphere* in which these nanoblogs exist. While blogs are individualistic and spread throughout the blogosphere (each blogger has his/her own blog) with their own interface and their regular readers, Twitter aggregates all the blog posts from each nanoblog and provides a single interface to access them. This forms a social bond between each nanoblogger, something that blog sites are not capable of doing today (though sites such as Blogger and Wordpress try). This is the social network effect.

Fan versus friend

The social effect of microblogs like Twitter is subtly different from that of social networks such as Facebook, Myspace, and Friendster. The connections in social networks are that of 'friends', that is, the relationship goes both ways. The *friend* you know in Facebook is most likely someone you knew before joining Facebook, and Facebook requires you to approve the connection. This is the *friend model*.

On the other hand the connections in microblogs can go either one way or both ways. When it is in the one-way mode, the connections are like being fans. A typical example — you might know Barack Obama but it is most unlikely that he knows you in return. This is the *fan model*. However, if he does know you, then connection becomes both ways and the model is similar to that of the social networks.

The differences are subtle but important. Facebook's model is reciprocal, that is the user needs to approve and agree that you are his friend before a connection is made, but Twitter's model is not. You can 'follow' any one that catches your fancy and the number of 'followers' can be quite exponential. While Facebook had a 5,000 friends limit until March 2009, Ashton Kutcher (@aplusk) was racing with CNN to have more than 1 million followers in April 2009 (which he eventually won). As of writing (October 2009) Ashton Kutcher leads the pack of close to 200 Twitter accounts with more than 1 million followers, with 3.8 million followers himself.

Of course, Facebook also have a fan model (after March 2009), which has a top account (Michael Jackson) reaching more than 10 million fans but if we compare the friend model in Facebook versus the fan model in Twitter you can see how the fan model has tremendous reach. The fact that Facebook modified their 5,000 friends limit and added features that support the fan model shows the importance of this model, and we can see how it had helped to push Twitter to its current heights.

Understanding user behavior

Regardless whether intentional or not (though I am inclined to think that it was), Twitter understood what users wanted. Blogs, though highly popular, were usually for the more verbose because not everyone can write lengthy blog posts or even write well. The need to share and to convey thoughts could be there but the process of translating it from the to-be-blogger's mind to a blog post usually took effort many people would normally consider work. Also writing long posts (or even short posts) takes time and that forms a barrier for many casual bloggers.

Using Twitter however, takes very little time and effort. The 140-character limitation is a double-edged sword — while it is a bane for people who need to write more, it also forced users to write succinctly and reduces the amount of time and effort needed to write. As there are no rules in writing as many 140-character tweets as you like, there is sufficient flexibility to extend the limitation. The barrier to blog and share with the world what you are doing at all times has been greatly reduced in Twitter.

In addition, some people do not find it comfortable to read lengthy blog posts on a computer screen while bite-sized tweets are more acceptable. This especially applies to reading on the mobile phone and on the go. Catching up with friends and knowing what they have been up to is something blogs and social networks have offered up until now. Twitter provides the means to access such updates for both friends and fans anywhere and easily. Social networks such as Facebook, LinkedIn, and others are catching up though. Many of these social networks also offer status update capabilities very much like Twitter and other microblogs.

Easy to share through text messaging

The need to share and convey meaning doesn't always occur in front of a laptop or a desktop computer. More often than not, it is those idle times and waiting moments, or when an idea strikes that the urge to share and communicate occurs. In this sense, Twitter's strategy of using texting as a major means of tweeting hit the bullseye. With billions of mobile phones in the world and tens of billions of text messages in the world flying around every month, Twitter was ensured an audience who is already familiar with their easy-to-use product. Users who are used to texting took to it like ducks to water — tweeting is merely an extension of their normal texting behavior, except that it provided a means to have a public one-to-many conversation instead of a one-to-one conversation. It is easy enough to see that the need to share coupled with the capability to actually do it quickly and easily at that time propelled Twitter into the stratosphere.

While it is easy enough to see how text messaging works for tweeting updates, Twitter actually sends updates to your mobile phone for you to read as well. However, as of writing, receiving updates only works for a few countries (in the U.S., UK, Canada, India, and New Zealand now but this could change rapidly) due to the costs involved.

Easy to access through multiple devices and applications

Twitter's mobility extends to not only text messaging but through its simple API — it enabled hundreds of different clients on multiple platforms. As long as connectivity over the Internet is available, it is easy enough to write a Twitter accessing client. At the same time, Twitter's APIs are easy enough to use that anyone can write a simple Twitter client.

RapLeaf, a social media company that conducted research on Twitter in August 2009 estimates over 1,900 Twitter clients in their survey of 4 million Twitter users. This of course does not include the myriad of applications that make use of Twitter APIs for discovery, statistics, and other purposes. By all standards, the current number is conservative as more new services and clients are being added daily.

Main features

As in the previous chapter, before we jump into designing the clone, let's look at the main features of a microblog. An open standard called *OpenMicroBlogging* exists but it is not widely adopted. In a market dominated by a single powerful player it is often difficult to introduce an open standard that allows interoperability, unless the dominant player is the one that came up with it.

In this chapter we will be discussing some of the main features common to many microblogs. As before, the main features represent the features that define a microblog. Inevitably the features are mostly Twitter features.

- Allow users to post status updates (known as 'tweets' in Twitter) to the public.

- Allow users to *follow* and *unfollow* other users. Users can follow any other user but it is not reciprocal.

- Allow users to send public messages directed to particular users using the @ replies convention (in Twitter this is known as *mentions*).

- Allow users to send direct messages to other users, messages are private to the sender and the recipient user only (direct messages are only to a single recipient).

- Allow users to *re-tweet* or forward another user's status in their own status update.

- Provide a public timeline where all statuses are publicly available for viewing.

- Provide APIs to allow external applications access.

There are a number of features that we have skipped in this chapter, which are normally part of most microblogs. These include search, trending topics, posting photos, and videos on the tweet.

Designing the clone

With the features we want for the clone well defined, let's delve into the functional design of our Twitter clone. We will be building a clone of Twitter called *Tweetclone*, which we will be hosting at the domain `http://tweetclone.saush.com`. Tweetclone contains a minimal feature set that is just enough to implement a simple Twitter clone.

Posting statuses

Let's start off with the main entity in the application. Tweets, generically known as statuses, are freely viewable by everyone. Each user must be logged in to post a status update (or to tweet) as in any normal blog. This means status updates belong to only one user at a time. This also means that we need a user to be registered and logged in (authenticated). Although this statement is simple, it is really quite crucial—it means we need to have a user authentication mechanism, unlike in Tinyclone in the previous chapter, where anyone can use it without logging in.

For many Internet applications, the username is not an important part of the functionality of the system (at least for the user himself). It is mainly used to authenticate the user at login and for the system to address the user. However, in microblogs such as Twitter and Tweetclone the username provides crucial information for the user himself. This is because users interact with other users using the username as the handle.

As a result, designing the username is important. Needless to say, the username needs to be unique. However, the username also needs to be editable by the user himself. At the same time, the username should be short (users don't like to type out long usernames and space is limited anyway). If a user can change his/her username at will, how can we identify him/her uniquely? In most cases we will identify him/her directly using a unique identifier, but in the cases where we need to use his/her nickname and if he/she changes it, he/she will not be able to access his/her tweets. This is actually the same behavior as in Twitter.

As for the status text, Twitter and some microblogs implement a 140-character limit. This is mainly because Twitter was originally built for SMS text messages. While this is not a hard-and-fast rule in microblogs, for faithful reproduction (aka cloning) purposes, we will implement the same limit in Tweetclone.

Following users

If posting statuses is the only thing users do in a microblog then microblogs are really nothing more than mini blogs with less text. What makes microblogs more than just blogs with less text are their social features. In fact, some suggest that microblogs such as Twitter are actually more similar to social networking services.

One of the main features in any social network involves modeling the interaction between its users. The two more commonly adopted models are the friend model and the fan model as described in a section above. Let's review the models again before we go through the design because this is a crucial part of a microblog.

In the friend model, users in the system already know each other and they connect to each other to renew that friendship or acquaintance. In this model, user Tom needs to accept Waldo's invitation to connect before the connection is made. Without that connection, Waldo will not get to have deeper information that is available on the system about Tom or be able to read Tom's status updates. Only minimal public information is provided, if any at all. Once that connection is made however, the relationship becomes mutual, Tom and Waldo have equal access to each other's information and status updates.

In the fan model on the other hand, Waldo doesn't need Tom to approve the connection. Waldo's connection to Tom is similar to a fan to a movie star; Waldo knows and follows Tom while Tom doesn't necessarily follow Waldo. In this case, the connection made is one-sided; Waldo knows about Tom's information and status updates while Tom doesn't get any information in return. However, Tom can follow Waldo in return without Waldo's approval too. This seemingly lop-sided relationship is not something new, even in other applications. It is widely used for example, in contact management systems where a user's contacts list (or address book, depending on the kind of application you're using) can contain contacts of friends, or contacts of people you know but who might not know you in return.

While both models seem similar and the difference trivial, the usage of systems based on either model is quite different. Users make use of systems built on the fan model, such as Twitter and the other microblogs, to make new friends and discover new things happening in the world around them. In fact, Twitter calls their search feature a 'discovery engine'. Twitter's live information stream coupled with a search engine allows its users to utilize Twitter as a real-time search engine. This has become enough of a threat that Google has responded by incorporating microblog search in its search engine.

In Tweetclone we will be implementing the fan model. This means users in Tweetclone have a one-way relationship with each other. If the users are friends, then two relationships will be built. The relationship is called *follows*, which is the more commonly known term used in Twitter. For example, Waldo and Ivan follow Tom; they are Tom's followers. At the same time Tom follows Ivan, so Tom is Ivan's follower. Tom has two followers and one follows, while Ivan has one follower and one follows, and Waldo has only one follows.

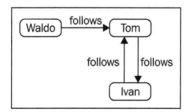

Sending publicly directed messages

A key feature in all microblogs is allowing users to send publicly directed messages to specific users. The message is actually a normal status update that is directed to specific users. From a user's point of view, this means that the status is publicly viewable by all users, but at the same time the recipient knows that the status update/message is intended for him/her. The normal convention used is to add the @ symbol in front of the user name. This convention is actually propagated from the IRC along with the namespace channel (also popularly known as the hash-tag). In Twitter, this feature is known as a *mention*.

The difference between a publicly directed message and a normal status update is that users are able to show just those messages that are directed to them. This means that in the system, we need to be able to indicate that a status update is directed to a user. Since a single public message can be directed at a number of users at the same time, the relationship between the status update and the user is one of many-to-many.

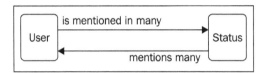

Sending privately directed messages

While the publicly directed messages are viewable by one and all, some microblogs, including Twitter, implement a private messaging system (known as *direct messages* in Twitter) that sends messages from one user to another, privately. Direct messages are directed from one user to another and only either one of the two users are able to view it. Direct messages are viewed separately altogether from the status updates.

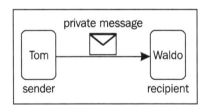

Direct messages have a sender and a recipient. In the preceding example, Tom sends the direct message to Waldo. Tom is the sender of the direct message while Waldo is the recipient.

Re-tweeting

Re-tweeting is a social network related feature and for a long time was not an official feature provided by Twitter. The basic premise of a re-tweet is very simple—the user copies another user's tweet and posts it as his/her tweet, sometimes adding his/her comments to it. The most common format of a re-tweet is to add RT to the front of the tweet, followed by the @ and the username though sometimes RT is placed at the back of the tweet, or 'via @username' is used instead.

In August 2009 Twitter announced *Project ReTweet*, which is basically Twitter's project to add re-tweeting into its platform, including its APIs. This simplifies the act of re-tweet, as well as making it consistent. Along with this feature Twitter also provided a set of Twitter APIs to go along with it. In November 2009, Twitter released the feature.

What is probably most controversial is of course that Twitter chose not to implement commenting on re-tweets. The community created convention of re-tweeting allows the user to add in their own comments or even modify it if they want to. The official Twitter feature doesn't allow this at all. On the other hand, with a more organized way of tweeting as well as an API, gathering re-tweeting statistics and discovering more information in Twitter is much easier.

In Tweetclone we will be implementing the simpler community convention based re-tweeting.

Public timeline

All tweets in most microblogs are, by default public, although in some microblogs you can block access to the tweets by making them private. Some microblogs like Identi.ca and Twitter publish public timelines that show all tweets from everyone. The public timeline is a simple feature. It's simply a list of all the latest tweets from all users in the system that is viewable without the user actually logging in.

API

Almost all microblogs (actually most web 2.0 styled web applications) have some **APIs** or **Application Programming Interfaces** that allow developers to access some parts of their service or data. While many popular web applications that provide API have clients, Twitter generated a whole sub-industry of client applications.

Twitter clients are so popular that they have been dubbed as the new 'Hello World' application (a 'Hello World' is an application that prints out 'Hello World' on a display device and is widely used as the introductory tutorial application for many programming language text books and tutorials).

Although there are many reasons why Twitter clients are so popular (mostly dealing with the popularity of the service itself), one of them is probably the ease of use of the APIs themselves. Twitter provided many of their original APIs without the need for authentication, and for those that do require authentication, simple HTTP Basic Authentication was used. Although Twitter also supported OAuth later as their recommended and more secured authentication service, Basic Authentication remained highly popular just because it's so easy to use. In fact Twitter recognizes this and for a very long time, both Basic Authentication and OAuth co-existed. In December 2009, Twitter announced that Basic Authentication would be turning off its Basic Authentication APIs in favor of OAuth by June 2010.

In terms of base functionality, a Twitter client is very simple. Twitter itself is built around the simple premise of asking: "What are you doing right now?" and letting the users answer. A Twitter client essentially needs to do two things — display the user's timeline and let him post tweets.

In the same spirit, Tweetclone will be implementing a small set of APIs. This small subset allows for a minimal Tweetclone client (which we will not implement, leaving it as an exercise for the reader). The APIs we will be implementing are as follows:

- Get all tweets for a user
- Post a tweet
- Get the public timeline

These APIs will be protected by HTTP Basic Authentication.

Authentication, access control, and user management

All applications require users (the definition of an application software is a computer program that supports or improves its users' work) but not all applications require their users to log in. The word processor desktop application and URL shortener web application in the previous chapter are examples of applications that do not require user login.

Applications normally require a user to log in when we need to identify the user and provide services that are specific to him only. This is true especially with web applications that support multiple users concurrently—if we have to provide a personalized service we need to identify him. The action of identifying a user is called *authentication*. Along with authentication is the idea of *access control*, which tells the application if an authenticated user is allowed to access certain resources, or not. The third leg of that supports user login in applications is *user management*, which is a set of functions that support the management of users, including user registration and password management.

Traditionally web application developers use existing libraries or write their own authentication, access control, and user management modules to support user login. The application would require users to register for an account then send a validation-cum-activation e-mail to the new user. Once the user receives and activates his/her account through the URL embedded in the e-mail, he/she would be allowed to enter his/her username and password into the application and be authenticated and identified. Other essential functions of user management include facilities to reset the password should the user forget, change his/her password, change his/her profile, settings, and so on.

As you can imagine, authentication, access control, and user management can be quite involved and complicated, especially when issues of security and privacy weigh in. When writing web applications (and even other types of applications) the authentication and user management modules take up a big chunk of critical work for developers and require continual maintenance and operations post-deployment, even with usage of external libraries.

Third party authentication and access control

At the same time, many larger software organizations started to tout their proprietary own authentication and access control mechanism. Microsoft started its Passport service in 1999 and received much criticism along the way (later it changed its name to Windows Live ID). Soon after, in September 2001, the Liberty Alliance (which many considered a counter to Passport) was started by Sun Microsystems, Oracle, Novell, and others to do federated identity management.

On the open front, two different technologies have surfaced to solve the issues of authentication and access control separately. OpenID is a popular digital identity used for authentication, originally developed for LiveJournal in 2005. Many large companies including Yahoo!, Google, PayPal, IBM, and Microsoft support it. As of November 2008, there are over 500 million OpenIDs on the Internet and about 27,000 sites have integrated it.

OAuth is a newer protocol used for access control, first drafted in 2007. It allows a user to grant access to information from one site (provider) to another site (consumer) without sharing his/her identity. OAuth is strongly supported by Google and Yahoo!, and is also used in Twitter, LinkedIn, and many other popular Internet applications.

As mentioned before, Google is an initial and strong supporter of OAuth but it also offers the older AuthSub web authentication as well as ClientLogin client authentication APIs in addition to being an OpenID provider (it calls its OpenID service Federated Login). Yahoo! started supporting OAuth officially in 2008, alongside its older BBAuth APIs and is also an OpenID provider. Facebook joined the race in 2008 with Facebook Connect, which does authentication as well as sharing Facebook information. MySpace also came in with their platform in 2008, originally called Data Availability, which quickly became MySpaceID.

In April 2009, Twitter started offering 'Sign In with Twitter', which true to its name, allows users to sign in with their Twitter accounts. Originally, Twitter used HTTP basic authentication to protect its resources but eventually support grew for OAuth. On top of all that, there is an extension to OpenID called OpenID OAuth Extension that combines OpenID's authentication with OAuth's access control, and Google, Yahoo!, and MySpace announced their support for it in September 2009.

As you can see there are really lots of players in the market. RPX, a popular authentication service provider, took advantage of these offerings and came up with a unified and simplified set of APIs to allow authentication with Yahoo!, Google, Windows Live ID, Facebook, AOL, MySpace, and various OpenID providers.

Authentication and user management

It's obvious from the preceding discussion that there are plenty of choices for a web developer today in terms of third party authentication and access control services. For smaller web applications (such as Tweetclone) it is foolish to write our own when we can pick and choose from a list. Also, from our requirements above you can realize that we don't need access control services, only authentication.

However, there is a slight twist to our requirements in Tweetclone. Before we jump into the explanation, let's look at third party authentication services from another angle. Looking from a different perspective, there are two types of third party authentication:

- Web authentication for web applications
- Client authentication for desktop or mobile client applications

The main difference between these two types of authentication is that Web authentication will redirect the user to provider's site for him/her to enter his/her username and password, then returns to the calling web application, usually with a success or failure token. Client authentication (usually) cannot do this, and would require the application to capture the username and password, which is sent by the client application to the provider. Obviously from a security point of view, web authentication is more secure and re-assuring to users since the user never need to pass the username and password to the application at all.

From the above you would realize that web authentication only works for web applications. This is the prickly point. If you remember from the section on designing APIs, we need to get the developer using our API to authenticate before using the API. However, he/she authenticates through his/her code only, and does not use a web interface. So how can we overcome this? Do we really need to write our own authentication and also user management module?

Not really. From our discussion above you will notice that out of the few providers, Google and Twitter both provide us with web as well as client authentication services. If we use either one of them, we can use the web authentication services for the Tweetclone web application and the client authentication services for the Tweetclone APIs. For Tweetclone we have chosen to use Google (because using Twitter authentications services would be too dependent on Twitter itself).

Also, for the web authentication, we have chosen to use RPX for Google to simplify the integration and also to allow for future flexibility (we will be using RPX in subsequent chapters too). This means that although RPX provides interfaces to a number of authentication providers, we will limit it to only Google.

As for user management, the functions are split between Google and Tweetclone. As the users are really Google users who happen to also use Tweetclone, the functions to change their profile, manage their passwords, and generally secure their account lies with Google. However, Tweetclone requires a user entity to manage the user-to-user relationships as well as tweet ownership and therefore we store some user information in Tweetclone. For example, we want to display some nice avatars on Tweetclone; the avatar information is going to be placed in our user profile and not in Google.

Scalability and stability

Two of the key issues that plague startups that become successful are the scalability and stability of the application. This is especially true with microblogs—the point in case is Twitter and their (in)famous and intermittent series of server failures throughout 2008 and 2009. Twitter was initially developed for internal use by a small company and its rapid growth wasn't anticipated. Spikes of utilization during large events and conferences such as Macworld, the Super Bowl, and Michael Jackson's death caused mini-meltdowns in which users were greeted by a stock image of a whale being lifted out of the sea by a flock of birds. This became the famous 'fail whale' and it is a warning sign for developers-to-be of large-scale Internet applications to be prepared for scalability.

While there are many techniques for scalability, we will focus on just one that is the most practically implemented at the start of deployment, and that is to deploy it on a cloud platform, Heroku.

Technologies and platforms used

We use a number of technologies in this chapter, mainly revolving around the Ruby programming language and its various libraries. In addition to Ruby and its libraries we also use a few mashups, which are described below. We have described Sinatra, DataMapper, and Haml in the previous chapters so we will not repeat this here. Please refer to *Chapter 1, Cloning Internet Applications* for the details if you need to refresh your memory.

JSON

JSON (JavaScript Object Notation) is a lightweight data-interchange format, often used within a web context. It is meant to be easy for humans to read as well as for machines to parse or create. As the name suggests, it was derived from Javascript for representing simple data structures and hashes. However, JSON itself is not programming language-specific and has many implementations in various languages. It is increasingly becoming the popular alternative to sending and receiving XML.

In this application we will be using the JSON gem, which is one of the most popular JSON Ruby libraries. Installing the JSON library is simple:

```
% sudo gem install json
```

To use the library you need to require it first:

```
require 'json'
```

There are primarily two uses of any JSON library — you either use it to parse JSON data or to create JSON formatted data from another format. Parsing is very easy with the JSON Ruby library:

```
obj = JSON.parse(json_data)
```

Creating is relatively easy as well:

```
JSON.generate(obj)
```

In this chapter and in many chapters, we often use generate JSON from the object itself using the to_json method.

Mashups

As with previous chapters, while the main features in the applications are all implemented within the chapters itself, sometimes we still depend on other services provided by generally well-known providers. In this chapter we use four services— RPX/Google for user web authentication, Google ClientLogin for API authentication, Gravatar for avatar services, and TinyURL for URL shortening.

RPX

RPX is an authentication provisioning service provided by JanRain, a technology startup with deep roots in the OpenID community. It doesn't do the actual authentication itself but acts as a proxy to a multitude of third party authentication providers such as Google, Yahoo!, MySpace, Windows Live ID, Facebook, Twitter, and a number of OpenID providers such as LiveJournal and Blogger. By wrapping around these third party providers it exposes a uniform interface that enables websites and applications to easily use any of the third party authentication providers. This is how it works:

1. The user chooses their identity provider from a sign-in interface provided by RPX. This sends some POST parameters to the RPX server, including a token URL, which is a URL that RPX will send to the user once they've been authenticated.

2. RPX initiates the authentication process with the chosen provider on behalf of the web application, including sending the user to the chosen provider.

3. The provider displays an authentication form to the user for him to authenticate himself (to the provider) and informs the user that he will be signing in to the web application.

4. Once the user is authenticated, the provider sends the user back to RPX, which in turn sends the user to the token URL specified earlier, along with a token parameter.

5. Armed with the token parameter and an API key that was given by RPX during registration, the web application sends a request to RPX for more information.

6. RPX returns the data accordingly if the token is valid. At this point in time, the user is authenticated and can be considered logged in.

To use RPX, we need to firstly register ourselves with RPX. RPX uses its own services for authentication so you can log in with any of the shown third party providers. Once you have registered, you need to create an application within RPX.

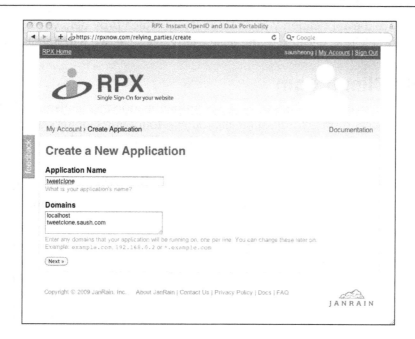

Once you have created the application you will be provided with an API key. This API key is what we will be using to interact with RPX at step 5 above.

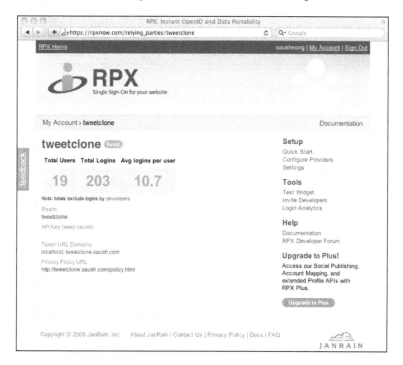

Once you have the application you can also set up which providers you want to allow. For Tweetclone, because of the reasons given above, we will only use Google.

Google ClientLogin

As explained above, Google has a couple of authentication mechanism. Google's ClientLogin mechanism is for *installed applications*, following Google's terminology. However, any application can use it, even web applications. For Tweetclone we use ClientLogin to authenticate for the APIs.

If you read the ClientLogin documentation in Google's ClientLogin for Installed Application page, you might see a complicated diagram that includes token exchange and CAPTCHA challenges.

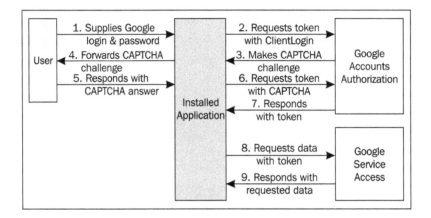

In actual usage this is not strictly necessary and even a bit misleading. If you use the generic service code in the *service* parameter, *xapi* (for GData services), you will not be challenged for a CAPTCHA. Naturally this is less secure but for our needs (for usage in an API) we will not be able to demand a CAPTCHA answer anyway so the flexibility suits us.

The generic URL for ClientLogin is:

```
https://www.google.com/accounts/ClientLogin
```

We need to send a POST request to the preceding URL, with the following minimal parameters:

Parameter	Description
accountType	Type of account to request authorization for. Possible values are GOOGLE (get authorization for a Google account only), HOSTED (get authorization for a hosted account only) and HOSTED_OR_GOOGLE (get authorization first for a hosted account; if attempt fails, get authorization for a Google account). For Tweetclone we will use GOOGLE.
email	User's full e-mail address. It must include the domain.
passwd	User's password.
service	This is the name of the service we are requesting. For the case of Tweetclone we are not requesting any service at all, so we stick with the generic 'xapi' service code.
source	This is a short string identifying your application, for logging purposes.

Gravatar

Gravatar is short for Globally Recognized Avatar, and is a free Internet application that allows you to map avatars (which are mid-to-small-sized thumbnail pictures representing yourself) to e-mails. The service itself is quite simple — it allows the user to add any number of avatar pictures and also any number of e-mail addresses that belong to you. You can map any of the pictures to any of the e-mail addresses.

We use Gravatar in Tweetclone because we need an avatar and because we don't have an authentication service and only keep a simple profile. We also use Gravatar centrally because not all third-party authentication providers will provide avatars.

Gravatar is very easily usable in web applications. An avatar in Gravatar is identified through its e-mail address, converted into lowercase, with whitespaces trimmed and then hashed with MD5. A typical avatar URL looks like the following:

```
http://www.gravatar.com/avatar/ee191858f0d96ad93098694537f71998
```

Note that the file extension is optional, and if it is required by some application, you can append any extension to it (Gravatar doesn't mind or care about the extension at all).

TinyURL

TinyURL is a URL shortening service that we cloned in *Chapter 2, URL Shorteners – Cloning TinyURL*. However, in Chapter 2 we did not implement an API, which is what we require in this chapter. We use TinyURL in Tweetclone to shorten and replace the URLs we encounter while parsing the status. TinyURL has a very simple API. Just execute the following in the web application:

```
http://tinyurl.com/api-create.php?url=<long url>
```

And you will be returned the shortened URL.

Heroku

Heroku is a Ruby-specific, cloud-computing platform that provides specialized Ruby hosting services for developers. It allows Ruby developers to easily and almost instantly deploy web applications to the Internet. Heroku supports Rack-based web applications so deploying our Sinatra applications to Heroku is a breeze. While Heroku charges for hosting, it also provides a free basic tier account. More information on how Heroku is used at the end of this chapter when we talk about deployment.

Building the clone

Now that we are done with the discussions on Twitter, its features and also the design of the clone, let's roll up our sleeves and get into the act of building it.

Modeling the data

The data model for Tweetclone is quite simple; it consists of two major classes — User and Status, and two minor classes that describe the relationships — Relationship and Mention.

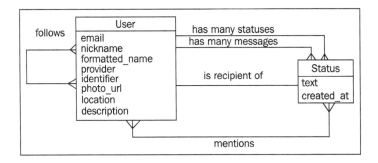

The `Relationship` class defines the many-to-many relationship between users, that is it defines who follows whom. The `Mention` class defines the many-to-many relationship between users and statuses (aka tweets). Each status can mention one or more users and each user can be mentioned in one or more statuses. A user can have one or more statuses, while only one user can be the recipient of a status. In addition to that, because we're modeling direct messages with statuses, a user can also have one or more direct messages.

In Tweetclone we have placed all the models in a single file called `models.rb`.

User

Let's define the `User` class first. The source code to define the DataMapper model of `User` is as follows:

```
class User
  include DataMapper::Resource

  property :id,            Serial
  property :email,         String, :length => 255
  property :nickname,      String, :length => 255
  property :formatted_name, String, :length => 255
  property :provider,      String, :length => 255
  property :identifier,    String, :length => 255
  property :photo_url,     String, :length => 255
  property :location,     String, :length => 255
  property :description,  String, :length => 255

  has n, :statuses
  has n, :direct_messages, :class_name => "Status"
  has n, :relationships
  has n, :followers, :through => :relationships, :class_name =>
"User", :child_key => [:user_id]
  has n, :follows, :through => :relationships, :class_name => "User",
:remote_name => :user, :child_key => [:follower_id]

  has n, :mentions
  has n, :mentioned_statuses, :through => :mentions, :class_name =>
'Status', :child_key => [:user_id], :remote_name => :status

  validates_is_unique :nickname, :message => "Someone else has taken
up this nickname, try something else!"

  def self.find(identifier)
    u = first(:identifier => identifier)
```

```
      u = new(:identifier => identifier) if u.nil?
      return u
    end

  def displayed_statuses
      statuses = []
      statuses += self.statuses.all(:recipient_id => nil, :limit => 10,
  :order => [:created_at.desc]) # don't show direct messsages
      self.follows.each do |follows| statuses += follows.statuses.
  all(:recipient_id => nil, :limit => 10, :order => [:created_at.desc])
  end if @myself == @user
      statuses.sort! { |x,y| y.created_at <=> x.created_at }
      statuses[0..10]
    end
  end
```

The properties of the User class are the profile of a user. We will be using it later when creating or modifying the user profile. The property to take note of in this is nickname. As mentioned during the design section, identifying the user is very important in Tweetclone. As we're using RPX, the unique identifying property is actually identifier, which for Google is the unique OpenID identifier with the following format:

```
https://www.google.com/accounts/o8/id?id=AItOawnFFjWL15Ie5xEw4EB4RBx
nd_ervO
```

However, it's impossible to use because it is not user-friendly (there is no way a user will remember the whole URL). Instead we use a nickname to identify the user, which is also why we need to make sure it is unique:

```
validates_is_unique :nickname, :message => "Someone else has taken up
this nickname, try something else!"
```

If you have gone to the Tweetclone site you will realize that the user sets the nickname when he/she first logs in. If the nickname is already taken, he/she will be asked to use something else. If he/she leaves the nickname empty, a random string will be set for him, based on the hash of the identifier, converted into an alphanumeric string.

```
user.update_attributes({:nickname => profile['identifier'].hash.
to_s(36), :email => profile['email'], :photo_url => photo, :provider
=> profile['provider']})
```

As mentioned above, a user can own multiple statuses and multiple messages, both of which are also modeled with the Status class.

```
has n, :statuses
has n, :direct_messages, :class_name => "Status"
```

We also define the two different relationships between users — follows, which is a list of users you follow and followers, a list of your fans. Implicitly we have also defined that if a user is in both these lists, he/she is a friend.

```
has n, :relationships
has n, :followers, :through => :relationships, :class_name => "User",
:child_key => [:user_id]
has n, :follows, :through => :relationships, :class_name => "User",
:remote_name => :user, :child_key => [:follower_id]
```

To keep track of the many-to-many relationships we define a separate class called Relationship. We define the user_id and follower_id properties here, which seems unusual because we use them in the belongs_to and has n relationships. However, this is necessary because we're defining a many-to-many self-referencing relationship.

```
class Relationship
  include DataMapper::Resource

  property :user_id, Integer, :key => true
  property :follower_id, Integer, :key => true
  belongs_to :user, :child_key => [:user_id]
  belongs_to :follower, :class_name => "User", :child_key =>
[:follower_id]
end
```

The user also keeps track of a list of statuses where he is mentioned. This will allow us to display the list of statuses where he is mentioned more efficiently.

```
has n, :mentions
has n, :mentioned_statuses, :through => :mentions, :class_name =>
'Status', :child_key => [:user_id], :remote_name => :status
```

As before, we use a separate class called Mention to keep track of the relationship. However, this class is simpler as it does not reference itself. Note that however we need to create a primary key property called id because DataMapper doesn't allow classes to be defined without a primary key. We could get away with this in the Relationship class because we defined a composite key.

```
class Mention
  include DataMapper::Resource
  property :id,          Serial
  belongs_to :user
  belongs_to :status
end
```

Next, we define a method to return a user, given the OpenID identifier. If the user exists, it is returned, and otherwise it will be created.

```
def self.find(identifier)
  u = first(:identifier => identifier)
  u = new(:identifier => identifier) if u.nil?
  return u
end
```

There is a method in DataMapper that allows the immediate creation of the object (and database record) if an object is not found — first_or_create. This method is not appropriate for our use here for a subtle reason — first_or_create will create the actual database record while the preceding method will only return a Ruby object without tying it to an actual record in the database. Why does this make a difference? It's because we will check if it is a new record later on, using the new_record? method on the object. If it's an object that is tied with an actual database record, it will be considered an existing record and we will never be able to update any further attributes.

```
user = User.find(profile['identifier'])
  if user.new_record?
    ...
    unless user.update_attributes({:nickname => profile['identifier'].
hash.to_s(36), :email => profile['email'], :photo_url => photo,
:provider => profile['provider']})
      flash[:error] = user.errors.values.join(',')
      redirect "/"
    end
```

Lastly, we need to define a method that retrieves all statuses that are relevant to this user. This means that we want to retrieve the tweets he posted as well as tweets of people he follows.

```
def displayed_statuses
    statuses = []
    statuses += self.statuses.all(:recipient_id => nil, :limit => 10,
:order => [:created_at.desc])
    self.follows.each do |follows| statuses += follows.statuses.
all(:recipient_id => nil, :limit => 10, :order => [:created_at.desc])
end if @myself == @user
    statuses.sort! { |x,y| y.created_at <=> x.created_at }
    statuses[0..10]
  end
```

First, we retrieve all of the user's own tweets in reverse chronological order, which means retrieving the statuses without recipients (statuses with recipients are direct messages).

```
statuses += self.statuses.all(:recipient_id => nil, :limit => 10,
:order => [:created_at.desc])
```

We add to this list of statuses the tweets of each person that the user follows, also in reverse chronological order.

```
self.follows.each do |follows| statuses += follows.statuses.
all(:recipient_id => nil, :limit => 10, :order => [:created_at.desc])
end if @myself == @user
```

After retrieving the statuses, we sort them in reverse chronological order again to get the actual order we want.

```
statuses.sort! { |x,y| y.created_at <=> x.created_at }
```

Finally, we return the first ten statuses only. As you will have realized, this is arbitrary and we did not implement a pagination system.

Status

Here's the source code for the `Status` class:

```
class Status
  include DataMapper::Resource

  property :id, Serial
  property :text, String, :length => 140
  property :created_at,  DateTime
  belongs_to :recipient, :class_name => "User", :child_key =>
[:recipient_id]
  belongs_to :user
  has n, :mentions
  has n, :mentioned_users, :through => :mentions, :class_name =>
'User', :child_key => [:user_id]

  before :save do
    @mentions = []
    case
    when text,starts_with('D ')
      process_direct_message
    when text.starts_with('follow ')
      process_follow
    else
      process
    end
  end

  after :save do
```

```
      unless @mentions.nil?
        @mentions.each {|m|
          m.status = self
          m.save
        }
      end
    end

    # general scrubbing
    def process
      # process url
      urls = self.text.scan(URL_REGEXP)
      urls.each { |url|
        tiny_url = open("http://tinyurl.com/api-create.
php?url=#{url[0]}") {|s| s.read}
        self.text.sub!(url[0], "<a href='#{tiny_url}'>#{tiny_url}</a>")
      }
      # process @
      ats = self.text.scan(AT_REGEXP)
      ats.each { |at|
        user = User.first(:nickname => at[1,at.length])
        if user
          self.text.sub!(at, "<a href='/#{user.nickname}'>#{at}</a>")
          @mentions << Mention.new(:user => user, :status => self)
        end
      }
    end

    # process direct messages
    def process_direct_message
      self.recipient = User.first(:nickname => self.text.split[1])
      self.text = self.text.split[2..-1].join(' ') # remove the first 2
words
      process
    end

    # process follow commands
    def process_follow
      Relationship.create(:user => User.first(:nickname => self.text.
split[1]), :follower => self.user)
      throw :halt # don't save
    end

    def to_json(*a)
      {'id' => id, 'text' => text, 'created_at' => created_at, 'user' =>
user.nickname}.to_json(*a)
    end
end
URL_REGEXP = Regexp.new('\b ((https?|telnet|gopher|file|wais|ftp) :
[\w/#~:.?+=&%@!\-] +?) (?=[.:?\-] * (?: [^\w/#~:.?+=&%@!\-]| $ ))',
Regexp::EXTENDED)
AT_REGEXP = Regexp.new('@[\w.@_-]+', Regexp::EXTENDED)
```

The `Status` class is quite simple compared with the `User` class; its main property is the status text, which we define to be of length 140 characters.

```
property :text, String, :length => 140
```

We also define the creation time of the status; this is important as we always sort the statuses in reverse chronological order.

```
property :created_at,  DateTime
```

Just as a user owns multiple statuses, we define the reverse relationship here and let the application know that a status belongs to a single user (this is the user that created the status).

```
belongs_to :user
```

Each status that is a direct message also belongs to a recipient.

```
belongs_to :recipient, :class_name => "User", :child_key =>
[:recipient_id]
```

Finally, each status can mention zero, one, or more users and has a many-to-many relationship with the user.

```
has n, :mentions
has n, :mentioned_users, :through => :mentions, :class_name => 'User',
:child_key => [:user_id]
```

Most of the logic processing in Tweetclone involves processing the tweet. Following typical object-oriented design, we place our logic in the `Status` class and add a `before` filter to process the tweet text prior to saving it to the database.

```
before :save do
  @mentions = []
  case
  when text.starts_with('D ')
    process_direct_message
  when text.starts_with('follow ')
    process_follow
  else
    process
  end
end
```

This block of code is executed when save is called. It methodically runs through the tweet to look for patterns in the tweet and calls various methods to process them accordingly. We implement the two common Twitter commands for sending direct messages and following users by interpreting the tweet that starts with *D* or *follow*.

When the tweet starts with *D*, we take the word after *D* and use that as the nickname of the user to send the direct message to. Then we clean up the text by removing *D* and the user nickname and run the catch-all `process` method.

```
def process_direct_message
  self.recipient = User.first(:nickname => self.text.split[1])
  self.text = self.text.split[2..-1].join(' ')
  process
end
```

When the tweet starts with *follow* we do the same thing. We get the nickname of the user to follow from the second word after *follow* and create a relationship between the owner of the status and the followed user. However, we stop processing at this point because we don't want to save the tweet (it's not really a tweet but a command to Tweetclone), so we throw a `halt` exception, which DataMapper will interpret, stopping the save from proceeding.

```
def process_follow
  Relationship.create(:user => User.first(:nickname => self.text.
split[1]), :follower => self.user)
  throw :halt
end
```

The `process` method contains the bulk of the logic to parse the tweet:

```
def process
  urls = self.text.scan(URL_REGEXP)
  urls.each { |url|
    tiny_url = open("http://tinyurl.com/api-create.php?url=#{url[0]}")
{|s| s.read}
    self.text.sub!(url[0], "<a href='#{tiny_url}'>#{tiny_url}</a>")
  }
  ats = self.text.scan(AT_REGEXP)
  ats.each { |at|
    user = User.first(:nickname => at[1,at.length])
    if user
      self.text.sub!(at, "<a href='/#{user.nickname}'>#{at}</a>")
      @mentions << Mention.new(:user => user, :status => self)
    end
  }
end
```

We also define a couple of regular expression constants that will be used to parse the tweets:

```
URL_REGEXP = Regexp.new('\b ((https?|telnet|gopher|file|wais|ftp) :
[\w/#~:.?+=&%@!\-] +?) (?=[.:?\-] * (?: [^\w/#~:.?+=&%@!\-]| $ ))',
Regexp::EXTENDED)
AT_REGEXP = Regexp.new('@[\w.@_-]+', Regexp::EXTENDED)
```

The first regular expression parses text looking for URLs while the second looks for any text that starts with @.

```
urls = self.text.scan(URL_REGEXP)
  urls.each { |url|
    tiny_url = open("http://tinyurl.com/api-create.php?url=#{url[0]}")
{|s| s.read}
    self.text.sub!(url[0], "<a href='#{tiny_url}'>#{tiny_url}</a>")>")
```

Using `URL_REGEXP`, we look for URLs and replace them with HTML anchor links to shortened URLs. For example, we might find:

```
http://maps.google.com/maps?f=q&source=s_q&hl=en&geocode=&q=singap
ore+flyer&vps=1&jsv=169c&sll=1.352083,103.819836&sspn=0.68645,1.38
2904&g=singapore&ie=UTF8&latlng=8354962237652576151&ei=Shh3SsSRDpb
4vAPsxLS3BQ&cd=1&usq=Singapore+Flyer
```

We would replace it with:

```
<a href=' http://tinyurl.com/mc42ar'> http://tinyurl.com/mc42ar</a>
```

This uses TinyURL's API, which simply produces a shortened URL when we pass it a long URL.

```
ats = self.text.scan(AT_REGEXP)
  ats.each { |at|
    user = User.first(:nickname => at[1,at.length])
    if user
      self.text.sub!(at, "<a href='/#{user.nickname}'>#{at}</a>")
      @mentions << Mention.new(:user => user)
    end
  }
```

Similarly, we use `AT_REGEXP` to look for mentions (such as `@tom`) and for each one of them we replace it with a link to their displayed statuses. We also create a Mention link from the parsed user to the status. For example, if we find `@tom` in the tweet, we will replace it with:

```
<a href='/tom'>@tom</a>
```

This also creates a Mention that links up the user Tom to this status.

Observant readers might notice that we created a `@mention` instance variable array at the start of the `before` filter and we're actually placing all created mentions into this array. Also, by calling the constructor for Mention instead of DataMapper's `create` method we are only creating Mention Ruby objects, and not actual database records. In any case, we're only passing the user object to the constructor and not the status. So we're not saving the Mention objects to the database yet, but why?

It is because the Status objects are not created yet (remember — we're still executing in the `before` filter), and any actual creation of the Mention objects will only link to `nil` when it comes to the Status object. Saving the link to the database will not work.

To overcome this, we store the Mention objects created during processing in the `@mention` instance variable, then run it through an `after` filter. The `after` filter will only run after Status is saved successful, so we can now safely create the Mention links to the users.

```
after :save do
    unless @mentions.nil?
      @mentions.each {|m|
        m.status = self
        m.save
      }
    end
  end
```

Building the application flow

Now that we have the data model in place and most of the processing logic, the next step is to build the application routing flow. We categorized the various application flows by functions, and we start with the important task of authenticating the users first.

In Sinatra, a *route* is an HTTP method paired with an URL matching pattern. Each route is associated with a block as shown in the following code snippet:

```
get '/' do
  .. show something ..
end

post '/' do
  .. create something ..
end
```

```
put '/' do
  .. update something ..
end

delete '/' do
  .. destroy something ..
end
```

The block associated with the route is known as the *route handler*. We have placed most of the routes and their associated handlers in a single source file called `tweetclone.rb`. However, we have also defined another source file called `helpers.rb` that contains all the Sinatra helper methods. `helpers.rb` is loaded from `tweetclone.rb`.

 You might be wondering what a Sinatra helper method is? Helper methods are re-usable methods used in route handlers and templates. Helper methods are installed into the `Sinatra::EventContext` so you can use them in the route handlers as well as the templates. In this chapter we use helper methods for common and reusable functions in the route handlers and the view templates.

Authenticating and managing users

As mentioned during the design section, we will be using RPX to authenticate users. This reduces the amount of work needed tremendously. Let's describe what will happen. The first and most basic route is the *index* route or /. If the user is already logged in and has a session, we will redirect him to his home page. Otherwise, we will prepare the token for RPX, which is a URL that RPX can call after it successfully authenticates the user.

```
get '/' do
  if session[:userid].nil? then
    @token = "http://#{env['HTTP_HOST']}/after_login"
    haml :login
  else
    redirect "/#{User.get(session[:userid]).nickname}"
  end
end
```

We use Haml for the view templates. As before (and therefore we will not show it again) we define a layout Haml template that will be used in all views, separate from the template below, which contains only the content. Sinatra looks for all view templates in a folder called `views` by default. Our login Haml template, called `login.haml` is found in the same place.

```
.span-24.top-padding.last
  .span-4.prepend-3
    %img.span-4{:src => '/sheep.gif'}
  .span-12
    %h1.title Tweetclone
    %h2.comic Cloning is the sincerest form of flattery
  .span-2.last
    %a.rpxnow{:onclick => "return false;", :href => "https://
tweetclone.rpxnow.com/openid/v2/signin?token_url=#{@token}" }
      %h3 Sign In

  -if flash[:error]
    .span-24.last
      .error
        = flash[:error]

  %hr.space

  .span-14.prepend-5
    %h2.alt

%script{:src => "https://rpxnow.com/openid/v2/widget", :type => "text/
javascript"}
%script{:type => "text/javascript"}
  RPXNOW.overlay = true;
  RPXNOW.language_preference = 'en';
```

Let's look at the code in detail. First of all, we need to embed the RPX Javascript to enable RPX authentication with Google.

```
%script{:src => "https://rpxnow.com/openid/v2/widget", :type => "text/
javascript"}
%script{:type => "text/javascript"}
  RPXNOW.overlay = true;
  RPXNOW.language_preference = 'en';
```

Next, we add an HTML anchor link that redirects us to RPX, passing in the token.

```
%a.rpxnow{:onclick => "return false;", :href => "https://tweetclone.
rpxnow.com/openid/v2/signin?token_url=#{@token}" }
```

This will redirect the user to the RPX site, which in turn redirects the user to the appropriate provider, in our case, Google. On completing authentication, RPX will call on Tweetclone at the URL (`after_login`) that was provided earlier on. RPX passes a `token` parameter to us in this call, which we will use to retrieve the user's profile.

We will define a separate helper method to do the work of retrieving the user's profile. All such methods are placed in the `helpers.rb` file:

```
def get_user_profile_with(token)
  response = RestClient.post 'https://rpxnow.com/api/v2/auth_info',
'token' => token, 'apiKey' => '<RPX API key>', 'format' => 'json',
'extended' => 'true'
  json = JSON.parse(response)
  return json['profile'] if json['stat'] == 'ok'
  raise LoginFailedError, 'Cannot log in. Try another account!'
end
```

We use the very useful Rest-Client library to easily send the POST request to RPX, passing in the token and requesting the information back in JSON format. If successful, RPX will return some information on the users, which we will use the Ruby JSON library to parse and return. Let's look at the *after_login* route next.

```
post '/after_login' do
  profile = get_user_profile_with params[:token]
  user = User.find(profile['identifier'])
  if user.new_record?
    photo = profile ['email'] ? "http://www.gravatar.com/
avatar/#{Digest::MD5.hexdigest(profile['email'])}" : profile['photo']
    unless user.update_attributes({:nickname => profile['identifier'].
hash.to_s(36), :email => profile['email'], :photo_url => photo,
:provider => profile['provider']})
      flash[:error] = user.errors.values.join(',')
      redirect "/"
    end
    session[:userid] = user.id
    redirect '/change_profile'
  else
    session[:userid] = user.id
    redirect "/#{user.nickname}"
  end
end
```

After getting the user profile from Google through RPX, we try to retrieve the user from our database, using the unique OpenID identifier. As mentioned before, if the user does not exist in Tweetclone yet, we'll create a new record. If it's a new record, we will update the rest of the attributes from the profile. This includes a photo link from Gravatar.

Gravatar uses e-mail addresses that are hashed using MD5 to uniquely identify a user's avatar. Since a user can have multiple e-mail addresses, he can have multiple avatars. However, in this case we're using only Google as the authentication provider and a user with a Google account must have an e-mail account as well, so it ends up that the Gravatar link created is always valid:

```
photo = profile ['email'] ? "http://www.gravatar.com/
avatar/#{Digest::MD5.hexdigest(profile['email'])}" : profile['photo']
```

Note that we can optionally take from the photo link if it is provided in the profile though Gmail doesn't provide that as of date. So what happens if the user is not a Gravatar user and therefore doesn't have a Gravatar avatar? In this case Gravatar returns a default avatar that looks like the following figure:

You will also notice that we set the nickname here as well. We hash the identifier returned by Google and convert it into an alphanumeric string, which we use as the nickname. This means if a user did not change his/her nickname later, this will be his/her nickname. Finally we set `session[:user_id]` with the user ID and redirect the user to change his/her profile.

The *profile* and *change_profile* routes do very little other than redirecting to their respective views. You might notice that the profile route uses a method called `load_users`, which takes in the user ID.

```
get '/change_profile' do  haml :change_profile end
get '/profile' do
  load_users(session[:userid])
  haml :profile
end
```

load_users is a convenient method found in `helpers.rb`. It retrieves the User object and also sets a few commonly used variables.

```
def load_users(id)
  @myself = User.get(id)
  @user = @myself
end
```

More security-minded users would realize that this is not very secured because the user ID is stored in the session. Also, anyone can game this clone by just using any user ID. In other words there are possible security holes. One of the ways to patch this particular hole is to use random unique session IDs that will shield the user ID and other application information. However, as mentioned in Chapter 1, we will not be dealing with such issues in this book. Repeating the caveat in Chapter 1, the code in this book is not production ready and is not intended to be. Anyone looking at simply taking the code in this book and using it in their application should be aware that the code in the clones only considered basic functional requirements and not issues relating to production quality software.

The *change_profile* route does the actual work of saving any changes on the user profile. You will realize that we don't actually change any information that is in the Google account itself; we're only changing our own data. In fact the user needs to go to Google to change his password. There are pros and cons to this approach. We trade off the complexities and risks of managing a user (in terms of security and privacy) for the downside of not owning your own user information and being dependent on another company for your users. In the case of Tweetclone it's a good trade-off since we still get some user information and there's a lot less code and risk to manage.

```
post '/save_profile' do
  user = load_users(session[:userid])
  unless user.update_attributes(:nickname => params[:nickname],
:formatted_name => params[:formatted_name], :location =>
params[:location], :description => params[:description])
    flash[:error] = user.errors.values.join(',')
    redirect '/change_profile'
  end
  redirect "/#{user.nickname}"
end
```

Finally, the logout route simply resets `session[:user_id]` and redirects the user back to the index route. Without the user ID, the index route shows the login view.

```
get '/logout' do
  session[:userid] = nil
  redirect '/'
end
```

Displaying and updating statuses

The main feature of Tweetclone, as in Twitter, is to post status updates and to display them. The main route for this is the *home* route (`/:nickname`). This is what the index route redirects to upon login. It shows the home page of the user and also a view of any other users that he/she is interested in.

```
get '/:nickname' do
  load_users(session[:userid])
  @user = @myself.nickname == params[:nickname] ? @myself : User.
first(:nickname => params[:nickname])
  @message_count = message_count
  if @myself == @user then
    @statuses = @myself.displayed_statuses
    haml :home
  else
    @statuses = @user.statuses
    haml :user
  end
end
```

We also need to get a count of direct messages that have been send to the user so we use another helper method in the `helpers.rb` file.

 Ruby on Rails developers might be puzzled when we refer to helpers here but they are not used the same way as Rails helpers. Rails helpers are methods used in views only, but Sinatra helpers can be used in routes and views alike; in a way Sinatra helpers are more powerful than Rails helpers.

Here we return the count of statuses that have a recipient who is the user (messages sent to the user) as well as statuses that the owner (that is sender) is the user.

```
def message_count
  Status.count(:recipient_id => session[:userid]) + Status.
count(:user_id => session[:userid], :recipient_id.not => nil) || 0
end
```

After loading the current user, we determine if the user is looking at himself/herself or at another user.

```
@user = @myself.nickname == params[:nickname] ? @myself : User.
first(:nickname => params[:nickname])
```

If he/she is looking at himself/herself, we will show him/her the home page (home. haml) with a list of displayed statuses. Otherwise we will show the user page (user. haml) with the viewed user's statuses. Remember that displayed_statuses retrieve the user's own tweets and also the tweets of any user he follows while statuses will only retrieve that particular user's own tweets.

```
if @myself == @user then
    @statuses = @myself.displayed_statuses
    haml :home
  else
    @statuses = @user.statuses
    haml :user
  end
```

Let's look at the home page first.

```
=snippet :'snippets/top'
.span-15.append-1
  =snippet :'snippets/update_box'
  %h2.comic Home
  =snippet :'snippets/statuses'
.span-5
  =snippet :'snippets/info_box'
.span-2.last
```

Well, it's that simple. We re-use snippets of common Haml code that are stored in the /views/snippets folder. This is basically the partial templates mechanism that is popularly used in many web frameworks. Although Sinatra does not support partials directly, it's very easy to re-create simple partials support by adding the following helper method:

```
def snippet(page, options={})
  haml page, options.merge!(:layout => false)
end
```

Again, yes, that's it! We simply run haml again on the given page, and include any parameters we pass to it, only telling the haml page not to use the default layout.

Let's look at the various snippets we're using in the home page. The top snippet is trivial, it's just a re-used Haml template for all logged in users to show the banner and the top-level menu.

```
.span-2
  %img{:src => '/sheephead.gif'}
.span-12
  %a{:href => '/'}
```

```
%h2.banner Tweetclone
.span-4.prepend-3.last
  %a{:href => '/'} [ home ]
  %a{:href => '/profile'} [ profile ]
  %a{:href => '/logout'} [ logout ]
```

The update_box snippet provides the user with a form and a text box to enter his tweet.

```
=snippet :'/snippets/text_limiter_js'
%h2.comic What are you doing?
%form{:method => 'post', :action => '/update'}
  %textarea.update.span-15#update{:name => 'status', :rows => 2,
:onKeyDown => "text_limiter($('#update'), $('#counter'))"}
  .span-6
    %span#counter
      140
    characters left
  .prepend-12
    %input#button{:type => 'submit', :value => 'update'}
```

The output of the snippet looks like the following:

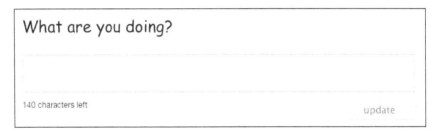

The *update_box* snippet also uses the *text_limiter_js* snippet to limit the text box to 140 characters.

```
:javascript
  function text_limiter(field,counter_field) {
    limit = 139;
    if (field.val().length > limit)
      field.val(field.val().substring(0, limit));
    else
      counter_field.text(limit - field.val().length);
  }
```

Although nominally a Haml file, in reality it is a Javascript function in disguise. Next we have the *statuses* snippet, which displays a list of statuses.

```
.statuses
  -@statuses.each do |status|
    %hr
    .span-2
      %img.span-2{:src => "#{status.user.photo_url}"}
    .span-10
      %a{:href => "/#{status.user.nickname}"}
        =status.user.nickname
       
      =status.text
    .span-3.last
      %a{:href =>"#", :onclick => "$('#update').
attr('value','@#{status.user.nickname} ');$('#update').focus();"}
(reply)
      %br
      %a{:href =>"#", :onclick => "$('#update').attr('value','D
#{status.user.nickname} ');$('#update').focus();"} (message)
      %br
      %a{:href =>"#", :onclick => "$('#update').attr('value','RT
@#{status.user.nickname}: #{status.text} ');$('#update').focus();"}
(retweet)

    %em.quiet
      =time_ago_in_words(status.created_at.to_time)
    %hr.space
```

Each status in the statuses snippet contains:

- An avatar of the user who posted that status
- That user's nickname and a link to his user page
- The text of the status
- A link to allow you to reply to that user
- A link to allow you to send a direct message to that user
- A link to retweet the status
- An indication of when that status was posted

This is how a single status update looks:

The links to reply, send direct message, and re-tweet are just shortcuts that pre-populate the update text box. For the reply link, this will place @ and the user's nickname in the text box. For the direct message link, this will place *D* followed by the user's nickname and for re-tweet, this will place *RT* then the whole status into the text box.

As for the time the status was posted, to create the friendly *time ago* text, we use a helper method to format the time accordingly:

```ruby
def time_ago_in_words(timestamp)
  minutes = (((Time.now - timestamp).abs)/60).round
  return nil if minutes < 0
  case minutes
  when 0                then 'less than a minute ago'
  when 0..4             then 'less than 5 minutes ago'
  when 5..14            then 'less than 15 minutes ago'
  when 15..29           then 'less than 30 minutes ago'
  when 30..59           then 'more than 30 minutes ago'
  when 60..119          then 'more than 1 hour ago'
  when 120..239         then 'more than 2 hours ago'
  when 240..479         then 'more than 4 hours ago'
  else                  timestamp.strftime('%I:%M %p %d-%b-%Y')
  end
end
```

Finally, we look at the *info_box* snippet, which is a right sidebar component that is found in a few other pages.

```haml
.span-2
  %a
    %img.span-2{:src => "#{@myself.photo_url}"}
.span-3.last
  .span-3
    %em #{@myself.nickname}
  .span-3
    %a{:href => '/follows'} #{@user.follows.count} following
  .span-3
```

```
   %a{:href => '/followers'} #{@user.followers.count} followers
   .span-3
     %a{:href => "/tweets"} #{@user.statuses.count} tweets
%hr.space
%a{:href => '/replies'}
  ="@#{@myself.nickname}"
%br
.span-4
  Direct messages
.span-1.last
  #{@message_count}
.span-5.last
  %a{:href => '/messages/sent'} [sent]
  %a{:href => '/messages/received'} [received]
%hr.space
.span-5.last
  %h3.comic Follows
  -@user.follows.each do |follow|
    %a{:href => "/#{follow.nickname}"}
      %img.smallpic{:src => "#{follow.photo_url}", :width => '24px',
:alt => "#{follow.nickname}"}
```

The sidebar shows the following information on the user:

- The user's avatar.

- The user's nickname.

- The number of users this user is following. This is a link to the list of users he/she follows.

- The number of users who follow this user. This is a link to the list of his/her followers.

- The number of tweets this user has posted. This is also a link to a list of his/her tweets.

- A list of tweets mentioning the user.

- The number of direct messages that the user has sent or received.

- A link to the list of direct messages the user has sent.

- A link to the list of direct messages the user has received.

- Avatars of users this user follows.

This is how the sidebar looks:

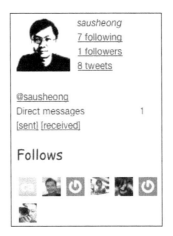

The snippet is quite self-explanatory so we won't go into it any further. We're done with the home page, so let's look at the other page the home route redirects to.

Unlike the home page, there are fewer re-usable codes in the user page, so there are more lines of code.

```
=snippet :'/snippets/top'
.span-15.prepend-2
  .span-2
    %img.span-2{:src => "#{@user.photo_url}"}
  .span-13.last
    %h1
      =@user.nickname
    -if @user != @myself
      -if @myself.follows.include? @user·
        %form{:method => 'post', :action => "/follow/#{@myself.
id}/#{@user.id}"}
          %input{:type => 'hidden', :name => '_method', :value =>
'delete'}
          %input#button{:type => 'submit', :value => 'unfollow'}
      -else
        %input#button{:type => 'button', :value => 'follow',
:onclick => "location.href='/follow/#{@user.nickname}'"}
  .span-15
    %h2
```

```
      =@user.statuses.pop.text unless @user.statuses.empty?
    %em.quiet
        =time_ago_in_words(@user.statuses.last.created_at.to_time)
unless @user.statuses.empty?
    %hr.space
    -@user.statuses.reverse.each do |status|
      %hr
      .span-2
        %img.span-2{:src => "#{status.user.photo_url}"}
      .span-10
        %a{:href => "/#{status.user.nickname}"}
          =status.user.nickname
        %hr.space
        =status.text
      %em.quiet
        =time_ago_in_words(status.created_at.to_time)
      %hr.space
.span-5
  .span-5.last (Name):#{@user.formatted_name}
  .span-5.last (Location): #{@user.location}
  .span-5.last (Bio):#{@user.description}
  .span-5.last
    %br
    #{@user.follows.count} following
    %br
    #{@user.followers.count} followers
    %br
    #{@user.statuses.count} tweets

  %hr.space
  .span-5.reset
    %h3
      Follows
    -@user.follows.each do |follow|
      %a{:href => "/#{follow.nickname}"}
        %img.smallpic{:src => "#{follow.photo_url}", :width => '24px',
:alt => "#{follow.nickname}"}
```

From the following screenshot you will notice that the user page has about the same layout as the home page but with less information. The one big difference is of course that the list of statuses belongs to only that user, and there is a big **follow** button for the viewing user to follow him. Also, instead of the update box, we have the last tweet posted by that user in larger font.

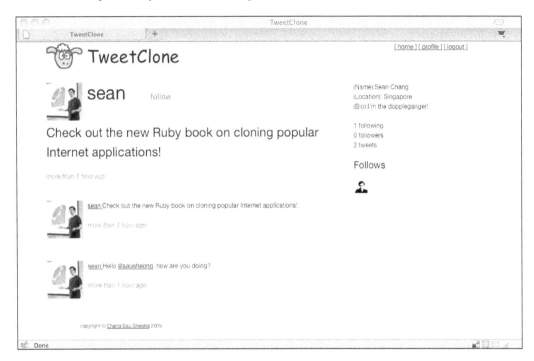

To post status updates, the user submits a post form to the *update* route. The route then takes in the status text and creates the Status object. Note that when the Status object is created and saved, the various processing logic in the `before` filter is called and executed. After the status is saved to the database, the user is redirected back to the home page, clearing the update text box.

```
post '/update' do
  user = User.get(session[:userid])
  Status.create(:text => params[:status], :user => user)
  redirect "/#{user.nickname}"
end
```

The rest of the status update and display routes are relatively simple. The *replies* route returns a list of statuses that mention the user and the logic is already in the models so there is little to do except to retrieve the data and send it to the replies page.

```
get '/replies' do
  load_users(session[:userid])
  @statuses = @myself.mentioned_statuses || []
  @message_count = message_count
  haml :replies
end
```

The replies page is rather simple as well.

```
=snippet :'snippets/top'
.span-15.append-1
  =snippet :'snippets/update_box'
  %h2.comic Tweets mentioning me
  =snippet :'snippets/statuses'
.span-5
  =snippet :'snippets/info_box'
.span-2.last
```

You might notice that the replies page is almost the same as the home page. The *tweets* route also does the same thing, except that it passes the statuses to the user page instead of the home page.

```
get '/tweets' do
  load_users(session[:userid])
  @status = @myself.statuses
  haml :user
end
```

Finally the *public_timeline* route is a simple implementation that retrieves all statuses from the database and shows them on a page that does not require any data from a logged in user.

```
get '/public_timeline' do
  @statuses = Status.all
  haml :public_timeline
end
```

This is the page for the public timeline:

```
.span-2
  %img{:src => '/sheephead.gif'}
.span-12
  %a{:href => '/'}
```

```
    %h2.banner Tweetclone
.span-4.prepend-3.last
  %a{:href => '/'} [ login ]
.span-15.append-1
  %h2.comic Recent Public Tweets
  .statuses
    -@statuses.reverse,each do |status|
      %hr
      .span-2
        %img.span-2{:src => "#{status.user.photo_url}"}
      .span-13.last
        %a{:href => "/#{status.user.nickname}"}
          =status.user.nickname
         
        =status.text
      %em.quiet
        =time_ago_in_words(status.created_at.to_time)
    %hr.space
.span-5
   
.span-2.last
```

Sending and displaying direct messages

Next we will look at how Tweetclone sends and displays direct messages. To recap, direct messages are stored in Tweetclone as statuses and the only difference between direct messages and a normal status is that it has a recipient (that is, it is directed at someone).

To display messages, we create the *get messages* route:

```
get '/messages/:direction' do
  load_users(session[:userid])
  @friends = @myself.follows & @myself.followers
  case params[:direction]
  when 'received' then @messages = Status.all(:recipient_id => @
myself.id); @label = "Direct messages sent only to you"
  when 'sent'    then @messages = Status.all(:user_id => @myself.id,
:recipient_id.not => nil); @label = "Direct messages you've sent"
  end
  @message_count = message_count
  haml :messages
end
```

First, we get a list of the user's *friends*, that is, a list of users who follow this user and whom this user also follows. This is simply the intersection of the *follows* list and the *followers* list. We will use this later to provide a list of users whom we can send messages to.

```
@friends = @myself.follows & @myself.followers
```

Then we check the requested direction. The direction parameter is used to determine if we want to display the user's sent messages or received messages. If we want the received messages, we retrieve all statuses which recipient is the user.

```
when 'received' then @messages = Status.all(:recipient_id => @myself.
id); @label = "Direct messages sent only to you"
```

If we want to display the user's sent messages, we retrieve all statuses that are owned by the user and have a recipient.

```
when 'sent'      then @messages = Status.all(:user_id => @myself.id,
:recipient_id.not => nil); @label = "Direct messages you've sent"
```

Once we have the messages, we send them to the view template.

```
=snippet :'snippets/top'
.span-15.append-1
  =snippet :'snippets/send_box'
  %h2.comic #{@label}
  =snippet :'snippets/messages'
.span-5
  =snippet :'snippets/info_box'
.span-2.last
```

As in the home page, it is made of reusable snippets. The two snippets that are different from the home page are the *send_box* snippet and the *message* snippet. The *send_box* snippet allows the user to send direct messages.

```
=snippet :'/snippets/text_limiter_js'
%form{:method => 'post', :action => '/message/send'}
  %h3
    Send
    %select{:name => 'recipient'}
      -@friends.each do |user|
        %option{:value => user.nickname} #{user.nickname}
    a message:
  %textarea.update.span-15#message{:name => 'message', :rows => 2,
:onKeyDown => "text_limiter($('#message'), $('#counter'))"}
```

```
.span-6
  %span#counter
    140
  characters left
.prepend-12
  %input#button{:type => 'submit', :value => 'send'}
```

We reuse the *text_limiter_js* snippet to limit the size of the direct message. We also provide a drop-down list box of friends whom the user can send to.

```
Send
  %select{:name => 'recipient'}
    -@friends.each do |user|
      %option{:value => user.nickname} #{user.nickname}
```

This is how the send message box looks:

The form will send a post to the *send message* route, which will create a Status object with the recipient passed in and redirect to the get messages route with the *sent* direction.

```
post '/message/send' do
  recipient = User.first(:nickname => params[:recipient])
  Status.create(:text => params[:message], :user => User.
get(session[:userid]), :recipient => recipient)
  redirect '/messages/sent'
end
```

Finally, the *messages* snippet is similar to the statuses snippet except it is focused on sending direct messages only.

```
.messages
  -@messages.each do |message|
    %hr
    .span-2
      %img.span-2{:src => "#{message.recipient.photo_url}"}
    .span-10
      %a{:href => "/#{message.recipient.nickname}"}
```

```
      =message.recipient.nickname
     
      =message.text
    .span-3.last
      %a{:href =>"#", :onclick => "$('#message').attr('value','D
#{message.recipient.nickname} ');$('#message').focus();"} (reply)
      %hr.space
      .span-13.pull-10.last
        %em.quiet
          =time_ago_in_words(message.created_at.to_time)
    %hr.space
```

Showing and forming relationships

Let's look at routes for showing and forming relationships next. Users related to each other through a *follow* relationship. If a user Tom follows you, he is your *follower*. Getting a list of your followers is quite simple; it's already in the User object, we just need to call the `followers` method to return a list of your followers.

```
get '/followers' do
  load_users(session[:userid])
  @users = @myself.followers
  @message_count = message_count
  haml :followers
end
```

The followers page then displays the list of followers.

```
=snippet :'snippets/top'
.span-15.append-1
  %h2.comic Your #{@users.count} followers.
  =snippet :'snippets/follow_users'
.span-5
  =snippet :'snippets/info_box'
.span-2.last
```

As before, we re-use some snippets and include the *follow_users* snippet here.

```
.users
  -@users.each do |user|
    %hr
    .span-2
      %img.span-2{:src => "#{user.photo_url}"}
      .small #{user.nickname}
    .span-10
      %a{:href => "/#{user.nickname}"}
        %h3 #{user.formatted_name} | #{user.location}
      =user.description
```

This snippet iterates the list of users retrieved by the *follower* route and displays their avatars and some profile information. In the same way, the *follows* route retrieves all users that the user follows and displays them in the *follows* page.

```
get '/follows' do
  load_users(session[:userid])
  @users = @myself.follows
  @message_count = message_count
  haml :follows
end
```

This is the *follows* page:

```
=snippet :'snippets/top'
.span-15.append-1
  %h2.comic You follow #{@users.count} people.
  =snippet :'snippets/follow_users'
.span-5
  =snippet :'snippets/info_box'
.span-2.last
```

As you can see the both the route and the page for both follower and follows routes are very similar. So why didn't we refactor them and combine them like in the get direct messages route? There is a specific reason for this. We didn't combine the route handlers because we wanted to explicitly show that there are two different routes. However, we could have both routes but still combine them in a single route handler except for the second reason.

As explain during the design section, the follow relationship is not reciprocal—if you follow someone it doesn't mean that he will follow you in return. In other words, the relationship is one-way only and a *friend* relationship is only formed when two one-way relationships are formed. This also means in terms of designing the application, the logic and flow of the application could be different for a follow and a follower relationship. This is why the route handlers are separated—it is to make the relationships clearly different, and also to allow flexibility of having separate routing logic in the future. Although this flexibility is not necessary in Tweetclone itself, it is good to remember that the design and implementation of any application should have the flow and relationship models clearly in mind.

In addition to clicking the button, we also provide a means to follow a user directly from the URL. For example, to follow a user with the nickname *tom* we go to the URL address `http://tweetclone.saush.com/follow/tom`. This is the create follow route.

```
get '/follow/:nickname' do
  user = User.first(:nickname => params[:nickname])
  rel = Relationship.first(:user => user :follower => @myself)
  Relationship.create(:user => user, :follower =>@myself) unless rel
  redirect "/#{params[:nickname]}"
end
```

Similarly, to delete a *follows* relationship, we pass in the follower ID and the ID of the user being followed to the *delete follow* route.

```
delete '/follow/:follower_id/:user_id' do
  Relationship.first(:follower_id => params[:follower_id], :user_id =>
params[:user_id]).destroy if @myself.id == :user_id
  redirect "/"
end
```

For example, if Tom currently follows Waldo but Tom wants to *unfollow* Waldo, we send an HTTP DELETE request to the URL address `http://tweetclone.saush.com/tom/waldo` to remove that *follow* relationship.

Notice that we did not do anything to secure the usage of these features. To re-iterate what was mentioned earlier, the code in this chapter and in the whole book has only feature considerations and not security or exception handling.

We're all done with the Tweetclone UI features. Let's move on to the API next.

Implementing the API

The first thing to realize when implementing APIs is that the consumers of the API are not end-users themselves but developers who use these APIs to build applications that interact with the end-users. As a result it is important to understand that the calls from to the APIs are probably not from the browser but a HTTP client library.

In Tweetclone we place all API routes in a file appropriately named `api.rb`, which is loaded from the main file `tweetclone.rb`. Before we jump into discussing the APIs themselves, it's important to discuss how these APIs are protected.

Many APIs use an industrial strength open specification called OAuth discussed in an earlier section. However, using OAuth can be a daunting task for beginners and as explained earlier, one of the possible reasons why Twitter APIs were so successful is that they allowed a simpler authentication method, the HTTP Basic Access Authentication. For Tweetclone we will follow Twitter's implementation of HTTP Basic Access Authentication.

> HTTP Basic Access Authentication is an authentication scheme that was first defined along with the HTTP/1.0 specification in RFC 1945 and further described in RFC 2616 (Hypertext Transfer Protocol – HTTP/1.1) and RFC 2617 (HTTP Authentication: Basic and Digest Access Authentication). It is a simple authentication mechanism that uses base64 encoding to send credentials to the server for validation. A typical HTTP basic access authentication flow goes like this:
>
> 1. The browser requests for a page from the server
>
>   If the page is protected by the HTTP basic access authentication, the server will send a *401 Not Found* response and the authentication realm such as the response header will contain this:
>
>   `WWW-Authenticate: Basic realm="Secure Area"`
>
>   The browser shows the authentication realm in a popup box, requesting for the username and password
>
> 2. When the user enters the username and password, the browser sends the same request again but this time it will add the header:
>
>   `Authorization: Basic <base-64 encoded`
>   `combination of username:password>`
>
> The server decodes the base-64 encoded *username:password* combination and determines if the username and password is correct. If it is, the server returns the protected resource, otherwise it will send another *401 Not Found* response.
>
> There are a few marked disadvantages in basic access authentication. Base-64 encoding is very easily decoded. In fact encoding it with base-64 is meant to convert non-HTTP compliant characters to HTTP compliant characters only. To avoid snooping on the network and finding out the username and password, HTTP basic access authentication is usually done over SSL, for example with HTTPS (though Twitter doesn't do this). Also another problem with HTTP basic access authentication is that once a user is logged in, there isn't the means provided by HTTP for the user to log out.

The mechanism works this way—all routes that need to be protected will call a helper method called `protected!` before anything else. This method responds to the client with a *401 Not Authorized* status code as well as a *WWW-Authenticate* header and the authentication realm, unless the client is already authorized.

```
def protected!
  response['WWW-Authenticate'] = %(Basic realm="Tweetclone") and
  throw(:halt, [401, "Not authorized\n"]) and
  return unless authorized?
end
```

We check the authorization by getting a new instance of Rack's basic access authentication request and making sure that it's really HTTP basic access authentication and that credentials are provided. Then we run a check on the authorization credentials.

```
def authorized?
  @auth ||= Rack::Auth::Basic::Request.new(request.env)
  @auth.provided? && @auth.basic? && @auth.credentials && check(@auth.
credentials)
end
```

The credentials are actually passed in as an array. Using Ruby's splat operator we extract the e-mail and password. Using the e-mail we retrieve the User from the database. Next we use RestClient and post a request to Google's ClientLogin account authentication, passing in the e-mail and the password. Google will respond to us with a HTTP response with some content in its body. While we can parse the response body to get more information, we really only want to check if the user and password combination is valid. To do this we just check and make sure the server returned a 200 OK. If that's the case, we will execute the rest of the code in the route.

```
def check(credentials)
  email, password = *credentials
  return false unless User.first(:email => email)
  response = RestClient.post 'https://www.google.com/accounts/
ClientLogin', 'accountType' => 'GOOGLE', 'Email' => email, 'Passwd' =>
password, :service => 'xapi', :source => Tweetclone'
  response.code == 200
end
```

As mentioned during the design section, we will only implement three functions:

- Get a user's status timeline
- Get everyone's status timeline
- Allow the user to post a status update

The routes for these functions are very simple. For the *user timeline* API route, we just extract the e-mail from the authentication credentials using the splat operator again. Then with the e-mail we extract the User as before, and then ask it to return a list of displayed statuses.

```
get '/api/statuses/user_timeline' do
  protected!
  email = *@auth.credentials
  user = User.first(:email => email)
  user.displayed_statuses.to_json if user
end
```

Note that the to_json method is called on the user's displayed statuses. Because we included the JSON gem in the definition, we can call to_json on objects. However, while the JSON gem recognizes standard Ruby classes, it doesn't recognize our specific classes like User or Status. To enable a JSON view of the Status object, we add a to_json method in the Status object.

```
def to_json(*a)
    {'id' => id, 'text' => text, 'created_at' => created_at, 'user' =>
user.nickname}.to_json(*a)
end
```

This simple method basically creates an array that describes the Status object, running to_json on it and returning the Status in JSON format. The *public_timeline* API route is even simpler; it simply returns all Status objects.

```
get '/api/statuses/public_timeline' do
  protected!
  Status.all.to_json
end
```

Finally, posting an update is very similar to getting a status. In this case we require the client to use HTTP POST instead of a HTTP GET. We extract the user first, and using the user and the text that is passed in, we create a Status object. If all goes well we stop here, otherwise we throw a halt and stop processing.

```
post '/api/statuses/update' do
  protected!
  email = *@auth.credentials
  user = User.first(:email => email)
 throw(:halt, [400, "Bad Request\n"])unless user and Status.
create(:text => params[:text], :user => user)
end
```

This wraps up our small set of APIs. We've covered building a clone of Twitter with limited features. Next we will discuss the different ways we can deploy the clone.

Deploying the clone

As in the previous chapter, we will deploy to the local machine (your desktop or laptop) and then to Heroku. The steps are quite similar except for one or two minor differences.

Deploying locally

For development purposes we would normally run it off the command line using the built-in web server. However, before we do this, we need to set up the database. Let's assume that for this application we have installed MySQL. At the command line go into the MySQL interactive command console:

```
$ mysql -u <username> -p <password>
```

Then just do a simple:

```
mysql> create database tweetclone;
```

This will just create the database. Next, go into IRB and run the following command:

```
> require 'models'
```

This will require the necessary classes for creating the database tables. Next, just run the following command:

```
> DataMapper.auto_migrate!
```

This will create the tables for the application. To run the application, we just need to run this at the command line:

```
$ ruby tweetclone.rb
```

Then go to `http://localhost:4567/` and you will see the login page:

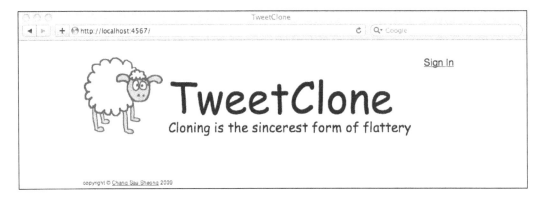

Try logging in. If you have added *localhost* to the list of applicable URLs in RPX you will be able to log in.

Deploying to the cloud

Alternatively we can also deploy to Heroku, the Ruby cloud-computing platform. As mentioned earlier, one of the simplest ways to scale your application is to let someone else do it for you. While ultimately a scalable Internet web application will probably need manual tweaking to squeeze out the performance, a painless and relatively cheap way of scaling is through using cloud platforms. Fortunately for Ruby developers there exists a simple-to-use cloud platform in Heroku.

Heroku provides a scalable platform, provisionless platform for Ruby developers. Heroku's platform is quite straightforward. The idea behind Heroku is that you upload a Ruby application into Heroku and it automatically deploys into EC2 and automatically scales.

Requests flow into Nginx used as a HTTP Reverse Proxy. Nginx then routes the requests into a Varnish based HTTP cache and injected into an Erlang based routing mesh that balances requests across a grid of 'dynos'. Dynos are a stack of: POSIX, Ruby VM, application server, Rack, middleware, framework, and finally the application itself. Applications are also provided with PostgreSQL and also memcached for persistence and caching respectively though nothing really stops us from persisting it outside of Heroku.

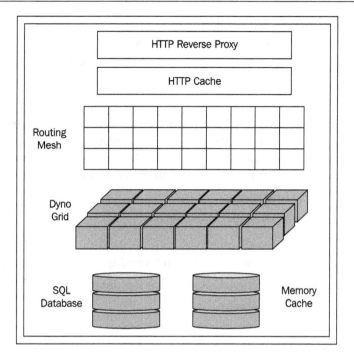

Deploying Sinatra applications to Heroku is very simple.

1. First, create a `config.ru` file. This is the Rack configuration file, which is actually just another Ruby script. All you need to have in this file is this:

    ```
    %w(sinatra tweetclone).each  {  |lib|  require lib}

    run Sinatra::Application
    ```

2. Install the Heroku gem. Then run the following command:

    ```
    $ sudo gem install heroku
    ```

    Heroku provides us with a set of useful tools packaged in a gem, very much like Capistrano.

3. Initialize an empty Git repository in the `tweetclone` folder:

    ```
    $ cd tweetclone
    tweetclone $ git init
    Initialized empty Git repository in .git/
    tweetclone $ git add .
    tweetclone $ git commit -m 'initial import'
    ```

    This just creates and initializes an empty git repository on your computer.

4. Create the Heroku application.

```
tinyclone $ heroku create tweetclone

Created http:// tweetclone.heroku.com/ | git@heroku.com: tweet-
clone.git

Git remote heroku added
```

You will be prompted for your username and password the first time you run a Heroku command. Subsequently this will be saved in `~/.heroku/credentials` and you won't be prompted anymore. It will also upload your public key to allow you to push and pull code.

5. Push your code to Heroku.

```
tweetclone$ git push heroku master
```

This will push your code and load your application into deployment. The application is now deployed, but you'll need to create the database as before.

6. Log in to the Heroku console and create the database

```
Tweetclone $ heroku console

Ruby console for tweetclone.heroku.com

>> DataMapper.auto_migrate!
```

Heroku allows you access to a console similar to IRB but with the environment of your deployment loaded up, just like `script/console` in Ruby on Rails. To create the database, just run `DataMapper.auto_migrate!` and it will create the database accordingly.

Tweetclone has just been deployed to the cloud. You can also change settings to point to a different domain. The final configuration of Tweetclone is at `http://tweetclone.saush.com`.

Summary

We have come a long way in this chapter. We ran through the history and ancestry of microblogs and also Twitter, the most popular microblog around. Then we jumped into the reasons why Twitter was so popular and also described the main features of Twitter.

Next, we went into designing a clone of Twitter, called Tweetclone. Tweetclone implemented most of the main features of Twitter, except for the search and search-related features, which will be covered in further depth in the chapter on search engines. This provided us with the outline and rationale of the application to be developed in the later section.

After the design we went into the implementation of Tweetclone. First we described and implemented the data model used in Tweetclone. Tweetclone consists of two major entities—the User and the Status. Next we described the flow of the application and how it is used. We went through authenticating and managing users, displaying and updating statuses, sending and displaying direct messages, and finally showing and forming relationships. After the application flow we went into how a simple set of APIs can be created for Tweetclone.

Finally we learnt how to deploy a Ruby cloud platform on a local machine as well as on Heroku.

4
Photo Sharing – Cloning Flickr

The World Wide Web was started as a means to share information amongst academics. While the original Web shared mostly text, the sharing of images came from the very roots of the World Wide Web. The original proposal of the HTML drafted in 1993 included the `img` tag that embeds images on the web page itself. From this basic lineage, photo sharing has become one of the most popular web services on the Internet as it became more commercial and mainstream.

In this chapter we will be creating a clone of Flickr, one of the most popular photo-sharing services around. We will start with a discussion on photo-sharing applications and then move on to the main features that make up such an application. After that we will proceed to design the application then show how it can be coded using the same technology stack we used in the previous chapters.

All about photo-sharing services

Photo sharing is one of the most popular services on the Internet and also one of its most useful services. Basically, photo sharing is about the uploading of digital photos by a user, to be shared with others either publicly or privately. The first photo-sharing applications appeared during the time when the World Wide Web itself was in its infancy, during the mid 1990s, but it was only after the dot-com bust that many of the current crop of photo-sharing applications started. One of the earliest photo-sharing applications is Webshots, which originated from a desktop screensaver software in 1995 and eventually migrated to the World Wide Web. Other popular photo-sharing services include Flickr, Photobucket, ImageShack, SmugMug, Snapfish, and Picasa, Google's photo-sharing service. In the past few years astonishingly (yet perhaps not) an entrant to the photo-sharing market is Facebook. As of writing, Facebook users upload an average of 3 billion photos every month and it is one of the largest photo-sharing applications around, despite being a new entrant.

Photo sharing as a market is pretty diverse and almost every one of the photo-sharing applications has its own signature strengths and focuses, so direct comparison is often meaningless. For example, while Facebook has many billions of images more than Flickr, its main premise is social networking while Flickr's main motivation is photo-sharing and social interaction through photos. As a result, Facebook doesn't allow sharing photos outside of Facebook users, and resizes all photos that are uploaded while Flickr allows anonymous sharing and viewing of photos and also maintains multiple sizes of the uploaded photo, including the original.

However, a good snapshot of popularity is through gauging the number of unique users of the service. We use Compete (`http://www.compete.com`) to analyse the number of users to the various popular photo-sharing applications. Note that we did not include Facebook in this comparison because it is impossible (without internal Facebook information) to determine from Compete the number of unique visitors to Facebook photos since they use a full URL to access their photo pages rather than a more general domain (such as `http://www.flickr.com`) or subdomain (such as `http://picasa.google.com`).

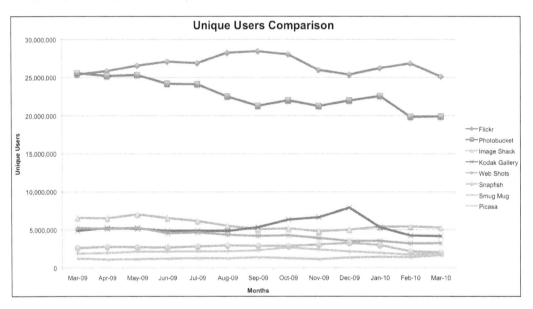

As we can see, Flickr ran closely with Photobucket for the honor of most popular photo-sharing application though for the past year or so, Photobucket seems to have fallen behind in the race. In this chapter we will be focusing on Flickr, one of the most popular and widely known photo-sharing applications around.

Flickr

Flickr was launched in February 2004 by Ludicorp, a Vancouver-based company. Flickr was originally created for Ludicorp's Game Neverending, a web-based massively multiplayer online game, but it became the main focus after the original project was shelved. In March 2005, Yahoo! acquired Ludicorp and Flickr and all content was migrated from servers in Canada to servers in the United States. On April 9, 2008, Flickr began to allow paid subscribers to upload videos, limited to 90 seconds in length and 150 MB in size. On March 2, 2009, Flickr added the ability to upload and view HD videos, and began allowing free users to upload normal-resolution video.

Flickr offers two types of accounts: Free and Pro. Free account users are allowed to upload 100 MB of images a month and two videos. If a free user has more than 200 photos on the site, they will only be able to see the most recent 200 in their photostream, though the photos uploaded are still there. Pro accounts allow users to upload an unlimited number of images and videos every month and receive unlimited bandwidth and storage.

Flickr uses tags to organize images and also sets, which are convenient categories that a photo can belong to. Sets may be grouped into collections, which can be nested. Photos in Flickr can be private to the user, private to family and friends or public to everyone, including anonymous viewers.

One of Flickr's stronger points is in the management of the copyright of the photos uploaded by its users. While many photo-sharing applications have little to no capabilities to manage the copyright of the uploaded photos, Flickr provides a friendly guide to both uploaders and viewers of photos to its site. Uploaders can choose copyright licenses that range from 'all rights reserved' to various combinations of Creative Commons licensing. As a result uploaders can choose to share their photos with various licences that are more assuring to viewers who fear that their activities might infringe any copyright materials.

Flickr focuses a lot on, and is very strong with, the user community. The social aspects of the site are probably the key features of Flickr. In fact, Flickr, at a certain level, can be considered as a social network that focuses on photos. Several features support this. Flickr has a concept of a *photostream*, which is a list of recent photos that have been uploaded and published to the site. Photostreams implies a need to continually take and upload photos and brings the sense of a photo blog to the site. In this sense, Flickr was designed to reward recent activity, something that is in line with the more recent social networks and microblogs such as Facebook and Twitter.

Main features

As in the previous chapter, before we jump into designing the clone, let's look at some major features of a photo-sharing application. Unlike in previous chapters, we will not list all major features of Flickr and clone those features. Instead, we will focus on a more generic photo-sharing application. However, the layout and design of the clone will reflect that of Flickr:

- Users can upload photos
- Users can create folders or albums to store photos
- Users can add title and captions to photos
- Users can comment on photos
- Photos can be annotated
- Photos have friendly URLs
- Photos can be publicly viewable by all or privately by the user only
- Photos can be edited and saved back to the site
- Users can share photos with other users through the site
- Users can share photos with anonymous users

As you might realize, the features are only a fraction of Flickr's features. However, the preceding features are enough to implement a no-frills photo-sharing application that provides respectable services.

Designing the clone

For this chapter, we will be building a no-frills photo-sharing application called *Photoclone*, hosted at the domain `http://photoclone.saush.com`.

Authentication, access control, and user management

Authentication and user management follow the similar route we went through in the Tweetclone. As before we will use RPX to proxy the third party authentication providers we want to use. However, unlike in Tweetclone we're not going to provide any APIs and therefore we're not going to use any client authentication. In this case we're not going to restrict ourselves to using Google's authentication mechanism as before.

This means that for user management, the functions are split between Google and Photoclone again. The functions to change their profile, manage their passwords, and generally secure their account lies with the authentication provider. However, Photoclone requires a user entity to manage the user-to-user relationships as well as photo ownership and therefore we store some user information in Photoclone. We also use the user information particularly the e-mail to get the avatar from Gravatar.

In Photoclone, access control is used to secure the user's right to view the photos. Photos can be public or private. Public photos are viewable by everyone while private photos can only be viewed by the owner/uploader. While Flickr has a concept of private for friends and family, Photoclone opts for a simpler design. If you follow a user, you will add his public photos in your shared photos list, basically a list of photos belonging to people you follow. This list is in the landing page (the page you 'land' on once you log in to the site). This allows you to have a clear view of the photos of people you follow.

Albums and photos

Photoclone uses a simple design to store and manage photos. An album is a container of photos. Each album belongs to a single user and can be shared through that user. Each album has a cover photo, which is the representative photo that is when displaying albums.

Uploading and storing photos

Uploading and storing photos properly is a critical part of any photo-sharing application. A good photo-sharing application should have a user-friendly photo uploading interface and speedy file transfer rates. This is especially true as digital cameras become more powerful and take pictures of larger sizes than ever.

Uploading for Photoclone is simple and follows a conventional HTML file upload format, which is a very familiar interface to most users. The upload page will allow six photos to be uploaded at the same time.

There can be multiple ways of storing photos for Photoclone. The easiest and most direct way is to store the photos locally in the same server that runs the application. As you can imagine while this is relatively easy to implement it has many flaws. The most obvious flaw is that the server will run out of disk space quickly if the application data grows. Scaling becomes an issue at a later stage because it will be difficult to run multiple servers easily to load balance. For smaller setups this is usually not a problem though.

Local storage of data can be implemented in one of two popular ways—either in the filesystem (in a directory structure or not) or as binary data in a database. There are many debates on the feasibility of storing large amounts of binary data in a database as compared to the filesystem. Here are some of the considerations of the pros and cons of storing photos as files in the filesystem or as binary data in a database.

Filesystem

- Speed of retrieving and displaying the photo is faster than if it's stored in the database
- Photos can be cached easily
- No large database files to contend with
- Lower memory consumption

Database

- Can be used over the network (though it will be slower)
- More security (not anyone can view the photos)
- Backup of files are all in a single place

Very often though, the solution ends up with the photos being stored in the filesystem but the database contains the metadata and pointers to the location where the files are stored.

Another way of storing photos is up in the *cloud* where services such as the Amazon Web Services (AWS) offer pay-per-use data storage facilities. The advantages of using cloud storage are:

- Very scalable, there is no limit to the amount of data you can store in the cloud
- Very little to no consideration for maintenance of servers or facilities
- Considerably cheaper than storing the data yourselves
- Can be used by multiple servers at the same time

As you can see the advantages of using cloud storage seems to be very similar to that of using the database. However, one major disadvantage is that depending on the location of the servers used in the cloud storage, the speed of uploading and storing photos can be quite slow.

In Photoclone we use a hybrid of cloud storage, filesystem, and database to enable optimal photo upload and display services keeping in mind the need for scaling as well budget. The design uses the Amazon Simple Storage Service (S3), which stores objects up to 8 GB in size in the cloud.

Objects stored in Amazon S3 are placed in containers aptly called *buckets*. In Photoclone, for easy management, we create a bucket for every user, when they first log in they store all their photos in this bucket. The files are uploaded into S3 and three different versions are created:

1. *Original* — this is the original photo that is uploaded. The extension of the file is changed to `.orig`.

2. *Display* — this is a photo that is resized to 500 pixels wide (with the necessary height in proportion), used for display in the main photo page. The extension of the file is changed to `.disp`.

3. *Thumbnail* — this is a thumbnail of the photo for quick display. The extension of the file is changed to `.thmb`.

A record is created for each photo that is uploaded and the database row ID becomes the name of the file. For example, when a photo is uploaded, a database record number 123 is created with the necessary metadata. The original file will be renamed `123.orig`, the display photo will be named `123.disp`, and the thumbnail photo will be named `123.thmb`. All three photos are then stored in S3.

However, to improve the performance of displaying the photos, we cache the photo locally in the same server. The caches are just that, under normal circumstances, photos that have been around for a period of time can be removed through a regularly running script. This will reduce the disk space needed on the server while keeping the bulk of the photos in S3.

You might realize that this design also facilitates easy scaling of Photoclone. Although the photos are served through cached files on the server, we can just as easily deploy new servers and serve out the same photos, as long as we have access to the same database.

Comments

An important part of any Web 2.0 site is the community element of the site. Central to building communities is providing a means for users to contribute back to the site, in this case commenting on photos that are shared by users. The commenting mechanism itself is quite simple. Each photo can have one or more comments and any user can create a comment. However, only the commentator can remove his own comments.

Annotations

Annotating photos is a common feature among the popular photo-sharing applications. Annotations allows the user to draw a rectangle around parts of the photo and attach notes to it. A photo can have one or more annotations on it, and are only applicable to the displayed photos. The annotations are not added in the photo image itself but added and displayed as a layer over the photo.

Editing photos

The ability to edit and modify photos online is not a common feature provided by most photo-sharing applications. However, we include this feature in because it is relatively easy to integrate a good online photo editor to provide this service. Amongst the better online photo editors that allow external integration include Picnik, FotoFlexer, and Pixlr. However, Picnik and FotoFlexer include mandatory advertisements in their integration. To provide a smoother user experience we integrate with Pixlr, which has a straightforward integration mechanism.

The integration involves sending the display photo to the Pixlr online photo editor. Once the user is satisfied with the changes, the photo is sent back to Photoclone to be saved.

Edited photos are linked back to their originals—each edited photo belongs to an original, so any photos that do not belong to an original is an original itself.

Friendly URLs

To share with non-users of Photoclone it's important that the URLs are friendly and easy to send out to anyone. Photoclone allows for sharing of user albums through the username like this:

```
http://photoclone.saush.com/user/sausheong
```

This will display all albums belonging to that user.

Sharing photos

Sharing photos is a main purpose of any photo-sharing application (hence the name). When it comes to basic features, storing and sharing photos with friends are the key purposes of any photo-sharing application and these two features are the highlight of Photoclone.

Sharing photos to non-users can be done through the user by passing the friendly URLs above to any one. That will share albums and photos that belong to a particular user to anyone. Only public photos will be shown in those albums. Sharing photos to users of the Photoclone can be done through photostreams. If you *follow* another user, you will see his/her photostream (the latest photos he/she uploaded).

One of the main features in any social network involves modeling the interaction between its users. The two more commonly adopted models are the *friend* model and the *fan* model as described in the previous chapter. Photoclone, like Tweetclone previously, uses the fan model of social interaction. We use the fan model because we want to share photos easily and quickly. While the friend model has more privacy control there is a delay between the time a user requests for a connection and his friend actually approving that connection. As a result the number of connections in a friend model network is much smaller than in the fan model.

A quick recap—the fan model, unlike the friend model, is a one-way user connection. A typical example—you might know Barack Obama but it is most unlikely that he knows you in return. The differences are subtle but important. While the friend model is reciprocal, that is the user needs to approve and agree that you are his/her friend before a connection is made, the fan model is not. You can follow anyone that catches your fancy and the number of followers any one person can have can be very large.

Photoclone uses a very simple mechanism for sharing photos. Instead of deliberately sharing with friends (which you can still do via friendly URLs), the sharing mechanism is inversed. Your fans are able to view your photos through their photostream whenever you upload new photos, without any directed effort on your part (sharing becomes very easy). Conversely, the more people you follow, the more pictures you can view in your photostream. This encourages users to follow more users.

Technologies and platforms used

We use a number of technologies in this chapter, mainly revolving around the Ruby programming language and its various libraries. In addition to Ruby and its libraries we also use a few mashups, which are described below. For more information on the technology stack used in this book (and in this chapter) please refer to Chapter 1.

Mashups

As with previous chapters, while the main features in the applications are all implemented within the chapters itself, sometimes we still depend on other services provided by other providers. In this chapter we use three services—RPX for user web authentication, Gravatar for avatar services, Amazon S3 for photo storage, and Pixlr for photo editing.

RPX

RPX is an authentication provisioning service provided by JanRain, a technology startup with deep roots in the OpenID community. It doesn't do the actual authentication itself but acts as a proxy to a multitude of third party authentication providers such as Google, Yahoo!, MySpace, Windows Live ID, Facebook, and Twitter, and a number of OpenID providers such as LiveJournal and Blogger. By wrapping around these third party providers it exposes a uniform interface that enables web sites and applications to easily use any of the third party authentication providers. RPX was previously discussed in more detail in Chapter 3.

Gravatar

Gravatar is short for Globally Recognized Avatar, and is a free Internet application that allows you to map avatars (which are mid to small-sized thumbnail pictures representing yourself) to e-mails. The service itself is quite simple — it allows the user to add any number of avatar pictures and also any number of e-mail addresses that belong to you. You can map any of the pictures to any of the e-mail addresses. We discussed Gravatar previously in Chapter 3.

Pixlr

Pixlr is one of many pieces of free online photo-editing software available on the Internet. Amongst its other more prominent competitors are FotoFlexer and Picnik. We chose Pixlr for Photoclone for a few reasons, including its neat look and feel, but mainly because other online photo editing software embeds advertising when used.

Pixlr has two photo editors — Pixlr Editor and Pixlr Express. Pixlr Editor is more sophisticated and complex, while Pixlr Express offers a simple way to edit photos. In Photoclone we will use Pixlr Express.

Pixlr has a small but effective set of APIs and it can be used in a few ways. Pixlr APIs can be used in many ways, including through HTTP GET and HTTP POST forms. However, for Photoclone we are going to use the Pixlr Javascript library.

The Javascript library allows us to call Pixlr in a few ways:

- As an overlay on top of the current page
- Opening up Pixlr in the same window
- Opening up Pixlr in another window

In Photoclone we will use the Javascript library to open Pixlr Express in the same window.

Amazon Web Services Simple Storage Service (S3)

Amazon.com is a successful Internet retailer that started from selling books through the Internet but has since extended its business to selling electronics, CDs, DVDs, and many other types of merchandise. In July 2002, Amazon.com launched the Amazon Web Services (AWS), a collection of web-based computing services. The AWS provided these services over the Internet, through HTTP, either REST or SOAP based interfaces. The services were billed per usage via various means, with a rather complicated billing calculation. AWS's revolutionary services were the pioneers of what eventually fell under the general umbrella of *cloud computing*.

One of the earliest services that were provided by AWS was the *Simple Storage Service* (S3). The AWS S3 was the first publicly available web service, first launched in 2006 in the U.S. and rolled out subsequently to Europe in 2007 and Asia/Singapore in 2010. Its basic premise is to provide unlimited storage space through a simple web service, charged per usage. The AWS S3 was built for scalability and high availability. Amazon claims to have more than 64 billion objects stored in its S3 servers as of August 2009.

AWS S3 allows users to store objects up to 5 GB in size, each accompanied by up to 2 KB of metadata. Objects are organized into buckets and identified within each bucket by a unique, user-assigned key. Buckets are organized within S3 to be unique although bucket names can be arbitrarily assigned by the user. A bucket can be stored in one of several regions including the U.S. Standard (Northern Virginia), EU (Ireland), the U.S-West (Northern California), and Singapore. Objects stored in a particular region never leave the region unless they are transferred out. Amazon provides authentication mechanisms — objects can be made private or public, and rights can be granted to specific users.

Buckets and objects can be created, listed, and retrieved using either a REST-style HTTP interface or a SOAP interface. Objects can be downloaded using various protocols including HTTP GET and Bittorrent.

Bucket names and keys (that identify objects that are stored) are chosen so that objects are addressable using HTTP URLs:

- `http://s3.amazonaws.com/bucket/key`
- `http://bucket.s3.amazonaws.com/key`

Before we can start using the AWS S3, we will need to register for an Amazon account at `htttp://aws.amazon.com` and then sign up for the S3 services at `http://aws.amazon.com/s3`. Each service is signed up individually so do not expect to sign up for all AWS services in one go. After you have signed up for AWS S3 services, you can go into your credentials and look for your access key and secret keys. You will need these to connect to AWS S3.

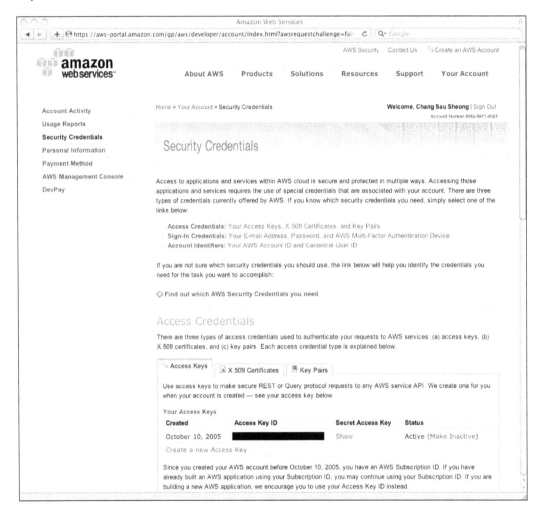

While using the AWS S3 can be quite involved, in Photoclone we will be using a Ruby gem called RightAWS to shield us from the mundane complexities and focus on just storing Photo objects in AWS S3.

RightAWS

RightAWS is a set of Ruby libraries used to access AWS, packaged in a gem and provided by RightScale, a company that provides cloud computing management services. RightScale has a fully automated management platform used to control and manage cloud services and is one of the more prominent companies providing services in this new domain. RightAWS provides access to more than AWS S3 but in Photoclone we only use the S3 interfaces.

Installing RightAWS is very simple:

```
$ gem install right_aws
```

For Photoclone we will only use its S3 interfaces and concentrate on using `RightAws::S3Interface`. To setup RightAWS services we need to provide the access key and secret keys that you got from the security credentials in AWS. In Photoclone we set up a constant with the connection to the `RightAWS::S3Interface`:

```
S3 = RightAws::S3Interface.new(S3_CONFIG['AWS_ACCESS_KEY'], S3_
CONFIG['AWS_SECRET_KEY'], {:multi_thread => true, :protocol => 'http',
:port => 80} )
```

Note that we are setting RightAWS to be multi-threaded because Photoclone is a web application and more than one user might be uploading or downloading photos at the same time; if it is single-threaded we won't get very far.

Building the clone

Now that we have a clear understanding of the clone we want to build, let's get into it. If you notice from the design discussion above, in terms of features the clone is relatively simple when compared with Flickr. However, you will realize to implement even just a portion of Flickr's core features does take some effort. In this chapter, the building of the clone will take up a significant part of the description. Now let's get on with it!

Configuration

Before we start building the application, let's configure AWS. From the preceding section you would have gotten the AWS access and secret keys. In `config.rb` we enter these keys.

```
S3_CONFIG = {}
S3_CONFIG['AWS_ACCESS_KEY'] = '<access key here>'
S3_CONFIG['AWS_SECRET_KEY'] = '<secret key here>'
```

Then in `models.rb`, we create a constant called `S3` that is an interface to S3. We set this interface to be multi-threaded and to use HTTP as its protocol. We need the interface to be multi-threaded because we need interface with S3 simultaneously.

```
S3 = RightAws::S3Interface.new(S3_CONFIG['AWS_ACCESS_KEY'], S3_
CONFIG['AWS_SECRET_KEY'], {:multi_thread => true, :protocol => 'http',
:port => 80} )
```

Modeling the data

The data model used in Photoclone is only slightly more complex than Tweetclone. While Tweetclone essentially has only two classes, describing Photoclone takes up two further classes:

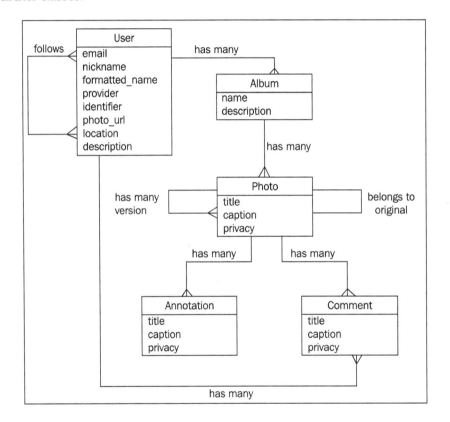

As you can see, the central model is the `Photo` class, which is the centerpiece of our design.

User

The User class is very similar to that used in Tweetclone, and we re-use much of the previous code. If you have read the previous chapter you can go lightly over this model.

```ruby
class User
  include DataMapper::Resource

  property :id,            Serial
  property :email,         String, :length => 255
  property :nickname,      String, :length => 255
  property :formatted_name, String, :length => 255
  property :provider,      String, :length => 255
  property :identifier,    String, :length => 255
  property :photo_url,     String, :length => 255
  property :description,   String, :length => 255

  has n, :relationships
  has n, :followers, :through => :relationships, :class_name =>
"User", :child_key => [:user_id]
  has n, :follows, :through => :relationships, :class_name => "User",
:remote_name => :user, :child_key => [:follower_id]

  has n, :albums
  has n, :photos, :through => :albums
  has n, :comments

  validates_is_unique :nickname, :message => "Someone else has taken
up this nickname, try something else!"
  after :create, :create_s3_bucket

  def self.find(identifier)
    u = first(:identifier => identifier)
    u = new(:identifier => identifier) if u.nil?
    return u
  end

  def follow(user)
    Relationship.create(:user => user, :follower => self)
  end

  def unfollow(user)
    Relationship.first(:user_id => user.id, :follower_id => self.id).
destroy
  end

  def create_s3_bucket
    S3.create_bucket("pc.#{id}")
  end
end
```

The properties of the `User` object are the profile of a user. We will be using it later when creating or modifying the user profile. The property to take note of in this is *nickname*. As mentioned during the design section, identifying the user is important in Photoclone because we need to share friendly URLs. As we're using RPX, the unique identifying property is actually *identifier*. However, besides being unfriendly (a typical identifier looks like this – `https://me.yahoo.com/a/C.UlGRU1t4SvPvc1bN6FBbvvw8QJyXc-#33d8b`) the identifier changes from provider to provider. Each provider uses a different way of identifying the user. As a result, we use the nickname to identify the user instead, which is also why we need to make sure it is unique:

```
validates_is_unique :nickname, :message => "Someone else has taken up
this nickname, try something else!"
```

If you have gone to the Photoclone site you will realize that the user sets the nickname when he/she first logs in. If the nickname is already taken, he/she will be asked to use something else. If he/she leaves the nickname empty, a random string will be set for him/her, based on the hash of the identifier, converted into an alphanumeric string.

```
user.update_attributes({:nickname => profile['identifier'].hash.
to_s(36), :email => profile['email'], :photo_url => photo, :provider
=> profile['provider']})
```

We also define the two different relationships between users — *follows*, which is a list of users you follow and *followers*, a list of your fans. Implicitly we have also defined that if a user is in both these lists, he/she is a friend.

```
has n, :relationships
has n, :followers, :through => :relationships, :class_name => "User",
:child_key => [:user_id]
has n, :follows, :through => :relationships, :class_name => "User",
:remote_name => :user, :child_key => [:follower_id]
```

To keep track of the many-to-many relationships we define a separate class called `Relationship`. We define the `user_id` and `follower_id` properties here, which seems unusual because we use them in the `belongs_to` and have *n* relationships. However, this is necessary because we're defining a many-to-many, self-referencing relationship.

```
class Relationship
  include DataMapper::Resource

  property :user_id, Integer, :key => true
  property :follower_id, Integer, :key => true
  belongs_to :user, :child_key => [:user_id]
  belongs_to :follower, :class_name => "User", :child_key =>
[:follower_id]
end
```

We define two convenient methods to allow a user to create or delete a
following relationship:

```
def follow(user)
  Relationship.create(:user => user, :follower => self)
end

def unfollow(user)
  Relationship.first(:user_id => user.id, :follower_id => self.id).
  destroy
end
```

A user has one or more albums and has access to the photos in the albums:

```
has n, :albums
has n, :photos, :through => :albums
has n, :comments
```

A user can also have one or more comments on the photos. Remember that users are
able to comment on any photo.

Next, we define a method to return a user, given the OpenID identifier. If the user
exists it is returned, and otherwise it will be created.

```
def self.find(identifier)
  u = first(:identifier => identifier)
  u = new(:identifier => identifier) if u.nil?
  return u
end
```

There is a method in DataMapper that allows for the immediate creation of the object
(and database record) if an object is not found — first_or_create. This method is
not appropriate for our use here for a subtle reason — first_or_create will create
the actual database record while the method above will only return a Ruby object
without tying it to an actual record in the database. Why does this make a difference?
It's because we will check if it is a new record later on, using the new_record?
method on the object. If it's an object that is tied with an actual database record,
it will be considered an existing record and we will never be able to update any
further attributes.

```
user = User.find(profile['identifier'])
  if user.new_record?
    ...
    unless user.update_attributes({:nickname => profile['identifier'].
hash.to_s(36), :email => profile['email'], :photo_url => photo,
:provider => profile['provider']})
      flash[:error] = user.errors.values.join(',')
      redirect "/"
    end
    ...
```

Finally, we create a bucket in S3 every time a new user record is created.

```
after :create, :create_s3_bucket
...
def create_s3_bucket
  S3.create_bucket("pc.#{id}")
end
```

Album

An album is a simple container for photos belonging to a user. Each photo has a cover photo, which is the photo used when displaying a list of photos. An empty album will show a default album icon instead. Each album can only belong to a single user.

Unlike sets in Flickr, photos can only belong to one album at a time.

```
class Album
  include DataMapper::Resource
  property :id,          Serial
  property :name,        String, :length => 255
  property :description, Text
  property :created_at, DateTime

  belongs_to :user
  has n, :photos
  belongs_to :cover_photo, :class_name => 'Photo', :child_key =>
[:cover_photo_id]

  def original_photos(viewer)
    criteria = {:photo_id => nil, :order => [:created_at.desc]}
    criteria[:privacy] = 'public' if viewer != user
    photos(criteria)
  end

  def edited_photos(viewer)
    criteria = {:photo_id.not => nil, :order => [:created_at.desc]}
    criteria[:privacy] = 'public' if viewer != user
    photos(criteria)
  end

  def public_photos
    photos(:photo_id => nil, :order => [:created_at.desc], :privacy
=> 'public')
  end

  def private_photos
    photos(:photo_id => nil, :order => [:created_at.desc], :privacy
=> 'private')
  end
end
```

Besides being a container for photos, an album also provides a number of convenience methods that return photos it contains.

Photo

A photo is the central class in Photoclone. Most of the application revolves around it and not surprisingly, this is the class with the most code. A Photo has a title, which is a brief one-liner that describes what the photo is about, and a caption that gives more information on the photo. There are two privacy settings for the photo—public or private. Public gives total access to one and all while private is only available for the user himself. While this seems a bit extreme, this design allows the easiest way to share photos yet retain privacy when needed.

A photo belongs to only one album, unlike in Flickr, where a photo can belong to any number of sets.

```
class Photo
  include DataMapper::Resource
  attr_writer :tmpfile
  property :id,          Serial
  property :title,       String, :length => 255
  property :caption,     String, :length => 255
  property :privacy,     String, :default => 'public'

  property :format,      String
  property :created_at,  DateTime

  belongs_to :album
  belongs_to :original, :class_name => 'Photo', :child_key => [:photo_
id]

  has n, :annotations
  has n, :comments
  has n, :versions, :class_name => 'Photo'

  after :save,    :save_image_s3
  after :destroy, :destroy_image_s3


  def filename_original; "#{id}.orig"; end
  def filename_display; "#{id}.disp"; end
  def filename_thumbnail; "#{id}.thmb"; end

  def url_thumbnail
```

```
      create_tmp_from_s3('thm')
      "/photos/#{id}.thm"
    end

    def url_display
      create_tmp_from_s3('tmp')
      "/photos/#{id}.tmp"
    end

    def previous_in_album(viewer)
      photos = viewer == album.user ? album.original_photos(viewer) :
album.public_photos
      index = photos.index self
      return nil unless index
      photos[index - 1] if index > 0
    end

    def next_in_album(viewer)
      photos = viewer == album.user ? album.original_photos(viewer) :
album.public_photos
      index = photos.index self
      return nil unless index
      photos[index + 1] if index < album.photos.length
    end

    def save_image_s3
      return unless @tmpfile
      S3.put(s3_bucket, filename_original, @tmpfile)

      img = Magick::Image.read(@tmpfile.open).first
      display = img.resize_to_fit(500)
      S3.put(s3_bucket, filename_display, display.to_blob)

      t = img.resize_to_fit(150)
      length = t.rows > t.columns ? t.columns : t.rows
      thumbnail =  t.crop(CenterGravity, length, length)
      S3.put(s3_bucket, filename_thumbnail, thumbnail.to_blob)
    end

    def destroy_image_s3
      S3.delete s3_bucket, filename_original
      S3.delete s3_bucket, filename_display
      S3.delete s3_bucket, filename_thumbnail
    end
```

```
def create_tmp_from_s3(type)
    tmp = File.dirname(__FILE__) + "/public/photos/#{id}.#{type}"
    return if File.exists? tmp
    File.open(tmp, 'w+') do |file|
        filename = (type == 'tmp' ? filename_display : filename_
thumbnail)
        S3.get(s3_bucket, filename) do |chunk|
            file.write chunk
        end
    end
end
def s3_bucket
    "pc.#{album.user.id}"
end

def self.random
    num_public_photos = all(:privacy => 'public').count
    return if num_public_photos == 0
    all(:privacy => 'public')[rand(num_public_photos)].url_display
end
end
```

Photos can be edited through Pixlr. Editing photos in Photoclone means that the photo itself is duplicated and the duplicate is sent to Pixlr. Once the user has completed modifying the duplicate, it can be sent back to Photoclone to be saved. When this happens, a new Photo object is created that is linked to the original Photo object.

```
belongs_to :original, :class_name => 'Photo', :child_key => [:photo_
id]
```

The original photo will then have another version added to its list of versions.

```
has n, :versions, :class_name => 'Photo'
```

After a user uploads a photo, Photoclone keeps three copies of it—the original copy, a scaled down copy for web display, and a thumbnail copy. All three copies are given a name according to the record ID of the record in the database, with different extensions signifying whether it is an original copy, the display copy, or a thumbnail copy.

```
def filename_original; "#{id}.orig"; end
def filename_display; "#{id}.disp"; end
def filename_thumbnail; "#{id}.thmb"; end
```

Saving an uploaded photo is relatively simple with the RightAWS S3 library. Notice that unlike the other models, the Photo model has a writable instance variable called `tmpfile`. Unlike properties, which are persisted as values in the database, this variable is transient; the data is not saved in the database. We use this transient variable to store the binary file data that has been uploaded to the server.

```
attr_writer :tmpfile
```

Let's look at how we can save the image to AWS S3.

```
def save_image_s3
  return unless @tmpfile
  S3.put(s3_bucket, filename_original, @tmpfile)

  img = Magick::Image.read(@tmpfile.open).first
  display = img.resize_to_fit(500)
  S3.put(s3_bucket, filename_display, display.to_blob)

  t = img.resize_to_fit(150)
  length = t.rows > t.columns ? t.columns : t.rows
  thumbnail =  t.crop(CenterGravity, length, length)
  S3.put(s3_bucket, filename_thumbnail, thumbnail.to_blob)
end
```

The first step is to check if there is any data in the transient `tmpfile` variable. If there isn't, we can't save anything. Then we use the `S3` constant we defined earlier in a configuration file, and save the data to S3.

```
S3.put(s3_bucket, filename_original, @tmpfile)
```

Note that the `s3_bucket` is basically derived from the user ID:

```
def s3_bucket
    "pc.#{album.user.id}"
end
```

`tmpfile` is actually binary data that is uploaded using the HTML file upload.

Basically file inputs in HTML forms lets users include entire files from their system through a form submission. The files could be text files, image files, or other data. The mechanism for a form-based file upload was originally proposed in RFC 1867 (published November 1995), as an extension to HTML 2.0 (RFC 1866), after its publication. Form-based file upload then was incorporated in HTML 3.2, which explicitly refers to RFC 1867 for further information on form-based file upload. RFC 1867 also introduced the `accept` attribute for the input element that enables file-type filtering based on MIME type. The `accept` attribute is a list of comma-separated media types. If an `accept` attribute is present, the browser should constrain the file patterns prompted for to match those with the corresponding appropriate file extensions for the platform.

In addition the `accept` attribute, the form should also set the `enctype` attribute, which specifies the encoding used by the form. A form without any file uploads will have the `enctype` attribute set by default to `application/x-www-form-urlencoded`, which is the well-known format of *name=value* pairs. For file uploads this is irrelevant, and we need to define the `enctype` to be `multipart/form-data`. This tells the server that the form data is encoded so that the data set as a whole is a multipart message containing a number of form fields as its components. This is not needed in normal forms but is necessary for forms containing file fields. The multipart structure means that each file comes in a package inside a larger package, with suitable content type information on the inner package.

The data is then sent to the server in its original formatting and it is up to the server to decipher it. In our case, Photoclone retrieves the data as a binary stream and this data stream is passed directly to S3 using the RightAWS library as the original copy.

After saving the original to S3, we generate the display copy using the RMagick. First, we open `tmpfile`. The variable `tmpfile` is a Tempfile object that is created from the uploaded data. Using RMagick, read in the data in `tmpfile` and create an RMagick image object. We resize this image object to fit in a width of 500 pixels, and using the `to_blob` method, we reconvert this image object into a binary stream and save it to S3.

```
img = Magick::Image.read(@tmpfile.open).first
display = img.resize_to_fit(500)
S3.put(s3_bucket, filename_display, display.to_blob)
```

Ruby comes with a `Tempfile` class that can be used to manage temporary files. Tempfile objects behave like any other I/O objects, though it does not directly inherit from I/O itself. Instead it delegates calls to a File object (which does inherit from I/O). Rack creates a Tempfile object when a file is uploaded through a form. We will look further into this in a later section.

We create the thumbnail in the same way, using the same RMagick image object. However instead of simply resizing the thumbnail, we crop it into a small square centering at the middle of the photo. We save the thumbnail into S3 as well.

```
t = img.resize_to_fit(150)
length = t.rows > t.columns ? t.columns : t.rows
thumbnail =  t.crop(CenterGravity, length, length)
S3.put(s3_bucket, filename_thumbnail, thumbnail.to_blob)
```

Now that we have the photos in S3, we need to display them for the user. To display the photos on the site, we need to have a URL to the photo.

```
def url_display
  create_tmp_from_s3('tmp')
  "/photos/#{id}.tmp"
end
```

This method returns the display photo URL. We call a common method called `create_tmp_from_s3` to create a temporary file. We create the temporary file first from S3 and then using this file as the display photo. If the file already exists, we don't re-create it of course. Otherwise, to create the temporary file, we use the S3 interface again and get the display photo from S3, then write it to a display temporary file with the extension `.tmp`.

```
def create_tmp_from_s3(type)
  tmp = File.dirname(__FILE__) + "/public/photos/#{id}.#{type}"
  return if File.exists? tmp
  File.open(tmp, 'w+') do |file|
    filename = (type == 'tmp' ? filename_display : filename_
thumbnail)
    S3.get(s3_bucket, filename) do |chunk|
      file.write chunk
    end
  end
end
```

We repeat this for thumbnails, using the same common method, except this time we use the extension `.thm` instead.

```
def url_thumbnail
    create_tmp_from_s3('thm')
    "/photos/#{id}.thm"
end
```

Now that we can upload photos, we would also want to delete photos when we don't need it. Note that we don't actually need to remove the temporary photo files locally; it should be cleared at regular intervals by a cache clearing script.

```
def destroy_image_s3
  S3.delete s3_bucket, filename_original
  S3.delete s3_bucket, filename_display
  S3.delete s3_bucket, filename_thumbnail
end
```

We also define some convenience methods in the Photo object to help us navigate the photos in the album by finding the photo before it in the album, and the photo after it. Which photos to view depends on who is viewing it (public photos are viewable by all, private photos only for the user).

```
def previous_in_album(viewer)
  photos = viewer == album.user ? album.original_photos(viewer) :
album.public_photos
  index = photos.index self
  return nil unless index
  photos[index - 1] if index > 0
end
```

```
def next_in_album(viewer)
  photos = viewer == album.user ? album.original_photos(viewer) :
album.public_photos
  index = photos.index self
  return nil unless index
  photos[index + 1] if index < album.photos.length
end
```

Finally for the login page, we generate a random public photo to be displayed.

```
def self.random
  num_public_photos = all(:privacy => 'public').count
  return if num_public_photos == 0
  all(:privacy => 'public')[rand(num_public_photos)].url_display
end
```

If the explanations in this section seem a bit vague, things will get clearer once we start discussing the flow of the application.

Annotation

Each photo can have one or more annotations. Annotations are implemented as a rectangular layer over the photo with white borders and text just below. The annotation has a description, an X and Y point that describes the upper-left corner of the layer, with a particular width and height. Each photo has one or more annotations.

```
class Annotation
  include DataMapper::Resource
  property :id,          Serial
  property :description, Text
  property :x,           Integer
  property :y,           Integer
  property :height,      Integer
  property :width,       Integer
  property :created_at,  DateTime

  belongs_to :photo
end
```

There isn't much to say about the Annotation model because it only stores the annotation information to be retrieved and displayed when viewing the photo. We will come to this in the following sections.

Comment

A user can comment on any public photos. The Comment class is very simple; the only property it has is the text description. A comment belongs to a user and a photo.

```
class Comment
  include DataMapper::Resource
  property :id,         Serial
  property :text,       Text
  property :created_at, DateTime
  belongs_to :user
  belongs_to :photo
end
```

As with the annotations there is nothing further to discuss about comments, the detailed explanation is made in a section below.

Building the application flow

Now that we have the models used in Photoclone let's look at how these models are used to build the web application. As before we start with authentication and user management.

Authenticating and managing users

As mentioned during the design section, we will be using RPX to authenticate users. This reduces the amount of work needed tremendously. Let's describe what will happen. The first and most basic route is the *index* route:

```
get '/' do
  if session[:userid].nil? then
    @token = "http://#{env['HTTP_HOST']}/after_login"
    haml :login
  else
    redirect "/#{User.get(session[:userid]).nickname}"
  end
end
```

If the user is already logged in and has a session, we will redirect him/her to his/her home page. Otherwise, we will prepare the token for RPX, which is a URL that RPX can call after it successfully authenticates the user. We use Haml for the view templates. As before we define a separate layout Haml template that will be used in all pages:

```
%html
  %head
    %title Photoclone
    %link{:rel => 'stylesheet', :href => '/css/blueprint/screen.css',
:type => 'text/css'}
    %link{:rel => 'stylesheet', :href => '/css/blueprint/plugins/
fancy-type/screen.css', :type => 'text/css'}
    %link{:rel => 'stylesheet', :href => '/css/additional.css', :type
=> 'text/css'}
    %script{:src => 'http://ajax.googleapis.com/ajax/libs/
jquery/1.3.2/jquery.min.js', :type => 'text/javascript'}
    %script{:src => '/js/select.js', :type => 'text/javascript'}
    %script{:src => '/js/notes.js', :type => 'text/javascript'}
  %body
    .container
      = yield
      %hr.space
      .span-24.last
        .small.span-5.prepend-19
```

```
        copyright &copy
        %a{:href => 'http://www.saush.com'} Chang Sau Sheong
        2009

  - unless @user
    %script{:src => "https://rpxnow.com/openid/v2/widget", :type =>
"text/javascript"}
    %script{:type => "text/javascript"}
      RPXNOW.overlay = true;
      RPXNOW.language_preference = 'en';
```

Unlike in Tweetclone where we put the RPX authentication script only in the login page, we place the script in the layout where it is used by every other page. The reason for the difference is simple—in Tweetclone, the only time the user needs to log in is at the login page. However, because of anonymous sharing of albums and photos, users are able to view pages in Photoclone without logging in. This means that for pages that are viewable by anonymous users, we need to have the facility for the user to log in, hence putting the RPX script in layout makes the most sense.

Sinatra looks for all view templates in a folder called `views` by default. Our login Haml template, called `login.haml`, is found in the same place:

```
.span-24
  .span-11
    %img.span-11{:src => '/images/login_logo.gif'}
    .span-9.prepend-2
      %h2{:style => 'margin-top:0; padding-top: 0;'} Sharing photos,
finding friends

      .subtitle Photoclone is a no-frills photo-sharing application
that allows you to share your photos with your friends!
      .subtitle You don't need to register any accounts, just use an
existing Google, Yahoo, Facebook or Twitter account!
  .span-2.prepend-10
    %a.rpxnow{:onclick => "return false;", :href => "https://
photoclone.rpxnow.com/openid/v2/signin?token_url=#{@token}" }
      %h3 Sign In

  -if flash[:error]
    .span-24
      .error
        = flash[:error]
  %img{:src => "#{Photo.random}"}
```

This is the RPX login light-box overlaying the front page:

To allow login, we add a HTML anchor link that redirects us to RPX, passing in the token.

```
%a.rpxnow{:onclick => "return false;", :href => "https://photoclone.
rpxnow.com/openid/v2/signin?token_url=#{@token}" }
```

This will redirect the user to the RPX site, which in turns redirects the user to the appropriate provider. On authentication completion, RPX will call on Photoclone at the URL (`after_login`) that was provided earlier on. RPX passes a `token` parameter to us in this call, which we will use to retrieve the user's profile.

We will define a separate helper method to do the work of retrieving the user's profile. All such methods are placed in the `helpers.rb` file:

```
def get_user_profile_with(token)
  response = RestClient.post 'https://rpxnow.com/api/v2/auth_info',
'token' => token, 'apiKey' => '<RPX API key>', 'format' => 'json',
'extended' => 'true'
  json = JSON.parse(response)
  return json['profile'] if json['stat'] == 'ok'
  raise LoginFailedError, 'Cannot log in. Try another account!'
end
```

We use the very useful Rest-Client library to easily send the POST request to RPX, passing in the token and requesting the information back in JSON format. If successful, RPX will return some information about the users, which we will use the Ruby JSON library to parse and return. Let's look at the *after_login* route next:

```
post '/after_login' do
  profile = get_user_profile_with params[:token]
  user = User.find(profile['identifier'])
  if user.new_record?
    photo = profile['email'] ? "http://www.gravatar.com/
avatar/#{Digest::MD5.hexdigest(profile['email'])}" : profile['photo']
    unless user.update_attributes({:nickname => profile['identifier'].
hash.to_s(36), :email => profile['email'], :photo_url => photo,
:provider => profile['provider']})
      flash[:error] = user.errors.values.join(',')
      redirect "/"
    end
    session[:userid] = user.id
    redirect '/change_profile'
  else
    session[:userid] = user.id
    redirect "/#{user.nickname}"
  end
end
```

After getting the user profile from the authentication provider through RPX, we try to retrieve the user from our database, using the unique identifier. As previously mentioned, if the user does not exist in Photoclone yet, we'll create a new record. If it's a new record, we will update the rest of the attributes from the profile. This includes a photo link from Gravatar.

Gravatar uses e-mail addresses that are hashed using MD5 to uniquely identify a user's avatar. As a user can have multiple e-mail addresses, he/she can have multiple avatars:

```
photo = profile['email'] ? "http://www.gravatar.com/
avatar/#{Digest::MD5.hexdigest(profile['email'])}" : profile['photo']
```

Note that we can optionally take from the photo link if it's provided in the profile, though Gmail doesn't provide that as of date. So what happens if the user is not a Gravatar user and therefore doesn't have a Gravatar avatar? In this case Gravatar returns a default avatar.

You will also notice that we set the nickname here as well. We hash the identifier returned by Google and convert it into an alphanumeric string, which we use as the nickname. This means if a user did not change his nickname later, this will be his nickname. Finally, we set `session[:userid]` with the user ID and redirect the user to change his profile.

The *profile* and *change profile* routes do very little other than redirecting to their respective views.

```
get '/change_profile' do  haml :change_profile end

get '/profile' do
  @myself = User.get(session[:userid]))
  @user = @myself
  haml :profile
end
```

The change profile route does the actual work of saving any changes on the user profile. You will realize that we don't actually change any information that is in the original account itself; we're only changing our own data. In fact the user needs to go back to the authentication provider to change his password. There are pros and cons to this approach as explained in the previous chapters. We trade off the complexities and risks of managing a user (in terms of security and privacy) for the downside of not owning your own user information and being dependent on another company for your users. In the case of Photoclone (and in fact for all other web applications in this book) it's a good trade-off since we still get some user information and there's a lot less code and risk to manage.

```
post '/save_profile' do
  user = User.get(session[:userid])
  unless user.update_attributes(:nickname => params[:nickname],
  :formatted_name => params[:formatted_name], :location =>
  params[:location], :description => params[:description])
    flash[:error] = user.errors.values.join(',')
    redirect '/change_profile'
  end
  redirect "/#{user.nickname}"
end
```

Finally, the *logout* route simply resets `session[:userid]` and redirects the user back to the index route. Without the user ID, the index route shows the login view.

```
get '/logout' do
  session[:userid] = nil
  redirect '/'
end
```

Coming back to the login page, you will notice that there is a random public photo each time Photoclone's login page is accessed. This random photo uses the `random` method in the Photo class.

```
%img{:src => "#{Photo.random}"}
```

This is how the front page looks:

This wraps up authentication and user management.

Landing page

Once a user logs in to Photoclone, he is brought to his own landing page, which contains the following:

- A logo and menu bar
- A photo avatar and a welcome greeting in multiple languages
- The recent photostream of the user
- The recent photostream of the people who the user follows

This is how the landing page looks:

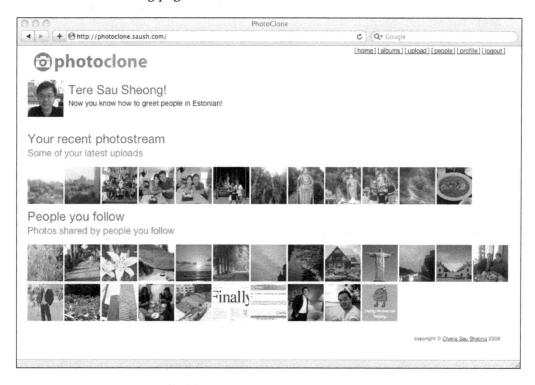

The *landing* route is quite simple:

```
get "/" do
  if session[:userid].nil? then
    haml :login
  else
    @user = User.get(session[:userid])
    @hello = HELLO[rand(HELLO.size)]
    haml :landing
  end
end
```

Note the `hello` variable. We will use this in a while. The landing page is found in `landing.haml`:

```
=snippet :'/snippets/top'

.span-24.last
  .span-2
    %img.span-2{:src => "#{@user.photo_url}"}
```

```
.span-20.last
  %h2{:style => 'margin-bottom: 0;'} #{@hello[:translation]} #{@
user.formatted_name}!
    %h4 Now you know how to greet people in  #{@hello[:lang]}!
%hr.space
.span-24.last
  %h2{:style => 'margin-bottom: 0;'} Your recent photostream
  %h3 Some of your latest uploads
  -unless @user.albums.empty?
    -@user.albums.photos(:photo_id => nil, :order => [:created_
at.desc])[0..11].each  do |photo|
      %a{:href => "/photo/#{photo.id}"}
        %img.span-2{:src => "#{photo.url_thumbnail}", :title =>
"#{photo.title}"}

  %h2{:style => 'margin-bottom: 0;'} People you follow
  %h3 Photos shared by people you follow
  - unless @user.follows.empty? and @user.follows.albums.empty?
    - @user.follows.albums.photos(:photo_id => nil, :order =>
[:created_at.desc], :privacy => 'public')[0..23].each  do |photo|
      %a{:href => "/photo/#{photo.id}"}
        %img.span-2{:src => "#{photo.url_thumbnail}", :title =>
"#{photo.title} (#{photo.album.user.nickname})"}
```

The logo and menu bar is a snippet using the same mechanism we first used in Tweetclone. We re-use snippets of common Haml code that are stored in /views/ snippets folder. This is basically the partial templates mechanism that is popularly used in many web frameworks. As mentioned in the previous chapter, although Sinatra does not support partials directly, it's very easy to re-create simple partials support by adding the following helper method:

```
def snippet(page, options={})
  haml page, options.merge!(:layout => false)
end
```

We simply run Haml again on the given page, and include any parameters we pass to it, only telling the Haml page not to use the default layout. The logo and menu bar is done with a snippet called top.haml:

```
.span-2
  %a{:href => '/'}
    %img{:src => '/images/logo.gif'}
- if @user
  .span-8.prepend-14.last
    %a{:href => '/'} [ home ]
    %a{:href => "/albums"} [ albums ]
```

```
    %a{:href => '/upload'} [ upload ]
    %a{:href => '/follows'} [ people ]
    %a{:href => '/profile'} [ profile ]
    %a{:href => '/logout'} [ logout ]
- else
  .span-2.prepend-20.last
    %a.rpxnow{:onclick => "return false;", :href => "https://
photoclone.rpxnow.com/openid/v2/signin?token_url=#{@token}" } sign in
```

Note that if the user has logged in, we will show the normal menu bar; if it's an anonymous user then we show a login link instead. Next are the photo avatar and the hello greetings:

```
.span-24.last
  .span-2
    %img.span-2{:src => "#{@user.photo_url}"}
  .span-20.last
    %h2{:style => 'margin-bottom: 0;'} #{@hello[:translation]} #{@
user.formatted_name}!
    %h4 Now you know how to greet people in  #{@hello[:lang]}!
```

Remember the `hello` variable we set earlier?

```
@hello = HELLO[rand(HELLO.size)]
```

This is trivially implemented with an array of hashes, using translation found from the Internet, stored in a file named `hello.haml`:

```
HELLO = []
HELLO << {:lang => 'Albanian', :translation => 'Tungjatjeta'} \
      << {:lang => 'Armenian', :translation => 'Barevdzes'} \
      << {:lang => 'Arabic', :translation => 'Marhaba'} \
      << {:lang => 'Austrian', :translation => 'Servas'} \
      << {:lang => 'Azerbaijani', :translation => 'Salaam aleihum'} \
      << {:lang => 'Basque', :translation => 'Kaixo'} \
      << {:lang => 'Belarussian', :translation => 'Dobri Dzen'} \
      << {:lang => 'Bengali', :translation => 'Namoshkar'} \
      << {:lang => 'Bulgarian', :translation => 'Min ga la baa'} \
      << {:lang => 'Cantonese', :translation => 'Nei ho'} \
      << {:lang => 'Mandarin', :translation => 'Ni hao'} \
      << {:lang => 'Croatian', :translation => 'Bok'} \
      << {:lang => 'Czech', :translation => 'Ahoj'} \
      << {:lang => 'Danish', :translation => 'Goddag'} \
      << {:lang => 'Dutch', :translation => 'Hallo'} \
      << {:lang => 'English', :translation => 'Hello'} \
      << {:lang => 'Farsi', :translation => 'Salaam'} \
```

```
<< {:lang => 'Finnish', :translation => 'Heippa'} \
<< {:lang => 'French', :translation => 'Bonjour'} \
<< {:lang => 'Estonian', :translation => 'Tere'} \
<< {:lang => 'Georgian', :translation => 'Gamarjobat'} \
<< {:lang => 'German', :translation => 'Hallo'} \
<< {:lang => 'Greek', :translation => 'Geia sou'} \
<< {:lang => 'Hindi', :translation => 'Namaste'} \
<< {:lang => 'Hungarian', :translation => 'Sziasztok'} \
<< {:lang => 'Gaelic', :translation => '    Dia duit'} \
<< {:lang => 'Italian', :translation => 'Ciao'} \
<< {:lang => 'Japanese', :translation => 'Konnichi wa'} \
<< {:lang => 'Korean', :translation => 'Ahnyong'} \
<< {:lang => 'Latin', :translation => 'Salve'} \
<< {:lang => 'Latvian', :translation => 'Sveiki'} \
<< {:lang => 'Lithuanian', :translation => 'Labas'} \
<< {:lang => 'Malayalam', :translation => 'Namaskaram'} \
<< {:lang => 'Norwegian', :translation => 'Hallo'} \
<< {:lang => 'Polish', :translation => 'Czesc'} \
<< {:lang => 'Portuguese', :translation => 'Ola'} \
<< {:lang => 'Russian', :translation => 'Privet'} \
<< {:lang => 'Spanish', :translation => 'Hola'} \
<< {:lang => 'Swedish', :translation => 'Hej'} \
<< {:lang => 'Turkish', :translation => 'Merhaba'} \
<< {:lang => 'Welsh', :translation => 'Dydd da'} \
```

We just randomly select a greeting and display it.

Displaying the user's own photostream is quite simple as well. If the album is not empty, we take the first 12 original photos belonging to the user and display them.

```
.span-24.last
  %h2{:style => 'margin-bottom: 0;'} Your recent photostream
  %h3 Some of your latest uploads
  -unless @user.albums.empty?
    -@user.albums.photos(:photo_id => nil, :order => [:created_
at.desc])[0..11].each  do |photo|
      %a{:href => "/photo/#{photo.id}"}
        %img.span-2{:src => "#{photo.url_thumbnail}", :title =>
"#{photo.title}"}
```

We can see an interesting DataMapper feature here. DataMapper provides a shortcut to access all photos belonging to a user, even though they are stored in separate albums like this:

```
@user.albums.photos
```

Finally, this is to show the photos in the photostreams of people the user follows:

```
%h2{:style => 'margin-bottom: 0;'} People you follow
  %h3 Photos shared by people you follow
  - unless @user.follows.empty? and @user.follows.albums.empty?
    - @user.follows.albums.photos(:photo_id => nil, :order =>
[:created_at.desc], :privacy => 'public', :limit => 24) each  do
|photo|
      %a{:href => "/photo/#{photo.id}"}
        %img.span-2{:src => "#{photo.url_thumbnail}", :title =>
"#{photo.title} (#{photo.album.user.nickname})"}
```

We take the first 24 public photos belonging to anyone that the user follows, ordered by the dates they were first uploaded and show them in a photostream.

Managing albums

Next, we look at the albums implementation. The albums are relatively simple to implement. The *albums* route returns the currently logged in user to the *manage album* page.

```
get "/albums" do
  @myself = @user = User.get(session[:userid])
  haml :"albums/manage"
end
```

We share the manage albums page with a number of other routes, so to identify which portions of the page to display we need to identify if the logged in user is the same as the user whose list of albums we want to view. The manage albums page uses two instance variables for this—myself indicates the logged in user and user indicates the user whose list of albums are being viewed.

```
=snippet :'/snippets/top'
.span-24
  .span-2
    %img.span-2{:src => "#{@user.photo_url}"}
  .span-9
    %h2{:style => 'margin-bottom: 0;'} #{@user == @myself ? 'Your' :
"#{@user.formatted_name}'s"} albums
    %h3
      = "You follow #{@user.formatted_name}" if @user != @myself and @
myself.follows.include? @user
%hr.space
.span-5
  %h3
    - if @user == @myself
```

```
      %a{:href => '/album/add'} [Add a new album]


-if @user.albums.empty? and @user == @myself
  .span-24
    %h3
      Looks like you don't have any albums yet. Do you want to
      %a{:href => '/album/add'}create one?


-@user.albums.each do |album|
  %hr
  .span-24
    .span-17
      %h3{:style => 'margin-bottom:5px;'}
        %a{:href => "/album/#{album.id}"} #{album.name}
      %h4 #{album.description}
      %hr.space
      - unless album.photos.empty?
      %h4{:style => 'font-style: italic;'} (#{album.photos.size}
photos in this album, last photo uploaded on #{album.photos.last.
created_at.strftime('%d-%b-%Y')})
    .span-3
      - if album.cover_photo
      %img.span-3{:src => "#{album.cover_photo.url_display}"}
      - elsif !album.photos.empty?
      %img.span-3{:src => "#{album.photos.first.url_display}"}
      - else
      %img.span-3{:src => "/images/album_icon.png"}
    .span-3
      - if @user == @myself
        - if album.photos.empty?
          %form{:id => "form_#{album.id}", :method => 'post', :action
=> "/album/#{album.id}"}
            %input{:type => 'hidden', :name => '_method', :value =>
'delete'}
            %a{:href => '#', :onclick => '$("#form_' + "#{album.id}" +
'").submit();'} [remove]
        %a{:href => "/album/#{album.id}/upload"} [upload]
```

This is how the manage albums page looks:

We use these two variables to format the view accordingly and display the appropriate messages:

```
%h2{:style => 'margin-bottom: 0;'} #{@user == @myself ? 'Your' : "#{@
user.formatted_name}'s"} albums
    %h3
      = "You follow #{@user.formatted_name}" if @user != @myself and @
myself.follows.include? @user
%hr.space
.span-5
  %h3
    - if @user == @myself
      %a{:href => '/album/add'} [Add a new album]
```

If the user has albums, we iterate through all his albums and display them accordingly.

```
-if @user.albums.empty? and @user == @myself
  .span-24
    %h3
      Looks like you don't have any albums yet. Do you want to
      %a{:href => '/album/add'}create one?

-@user.albums.each do |album|
  %hr
  .span-24
    .span-17
      %h3{:style => 'margin-bottom:5px;'}
        %a{:href => "/album/#{album.id}"} #{album.name}
      %h4 #{album.description}
      %hr.space
      - unless album.photos.empty?
        %h4{:style => 'font-style: italic;'} (#{album.photos.size}
photos in this album, last photo uploaded on #{album.photos.last.
created_at.strftime('%d-%b-%Y')})
```

We also display a cover photo. If there is a given cover photo (the user has explicitly set one of the photos as the cover photo) we will show that. Otherwise, we'll show the first photo in the list or a default album icon if the album is empty.

```
- if album.cover_photo
  %img.span-3{:src => "#{album.cover_photo.url_display}"}
- elsif !album.photos.empty?
  %img.span-3{:src => "#{album.photos.first.url_display}"}
- else
  %img.span-3{:src => "/images/album_icon.png"}
```

Lastly we'll only allow some actions if the current user is managing his own albums, and only allow the album to be deleted if the album is empty.

```
- if @user == @myself
  - if album.photos.empty?
    %form{:id => "form_#{album.id}", :method => 'post', :action => "/
album/#{album.id}"}
    %input{:type => 'hidden', :name => '_method', :value => 'delete'}
    %a{:href => '#', :onclick => '$("#form_' + "#{album.id}" + '").
submit();'} [remove]
  %a{:href => "/album/#{album.id}/upload"} [upload]
```

Note that delete uses the DELETE method and we are using the form submit hack to get around the problem of browsers not supporting any other HTTP methods other than GET and POST.

Since we're in the neighborhood of doing album deletes let's quickly jump into the *delete album* route:

```
delete "/album/:id" do
  album = Album.get(params[:id])
  user = User.get(session[:userid])
  if album.user == user
    if album.destroy
      redirect "/albums"
    else
      throw "Cannot delete this album!"
    end
  else
    throw "This is not your album, you cannot delete it!"
  end
end
```

Viewing someone else's albums uses the same manage albums page. The only difference is that the `myself` variable points to the logged in user and the `user` variable points to the user whose list of albums is being viewed.

```
get "/albums/:user_id" do
  @myself = User.get(session[:userid])
  @user = User.get(params[:user_id])
  haml :"albums/manage"
end
```

Creating the album is easy as well:

```
get "/album/add" do
  @user = User.get(session[:userid])
  haml :"/albums/add"
end
```

The *add album* page provides the user a form to add the album:

```
=snippet :'/snippets/top'
.span-24
  %h2 Create a new photo album
  Create an album here. You can add a cover photo later on if you
like.
.span-24
  %form{:method => 'post', :action => '/album/create'}
```

```
%p Name
%p
  %input.span-10{:type => 'text', :name => 'name'}
%p Description
%p
  %textarea.span-10{:name => 'description'}
%p
  %input{:type => 'submit', :value => 'create album'}
```

Actually creating the album is trivial:

```
post "/album/create" do
  album = Album.new
  album.attributes = {:name => params[:name], :description =>
params[:description]}
  album.user = User.get(session[:userid])
  album.save
  redirect "/albums"
end
```

As mentioned earlier, each album has a cover photo, which can be set explicitly. If the cover photo is not set, the first photo in the list of photos will be used instead, and if the album is empty a default album icon is used.

```
post "/album/cover/:photo_id" do
  photo = Photo.get(params[:photo_id])
  album = photo.album
  album.cover_photo = photo
  album.save!
  redirect "/album/#{album.id}"
end
```

There is not much in the *view album* route, which just allows an album and its contents to be displayed:

```
get "/album/:id" do
  @album = Album.get params[:id]
  @user = User.get session[:userid]
  haml :"/albums/view"
end
```

The *view album* page is more involved:

```
=snippet :'/snippets/top'
=snippet :'/snippets/album_inline_js'
.span-24
  .span-2
```

```
        %img.span-2{:src => "#{@album.user.photo_url}"}
      .span-20.last
        - if @user == @album.user
          %h2.edit_name{:style => 'margin-bottom: 0;'} #{@album.name}
          %h4.edit_area #{@album.description}
        - else
          %h2{:style => 'margin-bottom: 0;'} #{@album.name}
          %h4 #{@album.description}

  .span-24
    %h3
      - if @user == @album.user
        %a{:href => "/album/#{@album.id}/upload"} [Upload photos]
      - if @user
        %a{:href => "/albums/#{@album.user.id}"} [Back to albums]
      - else
        %a{:href => "/user/#{@album.user.nickname}"} [Back to albums]

%hr.space

- if @user
  .span-24
    %h3 Photos in this album
      - if @album.original_photos(@user).empty?
        %h4
          There are no photos in this album.
          %a{:href => "/album/#{@album.id}/upload"} Upload some photos?

      - @album.original_photos(@user).each   do |photo|
        %a{:href => "/photo/#{photo.id}"}
          %img.span-2{:src => "#{photo.url_thumbnail}"}
- else
  -@album.public_photos.each   do |photo|
    %a{:href => "/photo/#{photo.id}"}
      %img.span-2{:src => "#{photo.url_thumbnail}"}

%hr.space

%h3 Edited versions of photos in this album
- if @album.edited_photos(@user).empty?
  %h4 There are no edited versions of photos in this album
- @album.edited_photos(@user).each   do |photo|
  %a{:href => "/photo/#{photo.id}"}
    %img.span-2{:src => "#{photo.url_thumbnail}"}
```

This is how the view album page looks:

There are a few parts in this album view. Just below the common top menu bar is the photo avatar, followed by the title and description of the album. If you try the Photoclone site you might notice that the title and description of the album can be edited inline on the view album page itself. To provide the inline editing effect, we use Jeditable (`http://www.appelsiini.net/projects/jeditable`), a jQuery plugin, and create the snippet `album_inline_js.rb`.

```
%script{:type => "text/javascript", :src  => "/js/jeditable.mini.js"}
:javascript
$(document).ready(function() {
  $('.edit_name').editable('/album/name/#{@album.id}');
  $('.edit_area').editable('/album/description/#{@album.id}', {
    type    : 'textarea',
    submit  : 'OK',
    cancel  : 'Cancel',
    height  : 60
  });
});
```

First, we include the Jeditable plugin Javascript. Then we define two editable elements, one with the ID `edit_name` and the other with `edit_area`. We also tell jQuery to make an AJAX call to the edit *album property* route, given the property to edit and the album ID.

```
post "/album/:property/:photo_id" do
  album = Album.get params[:photo_id]
  if %w(name description).include? params[:property]
    album.send(params[:property] + '=', params[:value])
    album.save
  end
  album.send(params[:property])
end
```

Notice that we don't actually have an edit album name or edit album description route. Instead we have a single edit album property route with a `:property` parameter that is the property of the album we want to change. This next line is a little bit of metaprogramming we're sneaking in:

```
album.send(params[:property] + '=', params[:value])
```

Here we are actually calling the set property method in album. For example, if `params[:property]` is *name*, we're actually calling `album.name=` and the parameter is in `params[:value]`. This means we can set any property of the album we want with just this route and reduce the number of routes we need to create. However, because we don't want anyone to change any property they want, we restrict it to the `name` and `description` properties only. We will see this being used again later on when managing photos. The final line returns the newly set property back to the view template, which is then used by Jeditable to populate the text field or text area accordingly.

Next, if the owner of the album is the currently logged in user, we will allow for uploading new photos. Otherwise we will just allow for returning back to the albums list.

```
.span-24
  %h3
    - if @user == @album.user
      %a{:href => "/album/#{@album.id}/upload"} [Upload photos]
    - if @user
      %a{:href => "/albums/#{@album.user.id}"} [Back to albums]
    - else
      %a{:href => "/user/#{@album.user.nickname}"} [Back to albums]
```

Finally we show a list of photos in this album:

```
- if @user
  .span-24
    %h3 Photos in this album
    - if @album.original_photos(@user).empty?
      %h4
        There are no photos in this album.
        %a{:href => "/album/#{@album.id}/upload"} Upload some photos?

    - @album.original_photos(@user).each  do |photo|
      %a{:href => "/photo/#{photo.id}"}
        %img.span-2{:src => "#{photo.url_thumbnail}"}

- else
  -@album.public_photos.each  do |photo|
    %a{:href => "/photo/#{photo.id}"}
      %img.span-2{:src => "#{photo.url_thumbnail}"}
```

We show all original photos, public or private, if the user has logged in and is viewing his album. Otherwise we will only show public photos. Edited versions of the photos are shown regardless.

```
%h3 Edited versions of photos in this album
- if @album.edited_photos(@user).empty?
  %h4 There are no edited versions of photos in this album
- @album.edited_photos(@user).each  do |photo|
  %a{:href => "/photo/#{photo.id}"}
    %img.span-2{:src => "#{photo.url_thumbnail}"}
```

Note that if original or edited, photos can be set to private and will not be shown if the user has not logged in.

We want to allow anonymous users to view the albums and photos, so we provide friendly URLs to let anonymous users view albums belonging to the users. For this we have the *public albums* route:

```
get "/user/:username" do
  @viewed_user = User.first(:nickname => params[:username])
  redirect "/" if @viewed_user.nil?
  haml :"albums/public"
end
```

Instead of getting the viewed user by his/her ID, we get it through his/her nickname (this is why nicknames are important when the user first registers). Also instead of going to the manage albums page, we go a *public albums* page, which is specifically built for anonymous viewing.

```
=snippet :'/snippets/top'
.span-24
  .span-2
    %img.span-2{:src => "#{@viewed_user.photo_url}"}
  .span-9
    %h2{:style => 'margin-bottom: 0;'} #{@viewed_user.formatted_
name}'s albums
    %h3 #{@viewed_user.description}

%hr.space

-@viewed_user.albums.each do |album|
  %hr
  .span-24
    .span-17
      %h3{:style => 'margin-bottom:5px;'}
        %a{:href => "/album/#{album.id}"} #{album.name}
      %h4 #{album.description}
      %hr.space
      - unless album.photos.empty?
        %h4{:style => 'font-style: italic;'} (#{album.photos.size}
photos in this album, last photo uploaded on #{album.photos.last.
created_at.strftime('%d-%b-%Y')})
    .span-3
      - if album.cover_photo
        %img.span-3{:src => "#{album.cover_photo.url_display}"}
      - elsif !album.photos.empty?
        %img.span-3{:src => "#{album.photos.first.url_display}"}
      - else
        %img.span-3{:src => "/images/album_icon.png"}
```

Uploading photos

Let's look at one of the main features of Photoclone next. Uploading photos is critical in any photo-sharing application and it's no different in Photoclone. The upload photos route is as before, trivial as it simply shows the upload photos view.

```
get "/upload" do
  @user = User.get(session[:userid])
  @albums = @user.albums
  haml :upload
end
```

Here we show all albums belonging to the logged in user and allow him to choose which album he wants to upload to. However, at occasions we want to pre-choose the album he/she must upload to, in this case we use this route instead:

```
get "/album/:id/upload" do
  @user = User.get(session[:userid])
  @albums = [Album.get(params[:id])]
  haml :upload
end
```

In this route there is only one album to upload to and in this way we can share the same page.

```
=snippet :'/snippets/top'
.span-24
  %h2 Upload photos to an album
  - unless @albums.empty?
    .span-24
      %form{:method => 'post', :action => '/upload',
:enctype=>"multipart/form-data"}
        Upload photos to this album -
        %select.span-8{:name => 'album_id'}
          - @albums.each do |album|
            %option{:value => "#{album.id}"} #{album.name}
        %hr.space
        %ol
          %li
            %input{:type => 'file', :name => 'file1', :size => 60}
          %li
            %input{:type => 'file', :name => 'file2', :size => 60}
          %li
            %input{:type => 'file', :name => 'file3', :size => 60}
          %li
            %input{:type => 'file', :name => 'file4', :size => 60}
          %li
            %input{:type => 'file', :name => 'file5', :size => 60}
          %li
            %input{:type => 'file', :name => 'file6', :size => 60}

        %input{:type => 'submit', :value => 'upload'}
        %input{:type => 'button', :value => 'home', :onclick =>
"location.href='/'"}
    - else
      %h3
        Looks like you don't have any albums yet.
        %a{:href => "/album/add"} Create one
        before uploading photos!
```

There isn't much to the page itself. As discussed earlier in the models section we use the form field upload field to upload the photos. Most of the work is done by the model but the post route for uploading does some basic manipulation to get the pieces of data in place.

```
post "/upload" do
  album = Album.get params[:album_id]
  (1..6).each do |i|
    if params["file#{i}"] && (tmpfile = params["file#{i}"][:tempfile])
&& (name = params["file#{i}"][:filename])
      Photo.new(:title => name, :album => album, :tmpfile => tmpfile).
save
    end
  end
  redirect "/album/#{album.id}"
end
```

The parameters provided by most browsers are nested such that a parameter nested in the named parameter (in this case it is *file1*, *file2*, and so on) named `tempfile` will contain the binary data and parameter named `filename` will contain the name of the file that is uploaded. We just need to extract them and pass them to Photo, as we're saving a new record and the rest of the action happens in the model class.

Displaying photos

Displaying photos is another main feature of Photoclone. The next few features are related to viewing photos and manipulating photos and they start from viewing the photo. To explain them properly we will break them up into a few parts:

1. The action menu bar provides different actions for the user to manipulate the photo.

2. Displaying the photo including the title and caption, both of which can be edited inline.

3. Displaying photo metadata including editing the public/private indicator inline.

4. Displaying edited versions.

5. Navigation in the album to the next and previous photos.

6. Annotating the photo.

7. Commenting on the photo.

Annotating and commenting the photo will be left to the next two sections—we'll concentrate on the first five parts in this section. This is the how the *view photo* page finally looks after we're done:

Let's start with a quick look at the *view photo* route.

```
get "/photo/:id" do
  @photo = Photo.get params[:id]
  @user = User.get session[:userid]
  halt 403, 'This is a private photo' if @photo.privacy == 'Private'
and @user != @photo.album.user
```

```
    notes = @photo.annotations.collect do |n|
      '{"x1": "' + n.x.to_s + '", "y1": "' + n.y.to_s +
      '", "height": "' + n.height.to_s + '", "width": "' + n.width.to_s
+
      '","note": "' + n.description + '"}'
    end
    @notes = notes.join(',')
    @prev_in_album = @photo.previous_in_album(@user)
    @next_in_album = @photo.next_in_album(@user)
    haml :photo
  end
```

The view photo route is short, as with most of the other routes. After getting hold of the photo and the logged in user, we check if the photo is private. If it is, we throw a `halt` to inform the user that he/she is trying to view a private photo. Under normal circumstances this will not happen because we will not show thumbnail or any links to a private photo. However, this could happen if a previously public photo was bookmarked and subsequently made private, or an unauthorized user was really trying to view a private photo.

```
halt 403, 'This is a private photo' if @photo.privacy == 'Private' and
@user != @photo.album.user
```

The rest of the code deals with annotations and navigation so let's switch over to the view first. It is a rather large page and the most complex in Photoclone:

```
=snippet :'/snippets/top'
=snippet :'/snippets/annotations_js'
=snippet :'/snippets/editor_js'
=snippet :'/snippets/photo_inline_js'

.span-24
  %h3
    .span-4
      %a{:href => "/album/#{@photo.album.id}"} [Back to album]
    - if @user == @photo.album.user
      .span-4
        %a{:href => '#', :id => 'add_annotation' } [annotate photo]
      .span-3
        %a{:href => '#', :onclick => "pixlr.open({image:'http://
photoclone.saush.com/photos/#{@photo.id}.tmp', title:'#{@photo.title}
copy', service:'express'});"} [edit photo]
      .span-4
        %form{:id => "form_cover_photo", :method => 'post', :action =>
"/album/cover/#{@photo.id}"}
```

```
        %a{:href => '#', :onclick => '$("#form_cover_photo").
submit();'} [set album cover]
      .span-4
        %form{:id => "form_photo_#{@photo.id}", :method => 'post',
:action => "/photo/#{@photo.id}"}
          %input{:type => 'hidden', :name => '_method', :value =>
'delete'}
          %a{:href => '#', :onclick => '$("#form_photo_' + "#{@photo.
id}" + '").submit();'} [delete photo]

%hr.space
.span-24
  .span-13
    - if @user === @photo.album.user
      %h2.edit_title #{@photo.title}
    - else
      %h2 #{@photo.title}
    %img{:id => 'photo', :src => "#{@photo.url_display}"}
    - if @user === @photo.album.user
      %h4.edit_area #{@photo.caption}
    - else
      %h4 #{@photo.caption}

    #annotation_form
      %form{:id => 'annotation_add_form', :method => 'post', :action
=> "/annotation/#{@photo.id}"}
        %fieldset
          %legend
          %input{:name => 'annotation[x1]', :type => 'hidden', :id =>
'annotation_x1'}
          %input{:name => 'annotation[y1]', :type => 'hidden', :id =>
'annotation_y1'}
          %input{:name => 'annotation[height]', :type => 'hidden', :id
=> 'annotation_height'}
          %input{:name => 'annotation[width]', :type => 'hidden', :id
=> 'annotation_width'}
          %textarea{:name => 'annotation[text]', :id => 'annotation_
text'}
        .submit
          %input{:type => 'submit', :value => 'add'}
          %input{:type => 'button', :value => 'cancel', :id =>
'cancel_note'}
  .span-10
    %img.span-1{:src => "#{@photo.album.user.photo_url}"}
    Uploaded on #{@photo.created_at.strftime("%d %b %Y")} by
```

```
    - if @user user and !@user.follows.include?(@photo.album.user)
      %form{:id => "form_create_#{@photo.album.user.id}", :method =>
'post', :action => "/follow/#{@photo.album.user.id}"}
        %input{:type => 'hidden', :name => '_method', :value => 'put'}
        %a{:href => '#', :onclick => '$("#form_create_' + "#{@photo.
album.user.id}" + '").submit();'}
          =@photo.album.user.formatted_name
    - else
      =@photo.album.user.formatted_name
  %h4
    This photo is
    - if @user === @photo.album.user
      %b.edit_privacy #{@photo.privacy}
    - else
      %b #{@photo.privacy}
  - if @user === @photo.album.user
    %h3 Annotations
    - if @photo.annotations.empty?
      %h4 No annotations on this photo.
    - else
      - @photo.annotations.each do |note|
        .span-6
          =note.description
        .span-3
          %form{:id => "form_#{note.id}", :method => 'post', :action
=> "/annotation/#{note.id}"}
            %input{:type => 'hidden', :name => '_method', :value =>
'delete'}
            %a{:href => '#', :onclick => '$("#form_' + "#{note.id}"
+ '").submit();'} [remove]
        %hr.space


    - unless @photo.versions.empty?
      %h3 Edited versions
      - @photo.versions.each do |version|
        %a{:href => "/photo/#{version.id}"}
          %img.span-2{:src => "#{version.url_thumbnail}"}
    - if @photo.original
      %h3 Original photo
      %a{:href => "/photo/#{@photo.original.id}"}
        %img.span-3{:src => "#{@photo.original.url_display}"}


    %h3 #{@photo.album.name}

    - if @prev_in_album
```

```
      %a{:href => "/photo/#{@prev_in_album.id}"}
        %img.span-3{:src => "#{@prev_in_album.url_thumbnail}"}
    - else
      %img.span-3{:src => '/images/spacer.gif'}
    - if @next_in_album
      %a{:href => "/photo/#{@next_in_album.id}"}
        %img.span-3{:src => "#{@next_in_album.url_thumbnail}"}
    - else
      %img.span-3{:src => '/images/spacer.gif'}
    %br
    - if @prev_in_album
      %a{:href => "/photo/#{@prev_in_album.id}"}
        %img.span-2{:src => "/images/left_arrow.gif"}
    %a{:href => "/album/#{@photo.album.id}"}
      %img.span-2{:src => "/images/browse.gif"}
    - if @next_in_album
      %a{:href => "/photo/#{@next_in_album.id}"}
        %img.span-2{:src => "/images/right_arrow.gif"}


%hr.space

.span-24
  -@photo.comments.each do |comment|
    .span-13
      .span-2
        %img.span-2{:src => "#{comment.user.photo_url}"}
      .span-10
        .span-10
          %a.strong{:href => "/follow/#{comment.user.id}"} #{comment.
user.formatted_name} says:
        .span-10
          =comment.text
    .span-2
      - if @user == comment.user
        %form{:id => "form_comment_#{comment.id}", :method => 'post',
:action => "/comment/#{comment.id}"}
          %input{:type => 'hidden', :name => '_method', :value =>
'delete'}
          %a{:href => '#', :onclick => '$("#form_comment_' +
"#{comment.id}" + '").submit();'} [remove]
    %hr.space

.span-24
  %h3 Comments
  %form{:method => 'post', :action => "/comment/#{@photo.id}"}
```

```
%textarea.span-13.update{:name => 'text', :rows => '3'}
%br
%input{:type => 'submit', :value => 'post comment'}
```

As mentioned earlier, we'll be breaking this down in sequenced steps. First let's look at the action menu bar. This menu bar contains all the actions that can be done on the photo. However, the rest of the actions will be available only if the user owns the photo being viewed.

```
.span-24
  %h3
    .span-4
      %a{:href => "/album/#{@photo.album.id}"} [Back to album]
    - if @user == @photo.album.user
      .span-4
        %a{:href => '#', :id => 'add_annotation' } [annotate photo]
      .span-3
        %a{:href => '#', :onclick => "pixlr.open({image:'http://
photoclone.saush.com/photos/#{@photo.id}.tmp', title:'#{@photo.title}
copy', service:'express'});"} [edit photo]
      .span-4
        %form{:id => "form_cover_photo", :method => 'post', :action =>
"/album/cover/#{@photo.id}"}
          %a{:href => '#', :onclick => '$("#form_cover_photo").
submit();'} [set album cover]
        .span-4
          %form{:id => "form_photo_#{@photo.id}", :method => 'post',
:action => "/photo/#{@photo.id}"}
            %input{:type => 'hidden', :name => '_method', :value =>
'delete'}
            %a{:href => '#', :onclick => '$("#form_photo_' + "#{@photo.
id}" + '").submit();'} [delete photo]
```

Next, we look at displaying the photo and doing inline editing of the title and caption:

```
.span-24
  .span-13
    - if @user === @photo.album.user
      %h2.edit_title #{@photo.title}
    - else
      %h2 #{@photo.title}
    %img{:id => 'photo', :src => "#{@photo.url_display}"}
    - if @user === @photo.album.user
      %h4.edit_area #{@photo.caption}
    - else
      %h4 #{@photo.caption}
```

As with editing the album title and description, we use Jeditable to allow inline editing of the photo's title and caption. We use a similar snippet called `photo_inline_js.rb` to add in the necessary JavaScript setup for Jeditable.

```
%script{:type => "text/javascript", :src  => "/js/jeditable.mini.js"}
:javascript
  $(document).ready(function() {
    $('.edit_title').editable('/photo/title/#{@photo.id}');
    $('.edit_area').editable('/photo/caption/#{@photo.id}', {
      type    : 'textarea',
      submit  : 'OK',
      cancel  : 'Cancel',
      height  : 60
    });
    $('.edit_privacy').editable('/photo/privacy/#{@photo.id}', {
      data    : " {'public':'public','private':'private'}",
      type    : 'select',
      submit  : 'OK',
      style   : 'display: inline'
    });
  });
});
```

Note that `edit_title` links to the edit photo title route while `edit_area` links to the *edit photo property* route. As with editing the album, we use a single route for both actions.

```
post "/photo/:property/:photo_id" do
  photo = Photo.get params[:photo_id]
  if %w(title caption).include? params[:property]
    photo.send(params[:property] + '=', params[:value])
    photo.save
  end
  photo.send(params[:property])
end
```

The last editable class refers to a privacy editable field, which we will discuss next.

```
%h4
  This photo is
  - if @user === @photo.album.user
    %b.edit_privacy #{@photo.privacy}
  - else
    %b #{@photo.privacy}
```

Remember that `privacy` is an attribute of photo. This means that we can use the same edit photo route above to perform the actual edit. However, if you click on the **public** button on the page, you might notice that instead of turning into a text field or a text area, it turns into a drop down select field. We supply the default data here directly in the script.

We also provide some metadata on the time the photo was uploaded and the user who uploaded it. The user can optionally follow this user if he/she is not already in his/her list of people followed.

```
.span-10
    %img.span-1{:src => "#{@photo.album.user.photo_url}"}
    Uploaded on #{@photo.created_at.strftime("%d %b %Y")} by
    - if @user and !@user.follows.include?(@photo.album.user)
        %form{:id => "form_create_#{@photo.album.user.id}", :method =>
'post', :action => "/follow/#{@photo.album.user.id}"}
            %input{:type => 'hidden', :name => '_method', :value => 'put'}
            %a{:href => '#', :onclick => '$("#form_create_' + "#{@photo.
album.user.id}" + '").submit();'}
                =@photo.album.user.formatted_name
    - else
        =@photo.album.user.formatted_name
```

Just below the metadata we show a list of annotations on the photo and below that is a list of edited versions of the photo. The navigation amongst photos in the same album goes below the edit versions.

Remember we have these two variables in the route:

```
@prev_in_album = @photo.previous_in_album(@user)
@next_in_album = @photo.next_in_album(@user)
```

These two variables are used to determine the next and previous photos to view. The logic is in the Photo model but here we determine the layout:

```
%h3 #{@photo.album.name}

    - if @prev_in_album
        %a{:href => "/photo/#{@prev_in_album.id}"}
            %img.span-3{:src => "#{@prev_in_album.url_thumbnail}"}
```

```
- else
  %img.span-3{:src => '/images/spacer.gif'}
- if @next_in_album
  %a{:href => "/photo/#{@next_in_album.id}"}
    %img.span-3{:src => "#{@next_in_album.url_thumbnail}"}
- else
  %img.span-3{:src => '/images/spacer.gif'}
%br
- if @prev_in_album
  %a{:href => "/photo/#{@prev_in_album.id}"}
    %img.span-2{:src => "/images/left_arrow.gif"}
%a{:href => "/album/#{@photo.album.id}"}
  %img.span-2{:src => "/images/browse.gif"}
- if @next_in_album
  %a{:href => "/photo/#{@next_in_album.id}"}
    %img.span-2{:src => "/images/right_arrow.gif"}
```

Note that the previous and next photos in the list represent a last-in-first-out structure. The last uploaded photo is considered the first photo to view while the next photo goes to the second to last.

Just below the thumbnails of the previous and next photos, we have a clearer navigation guide, with arrows that point in either direction, and a central link that points back to the album. As with web design it is always good to have multiple links to the same page, to enforce interactivity of elements on the page as well as to place navigation where it is most natural.

The navigation for photos before and after depends on the user that is viewing the photo.

```
def previous_in_album(viewer)
  photos = viewer == album.user ? album.original_photos(viewer) :
album.public_photos
  index = photos.index self
  return nil unless index
  photos[index - 1] if index > 0
```

```
end

def next_in_album(viewer)
  photos = viewer == album.user ? album.original_photos(viewer) :
album.public_photos
  index = photos.index self
  return nil unless index
  photos[index + 1] if index < album.photos.length
end
```

Also, we only show original photos and not edited photos.

Annotating photos

To annotate on a photo, we place a Javascript layer on top of the photo and draw a white box around the item that that user marked. For this we use the ImgNotes jQuery plugin by Tarique Sani that in turn uses another jQuery plugin called ImgAreaSelect by Michał Wojciechowski. There are a few files we will need for this. In the `public/js` folder we add `notes.js` and `select.js`, from the ImgNotes and ImgAreaSelect jQuery plugins respectively. The links to these two scripts are in `layout.rb`.

```
%script{:src => '/js/select.js', :type => 'text/javascript'}
%script{:src => '/js/notes.js', :type => 'text/javascript'}
```

The two important functions in the two files of note are `img_annotations` in the `notes.js` and `imgAreaSelect` in `select.js`. To add in the annotation feature, we include a snippet called `annotations_js` in the view photo page:

```
=snippet :'/snippets/annotations_js'
```

This snippet allows us to provide annotations to photos:

```
:javascript
  notes = [ #{@notes} ];

  $(window).load(function () {
  $('#photo').img_annotations();

  $('#cancel_note').click(function(){
    $('#photo').imgAreaSelect({ hide: true });
    $('#annotation_form').hide();
  });

  $('#add_annotation').click(function(){
    $('#photo').imgAreaSelect({ onSelectChange: show_add_annotation,
x1: 120, y1: 90, x2: 280, y2: 210 });
      return false;
```

```
      });
   });

   function show_add_annotation (img, area) {
      imgOffset = $(img).offset();
      form_left  = parseInt(imgOffset.left) + parseInt(area.x1);
      form_top   = parseInt(imgOffset.top) + parseInt(area.y1) +
   parseInt(area.height)+5;

      $('#annotation_form').css({ left: form_left + 'px', top: form_top
   + 'px'});
      $('#annotation_form').show();
      $('#annotation_form').css("z-index", 10000);
      $('#annotation_x1').val(area.x1);
      $('#annotation_y1').val(area.y1);
      $('#annotation_height').val(area.height);
      $('#annotation_width').val(area.width);
   }
```

`notes` is a JavaScript variable used store the list of notes added to the photo:

```
   notes = [ #{@notes} ];
```

The data looks something like this:

```
   notes = [ {"x1": "63", "y1": "39", "height": "239", "width":
   "384","note": "La Rotonde lits up prettily at night!"},{"x1": "325",
   "y1": "8", "height": "74", "width": "146","note": "Great Provencal
   evening"} ];
```

`x1` and `y1` are the coordinates of the upper-left corner of the white box while `height` and `width` define the height and width of the box. The `note` field is the actual text to be displayed. We indicate the image to be annotated to be the element that has a class ID `photo`.

```
   $('#photo').img_annotations();
```

Remember the function `img_annotations`, which we are using here. When we click on an element that has the class ID `add_annotation`, we use the `imgAreaSelect` function to draw the white select box and at the same time, call the `show_add_anno-tation` function.

```
   $('#add_annotation').click(function(){
      $('#photo').imgAreaSelect({ onSelectChange: show_add_annotation, x1:
   120, y1: 90, x2: 280, y2: 210 });
      return false;
   });
});
```

The `show_add_annotation` function in turn shows a form just below the white box, and pre-populates certain dimensions data into that form:

```
function show_add_annotation (img, area) {
   imgOffset = $(img).offset();
   form_left  = parseInt(imgOffset.left) + parseInt(area.x1);
   form_top   = parseInt(imgOffset.top) + parseInt(area.y1) +
parseInt(area.height)+5;

   $('#annotation_form').css({ left: form_left + 'px', top: form_top +
'px'});
   $('#annotation_form').show();
   $('#annotation_form').css("z-index", 10000);
   $('#annotation_x1').val(area.x1);
   $('#annotation_y1').val(area.y1);
   $('#annotation_height').val(area.height);
   $('#annotation_width').val(area.width);
}
```

The annotation form is the form that allows the user to write the annotation text and it is a basic HTML form with a **submit** and a **cancel** button:

```
#annotation_form
   %form{:id => 'annotation_add_form', :method => 'post', :action => "/
annotation/#{@photo.id}"}
    %fieldset
      %legend
      %input{:name => 'annotation[x1]', :type => 'hidden', :id =>
'annotation_x1'}
      %input{:name => 'annotation[y1]', :type => 'hidden', :id =>
'annotation_y1'}
      %input{:name => 'annotation[height]', :type => 'hidden', :id =>
'annotation_height'}
      %input{:name => 'annotation[width]', :type => 'hidden', :id =>
'annotation_width'}
      %textarea{:name => 'annotation[text]', :id => 'annotation_text'}
     .submit
      %input{:type => 'submit', :value => 'add'}
      %input{:type => 'button', :value => 'cancel', :id => 'cancel_
note'}
```

The **cancel** button calls the `cancel_note` function to hide the form once more:

```
$('#cancel_note').click(function(){
   $('#photo').imgAreaSelect({ hide: true });
   $('#annotation_form').hide();
});
```

This is how an annotated photo looks:

When the user enters the note he/she wants to make on the photo and clicks on the **add** button, the data will be sent to the *add annotation* route:

```
post "/annotation/:photo_id" do
  photo = Photo.get params[:photo_id]
  note = Annotation.create(:x => params["annotation"]["x1"],
                           :y => params["annotation"]["y1"],
                           :height => params["annotation"]["height"],
                           :width => params["annotation"]["width"],
                           :description => params["annotation"]
["text"])
  photo.annotations << note
  photo.save
  redirect "/photo/#{params[:photo_id]}"
end
```

The annotation is created and added to the photo and the user is redirected back to the view photo route:

```
%h3 Annotations
  - if @photo.annotations.empty?
    %h4 No annotations on this photo.
  - else
```

```
- @photo.annotations.each do |note|
  .span-6
    =note.description
  .span-3
    %form{:id => "form_#{note.id}", :method => 'post', :action =>
"/annotation/#{note.id}"}
      %input{:type => 'hidden', :name => '_method', :value =>
'delete'}
      %a{:href => '#', :onclick => '$("#form_' + "#{note.id}" +
'").submit();'} [remove]
```

The page with the annotated photo looks like this:

To remove the annotation, the user can click on the **[remove]** link at the list of annotations to the right. This will simply remove the annotation and reload the same page.

```
delete "/annotation/:id" do
  note = Annotation.get(params[:id])
  photo = note.photo
  if note.destroy
    redirect "/photo/#{photo.id}"
  else
      throw "Cannot delete this annotation!"
  end
end
```

Commenting on photos

Commenting on photos is a relatively simple feature to implement. Right at the bottom of `photo.haml` is the comment form for each photo:

```
.span-24
  %h3 Comments
  %form{:method => 'post', :action => "/comment/#{@photo.id}"}
    %textarea.span-13.update{:name => 'text', :rows => '3'}
    %br
    %input{:type => 'submit', :value => 'post comment'}
```

Posting to the comment route will add a comment to the photo:

```
post "/comment/:photo_id" do
  photo = Photo.get params[:photo_id]
  comment = Comment.create(:text => params[:text])
  comment.user = User.get session[:userid]
  photo.comments << comment
  photo.save
  redirect "/photo/#{params[:photo_id]}"
end
```

After creating the comment, it will appear at the bottom of the view photo page:

```
.span-24
  -@photo.comments.each do |comment|
    .span-13
      .span-2
        %img.span-2{:src => "#{comment.user.photo_url}"}
      .span-10
        .span-10
```

```
      %a.strong{:href => "/follow/#{comment.user.id}"} #{comment.
user.formatted_name} says:
          .span-10
          =comment.text
      .span-2
        - if @user == comment.user
          %form{:id => "form_comment_#{comment.id}", :method => 'post',
:action => "/comment/#{comment.id}"}
            %input{:type => 'hidden', :name => '_method', :value =>
'delete'}
            %a{:href => '#', :onclick => '$("#form_comment_' +
"#{comment.id}" + '").submit();'} [remove]
      %hr.space
```

Only the user who created the comment can delete the comment he wrote:

```
delete "/comment/:id" do
  comment = Comment.get(params[:id])
  photo = comment.photo
  commentor = comment.user
  user = User.get session[:userid]
  comment.destroy if user == commentor
  redirect "/photo/#{photo.id}"
end
```

Editing photos

We use Pixlr as the editor to modify the photos we create. The photo editing
mechanism works in the following way:

1. The user clicks on the edit photo link.
2. Photo data is sent to the Pixlr photo editor and the user is directed to
   it as well.
3. The user modifies the photo on the Pixlr editor.
4. When the user is done with the changes, he saves the photo and the data is
   sent back to Photoclone.
5. Photoclone saves it as an edited version and links it to the original photo.

Let's start with the link that triggers sending the photo to Pixlr:

```
%a{:href => '#', :onclick => "pixlr.open({image:'http://photoclone.
saush.com/photos/#{@photo.id}.tmp', title:'#{@photo.title} copy',
service:'express'});"} [edit photo]
```

The link calls the Pixlr JavaScript library function open to send the temporary display photo to the Pixlr editor; in this our case we're using the Pixlr Express editor. The title of the photo is appended with the word *copy*. Let's look closer. Before we can use the link, we need to include the snippet `editor_js` in `photo.haml`:

```
=snippet :'/snippets/editor_js'
```

The snippet is a bunch of settings that tells Pixlr how we want it to behave:

```
%script{:type => "text/javascript", :src  => "/js/pixlr_minified.js"}
:javascript
  pixlr.settings.target = 'http://photoclone.saush.com/photo/save_
edited/#{@photo.id}';
  pixlr.settings.exit = "http://photoclone.saush.com/photo/#{@photo.
id}";
  pixlr.settings.credentials = true;
  pixlr.settings.method = 'post';
  pixlr.settings.locktarget = true;
```

First, the snippet adds in a minified version of the Pixlr Javascript library. The `target` setting is the URL that Pixlr will call and send the edited photo data to. The `exit` setting is the URL that Pixlr will redirect to (without sending any data) if the user chooses to exit from the Pixlr photo editor. The `credentials` setting is used for reducing the number of round-trips needed to the Pixlr server. If we set it to `true`, we need a `crossdomain.xml` file in the root folder of the server (in this case it is the `public` folder), which simply indicates that our server allows access for Pixlr. This file is required by the Flash component used by Pixlr.

```
<?xml version="1.0"?>
<!DOCTYPE cross-domain-policy SYSTEM "http://www.adobe.com/xml/dtds/
cross-domain-policy.dtd">
<cross-domain-policy>
  <allow-access-from domain="pixlr.com" />
  <site-control permitted-cross-domain-policies="master-only"/>
  <allow-http-request-headers-from domain="pixlr.com" headers="*"
secure="true"/>
</cross-domain-policy>
```

The `method` setting tells Pixlr that we'll be sending the data through HTTP POST. Lastly, the `locktarget` setting tells Pixlr to stop the user from saving the photo to his/her computer because we want the user to save the photo back to Photoclone.

This is how the Pixlr Express photo editor looks with the photo redirected
from Photoclone:

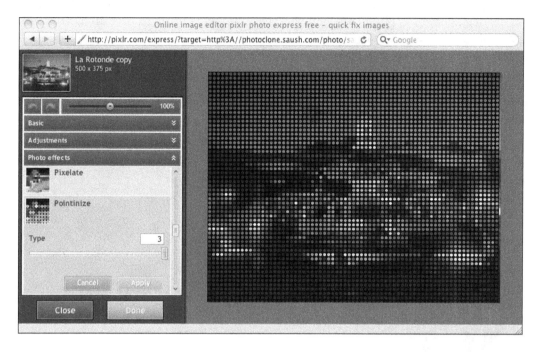

Once the user is satisfied with his/her changes and saves them by clicking on the
Done button, the photo will be sent back to the *save edited photo* route:

```
post "/photo/save_edited/:original_photo_id" do
  if params[:original_photo_id] && params["image"] && (tmpfile =
params["image"][:tempfile]) && (name = params["image"][:filename])
    original_photo = Photo.get params[:original_photo_id]
    new_photo = Photo.new(:title => name, :album => original_photo.
album, :tmpfile => tmpfile)
    original_photo.versions << new_photo
    original_photo.save
  end
  redirect "/photo/#{original_photo.id}"
end
```

This is very similar to the code we saw in the photo upload; in fact the methods
we used are the same, except this time we save the edited photo as a version
of the original.

Sharing photos

Sharing photos is a primary function of a photo-sharing application. As mentioned in the design section, Photoclone enables sharing photos through friendly URLs and photostreams. We saw how Photoclone implements friendly URLs in the preceding user management section; let's take a look at how photostreams are implemented by examining how Photoclone enables users to search and follow other users.

This is the *view users* page, which shows a list of people who follow you and a list of people who you follow:

Photoclone has a single page that shows the user a list of users they follow and the users following him/her. The route used for this page is the *follows* route:

```
get "/follows" do
  @user = User.get session[:userid]
  @follows = @user.follows
  @followers = @user.followers
```

```
    if params[:query]
      @search_results = User.all(:nickname.like => params[:query] + '%')
    end
    haml :'follows/manage'
  end
```

This route retrieves the logged in user and extracts the people following him/her as well as people he/she is following:

```
=snippet :'/snippets/top'
.span-24
  .span-2
    %img.span-2{:src => "#{@user.photo_url}"}
  .span-9
    %h2{:style => 'margin-bottom: 0;'} People you follow
    %h3 View photos shared by people you follow!
  .span-7.prepend-5
    %form{:method => 'get'}
      %input{:type => 'text', :name => 'query'}
      %input{:type => 'submit', :value => 'search people'}

- if @search_results
  %hr.space
  .span-24
    %h3 People who match your search criteria
    - @search_results.each do |res|
      .span-3.picbox
        %a{:href => "/albums/#{res.id}"}
          %img.span-2{:src => "#{res.photo_url}"}
          %h4{:style => 'margin-bottom:5px;'} #{res.nickname}
        - unless res == @user or @user.follows.include? res
          %form{:id => "form_create_#{res.id}", :method => 'post',
:action => "/follow/#{res.id}"}
            %input{:type => 'hidden', :name => '_method', :value =>
'put'}
            %a{:href => '#', :onclick => '$("#form_create_' + "#{res.
id}" + '").submit();'} [follow]
          %hr.space

%hr.space
.span-24
  %h3 People I follow
  - if @follows.empty?
    %h4 You are not following anyone right now. Search for someone and
follow them to view their photos!
```

```
   - else
     .span-24
       -@follows.each do |follow|
         .span-3.picbox
           %a{:href => "/albums/#{follow.id}"}
             %img.span-2{:src => "#{follow.photo_url}"}
             %h4{:style => 'margin-bottom:5px;'} #{follow.nickname}
           %form{:id => "form_delete_#{follow.id}", :method => 'post',
:action => "/follow/#{follow.id}"}
             %input{:type => 'hidden', :name => '_method', :value =>
'delete'}
             %a{:href => '#', :onclick => '$("#form_delete_' +
"#{follow.id}" + '").submit();'} [unfollow]
           %hr.space

%hr.space
.span-24
  %h3 People following you
  - if @followers.empty?
    %h4 No one is following you at the moment. Tell them about it!
  - else
    .span-24
      -@followers.each do |follower|
        .span-3
          %a{:href => "/albums/#{follower.id}"}
            %img.span-2{:src => "#{follower.photo_url}"}
            %h4{:style => 'margin-bottom:5px;'} #{follower.nickname}
            - unless @user.follows.include? follower
              %form{:id => "form_follower_create_#{follower.id}",
:method => 'post', :action => "/follow/#{follower.id}"}
                %input{:type => 'hidden', :name => '_method', :value
=> 'put'}
                %a{:href => '#', :onclick => '$("#form_follower_
create_' + "#{follower.id}" + '").submit();'} [follow]
          %hr.space
```

For every user that the logged in user follows, there is an option for the user to stop following that person.

```
%form{:id => "form_delete_#{follow.id}", :method => 'post', :action =>
"/follow/#{follow.id}"}
          %input{:type => 'hidden', :name => '_method', :value =>
'delete'}
          %a{:href => '#', :onclick => '$("#form_delete_' +
"#{follow.id}" + '").submit();'} [unfollow]
```

To stop following a user, we simply use the unfollow method (remember the two convenience methods mentioned in the authentication and user management section) on the person being followed:

```
delete "/follow/:user_id" do
  me = User.get session[:userid]
  person = User.get params[:user_id]
  me.unfollow person
  redirect "/follows"
end
```

Similarly, for every user that is following the logged in user, there is an option for him/her to follow that user in return (unless he is already following that user):

```
%form{:id => "form_follower_create_#{follower.id}", :method => 'post',
:action => "/follow/#{follower.id}"}
%input{:type => 'hidden', :name => '_method', :value => 'put'}
    %a{:href => '#', :onclick => '$("#form_follower_create_' +
"#{follower.id}" + '").submit();'} [follow]
```

To follow a user, we use the follow method on that person:

```
put "/follow/:user_id" do
  me = User.get session[:userid]
  person = User.get params[:user_id]
  me.follow person
  redirect "/follows"
end
```

Photoclone also implements a simple search function:

```
%form{:method => 'get'}
  %input{:type => 'text', :name => 'query'}
  %input{:type => 'submit', :value => 'search people'}
```

This simple search box goes out to the follows route, which does a SQL search on the user's nickname:

```
if params[:query]
  @search_results = User.all(:nickname.like => params[:query] + '%')
end
```

The search results are then displayed above the other lists. As before we allow an option for the user to follow people from the search results:

```
.span-24
    %h3 People who match your search criteria
    - @search_results.each do |res|
```

```
.span-3.picbox
  %a{:href => "/albums/#{res.id}"}
    %img.span-2{:src => "#{res.photo_url}"}
    %h4{:style => 'margin-bottom:5px;'} #{res.nickname}
  - unless res == @user or @user.follows.include? res
    %form{:id => "form_create_#{res.id}", :method => 'post',
:action => "/follow/#{res.id}"}
      %input{:type => 'hidden', :name => '_method', :value =>
'put'}
      %a{:href => '#', :onclick => '$("#form_create_' + "#{res.
id}" + '").submit();'} [follow]
```

These are the results from our search, also displayed in the view users page:

And that is it! A minimalist and simple Flickr clone. We have covered quite a lot of ground in building Photoclone. The next step is to deploy it.

Deploying the clone

Unlike as in the previous chapters, we will only see how we deploy to a normal server, and not to Heroku. This is because while we store most of our data on Amazon, for fast processing we actually keep temporary cached files in the same server. Unfortunately Heroku doesn't provide for non-database file storage (we are not allowed access to the file server). While there are a few other ways of deploying Photoclone on a non-dedicated server, the steps are almost the same. We will only describe one way of deploying the service.

Deploying on a server

For development purposes we would normally run it off the command line using the built-in web server. However, before we do this, we need to set up the database. For this application we would need to have MySQL already installed. At the command line go into the MySQL interactive command console:

```
$ mysql -u <username> -p <password>
```

Then just do a simple command:

```
mysql> create database photoclone;
```

This will just create the database. Next, go into IRB and run the following command:

```
> require 'models'
```

This will get the necessary classes for creating the database tables. Next, just run the following command:

```
> DataMapper.auto_migrate!
```

This will create the tables for the application. To run the application, we just need to run this at the command line:

```
$ ruby photoclone.rb
```

Then go to `http://localhost:4567/` and you will see the login page. Try logging in. If you have added *localhost* to the list of applicable URLs in RPX you will be able to log in.

Summary

We have gone through a lot in this chapter. We began by introducing photo-sharing applications in general and then Flickr specifically. We walked through what made Flickr work and discussed the main features of a photo-sharing application. After that we went through the design of implementing those main features. Before jumping into describing how we implemented the design, we went on a tour of the technologies we used in building the clone. In particular we discussed the three main technologies used — RPX for authentication, Pixlr for photo editing, and AWS S3 for permanent photo storage. We spent the bulk of this chapter explaining how we built Photoclone, a photo-sharing application that has those set of features. We went through the data model used in Photoclone, where the bulk of logic resided and then the major application flow in Photoclone. Finally, we wrapped up with a simple description of how Photoclone can be deployed.

5
Social Networking Services – Cloning Facebook 1

One of the most dominant Internet services today is the social networking service. According to a report by the Nielsen Company, in January 2010, the amount of time an average person spent on Facebook is more than seven hours per month, which amounts to more than 14 minutes per day. If you lump together the time spent on Google, Yahoo!, YouTube, Bing, Wikipedia, and Amazon, it still doesn't beat Facebook! By March 2010, Facebook accounted for more than seven percent of all Internet traffic in the United States, surpassing visits to Google. Social networking services have risen in the past few years to be more than just a passing fad, to be an important communications tool as well as a part of daily life.

We will be building our last and most complex clone based on Facebook, the most popular social networking service as of date. The clone we will build here will be described over this and the next chapter. In this chapter we will cover basic information about social networking services, main features of the clone that we will build, as well as the description of the data model we will be using for the clone.

All about social networking services

A social networking service is an Internet service that models social relationships among people. Essentially it consists of a user profile, his or her social links, and a variety of additional services. Most social networking services are web-based and provide various ways for users to interact over the Internet, including sharing content and communications.

Early social networking websites started in the form of generalized online communities such as The WELL (1985), theglobe.com (1994), GeoCities (1994), and Tripod (1995). These early communities focused on communications through chat rooms, and sharing personal information and topics via simple publishing tools. Other communities took the approach of simply having people link to each other via e-mail addresses. These sites included Classmates (1995), focusing on ties with former schoolmates, and SixDegrees (1997), focusing on indirect ties.

SixDegrees.com in a way was the first to bring together the first few defining features of a social networking service. The basic features of the first online social networking services include user profiles, adding friends to a friends list, and sending private messages. Unfortunately, SixDegrees was too advanced for its time and eventually closed in 2001.

Interestingly the most popular social networking service in Korea, CyWorld, was started around this time in 1999. The original intention for CyWorld was to develop an online dating service similar to Match and provide an open public meeting place for users to meet online. In 2001, CyWorld launched the minihompy service, a feature that allows each user to create a virtual homepage. This was highly successful as celebrities and politicians took to this platform to reach out to their fans and audience. CyWorld also eventually included a virtual currency called "dottori" in 2002 and a mobile version in 2004. Up to 2008, CyWorld had more than one third of Korea's entire population as members with a strong penetration of ninety percent in the young adults market.

Between 2002 and 2004, a few social networking services became highly popular. Friendster, started by Jon Abraham in 2002 to compete with Match.com, was highly successful initially. However due to platform and scalability issues, its popularity plummeted as newer social networking services were launched. MySpace, launched in 2003, was started as a Friendster alternative and became popular with independent rock bands from Los Angeles as promoters used the platform to advertise VIP passes for popular clubs. Subsequently, MySpace facilitated a two-way conversation between bands and their fans, and music became the growth engine of MySpace. MySpace also introduced the concept of allowing users to personalize their pages and to generate unique layouts and backgrounds. Eventually MySpace became the most dominant social networking service in U.S. until Facebook took over in 2009.

Mixi is the largest online social networking service in Japan with a total of 20 million users to date and over ninety percent of users being Japanese. Launched in February 2004 by founder Kenji Kasahara, the focus of Mixi is to enable users to meet new people who share common interests. An interesting feature of Mixi (counterintuitive) is that it's an *invitation by friend* social network, which means that a new user can only join Mixi through an invitation by an existing user. This feature is only found in niche and private social networks such as `http://www.asmallworld.net`, a successful social networking service that caters to celebrities and high net worth individuals. This invitation-based model holds the user responsible for who they invite, and thus reduces unwanted behavior within the network, reflecting Japanese culture itself.

Social networking began to emerge as a part of business Internet strategy at around 2005 when Yahoo! launched Yahoo! 360, its first attempt at a social networking service. In July 2005 News Corporation bought MySpace. It was around this time as well that the first mainland Chinese social networks started. The three most notable examples in chronological order are 51.com (2005), Xiaonei (2005), and Kaixin001 (2008). 51.com drew its inspiration from CyWorld, and later MySpace and QQ. On the other hand, Xiaonei has a user interface that follows Facebook, though it also offers the user flexibility to change the look and feel, similar to MySpace. Kaixin001, the latest social networking platform in China with the fastest growing number of users, started in 2008 and the platform and user interface are remarkably similar to Facebook.

It was also around this time that more niche social networking services focusing on specific demographics sprang up, with the most successful example being LinkedIn, which focused on business professionals. At the same time media content sharing sites began slowly incorporated social networking service features and became social networking services themselves. Examples include QQ (instant messaging), Flickr (photo-sharing), YouTube (video-sharing), and Last.FM (music sharing).

As mentioned earlier, as of early 2010 social networking services are the dominant service and purpose for many users on the Internet, with Internet traffic in US surpassing the previous giant of the Internet.

Facebook

Facebook is the most dominant social networking service till date, with 400 million active users, 5 billion pieces of content shared each week, and more than 100 million active users concurrently accessing Facebook through their mobile devices.
It is also the most widespread, with 70 percent of its users from outside of US, its home market.

Mark Zuckerberg and some of his Harvard college roommates launched Facebook in February 2004. Initially intended as an online directory for college students (the initial membership was limited to Harvard College students) it was later expanded to include other colleges, then high schools, and finally anyone around the world who is 13 years old and above.

Facebook features are typically that of many social networks that were created around that time. The more prominent ones are the Wall (a space on every user's profile five friends to post messages on), pokes (which allows users to virtually *poke* each other, that is to notify a user that they have been *poked*), photo uploading, sharing, and status updates, which allow users to inform their friends of their whereabouts and what they were doing. Over time, Facebook included features to form virtual groups, to blog, to start events, chat with instant messaging, and even send virtual gifts to friends.

Facebook launched Facebook Platform in May 2007, providing a framework for software developers to create applications that interact with Facebook. It soon became wildly popular, and within a year 400,000 developers have registered for the platform, and built 33,000 applications. As of writing date there are more than 500,000 active applications in Facebook, developed by more than 1 million developers and there are more than 250 applications with more than 1 million monthly active users!

In this chapter we will be cloning Facebook and creating an application called Colony, which has the basic but essential features of Facebook.

Main features

Online social networking services are complex applications with a large number of features. However, these features can be roughly grouped into a few common categories:

- User
- Community
- Content-sharing
- Developer

User features are features that relate directly to and with the user. For example, the ability to create and share their own profiles, and the ability to share status and activities are user features. Community features are features that connect users with each other. An example of this is the friends list feature, which shows the number of friends a user has connected with in the social network.

Content sharing features are quite easy to understand. These are features that allow a user to share his self-created content with other users, for example photo sharing or blogging. Social bookmarking features are those features that allow users to share content they have discovered with other users, such as sharing links and tagging items with labels. Finally, developer features are features that allow external developers to access the services and data in the social networks.

While the social networking services out in the market often try to differentiate themselves from each other in order to gain an edge over their competition, in this chapter we will be building a stereotypical online social networking service. We will be choosing only a few of the more common features in each category, except for developer features, which for practical reasons will not be implemented here.

Let's look at these features we will implement in Colony, by category.

User

User features are features that relate directly to users:

- Users' activities on the system are broadcast to friends as an activity feed.
- Users can post brief status updates to all users.
- Users can add or remove friends by inviting them to link up. Friendship in both ways need to be approved by the recipient of the invitation.

Community

Community features connect users with each other:

- Users can post to a wall belonging to a user, group, or event. A wall is a place where any user can post on and can be viewed by all users.
- Users can send private messages to other users.
- Users can create events that represent an actual event in the real world. Events pull together users, content, and provide basic event management capabilities, such as RSVP.
- Users can form and join groups. Groups represent a grouping of like-minded people and pulls together users and content. Groups are permanent.
- Users can comment on various types of shared and created content including photos, pages, statuses, and activities. Comments are textual only.
- Users can indicate that they like most types of shared and created content including photos, pages, statuses, and activities.

Content sharing

Content sharing features allow users to share content, either self-generated or discovered, with other users:

- Users can create albums and upload photos to them
- Users can create standalone pages belonging to them or attached pages belonging to events and groups

You might notice that some of the features in the previous chapters are similar to those here. This should not be surprising. Online social networking services grew from existing communications and community services, often evolving and incorporating features and capabilities from those services. The approach adopted in this book is no different. We will be using some of the features we have built in the previous chapter and adapt them accordingly for Colony.

> For the observant reader you might notice that the previous chapters have clones that end with *clone*. The original name of this clone during writing was *Faceclone*, but apparently Facebook has trademarked *Face* for many of its applications. In order to avoid any potential trademark issues, I chose *Colony* instead.

Designing the clone

Now that we have the list of features that we want to implement for Colony, let's start designing the clone. The design and implementation of this clone will be described over this and the next chapter. We will start with the data model in this chapter and move on to describing the application flow and deployment with the next chapter.

Authentication, access control, and user management

Authentication, access control, and user management are handled much the same as in previous chapters. As with the other clones, authentication is done through RPX, which means we delegate authentication to a third party provider such as Google, Yahoo!, or Facebook. Access control however is still done by Colony, while user management functions are shared between the authentication provider and Colony.

Access control in Colony is done on all data, which prevents user from accessing data that they are not allowed to. This is done through control of the user account, to which all other data for a user belongs. In most cases a user is not allowed access to any data that does not belong to him/her (that is not shared to everyone). In some cases though access is implicit; for example, an event is accessible to be viewed only if you are the organizer of the event. Note that unlike Photoclone, which has public pages, there are no public pages in Colony.

As before, user management is a shared responsibility between the third party provider and the clone. The provider handles password management and general security while Colony stores a simple set of profile information for the user.

Status updates

Allowing you to send status updates about yourself is a major feature of all social networking services. This feature allows the user, a member of the social networking service, to announce and define his presence as well as state of mind to his network. If you have gone through the Twitter clone chapter, you might notice that this feature is almost the same as the one in Tweetclone.

The major difference in the features is in *who* can read the statuses, which can be quite subtle yet obvious to someone who has read the previous chapters. In Tweetclone, the user's followers can read the statuses (which is really just anyone who chooses to follow him or her) while in Colony, only the user's friends can read the statuses. Remember that a user's friend is someone validated and approved by the user and not just anyone off the street who happens to follow that user.

Status updates belong to a single user but are viewable to all friends as a part of the user's activity feed.

User activity feeds and news feeds

Activity feeds, activity streams, or life streams are continuous streams of information on a user's activities. Activity feeds go beyond just status updates; they are a digital trace of a user's activity in the social network, which includes his status updates. This include public actions like posting to a wall, uploading photos, and commenting on content, but not private actions like sending messages to individuals. The user's activity feed is visible to all users who visit his user page.

Activity feeds are a subset of news feeds that is an aggregate of activity feeds of the user and his network. News feeds give an insight into the user's activities as well as the activities of his network. In the design of our clone, the user's activity feed is what you see when you visit the user page, for example `http://colony.saush.com/user/sausheong`, while the news feed is what you see when you first log in to Colony, that's the landing page. This design is quite common to many social networking services.

Friends list and inviting users to join

One of the reasons why social networking services are so wildly successful is the ability to reach out to old friends or colleagues, and also to see friends of your friends. To clone this feature we provide a standard friends list and an option to search for friends. Searching for friends allows you to find other users in the system by their nicknames or their full names. By viewing a user's page, we are able to see his friends and therefore see his friend's user pages as well.

Another critical feature in social networking services is the ability to invite friends and spread the word around. In Colony we tap on the capabilities of Facebook and invite friends who are already on Facebook to use Colony. While there is a certain amount of irony (using another social networking service to implement a feature of your social networking service), it makes a lot of practical sense, as Facebook is already one of the most popular social networking services on the planet. To implement this, we will use Facebook Connect. However, this means if the user wants to reach out and get others to join him in Colony he will need to log into Facebook to do so.

As with most features, the implementation can be done in many ways and Facebook Connect (or any other type of third-party integration for that matter) is only one of them. Another popular strategy is to use web mail clients such as Yahoo! Mail or Gmail, and extract user contacts with the permission of the user. The e-mails extracted this way can be used as a mailing list to send to potential users. This is in fact a strategy used by Facebook.

Posting to the wall

A wall is a place where users can post messages. Walls are meant to be publicly read by all visitors. In a way it is like a virtual cork bulletin board that users can pin their messages on to be read by anyone. Wall posts are meant to be short public messages. The Messages feature can be used to send private messages.

A wall can belong to a user, an event, or a group and each of these owning entities can have only one wall. This means any post sent to a user, event, or group is automatically placed on its one and only wall.

A message on a wall is called a *post*, which in Colony is just a text message (Facebook's original implementation was text only but later extended to other types of media). Posts can be remarked on and are not threaded. Posts are placed on the wall in a reverse chronological order in a way that the latest post remains at the top of the wall.

Sending messages

The messaging feature of Colony is a private messaging mechanism. Messages are sent by senders and received by recipients. Messages that are received by a user are placed into an inbox while messages that the user sent are placed into a sent box. For Colony we will not be implementing folders so these are the only two message folders that every user has.

Messages sent to and received from users are threaded and ordered by time. We thread the messages in order to group different messages sent back and forth as part of an ongoing conversation. Threaded messages are sorted in chronological order, where the last received message is at the bottom of the message thread.

Attending events

Events can be thought of as locations in time where people can come together for an activity. Social networking services often act as a nexus for a community so organizing and attending events is a natural extension of the features of a social networking service. Events have a wall, venue, date, and time where the event is happening, and can have event-specific pages that allow users to customize and market their event.

In Colony we categorize users who attend events by their attendance status. *Confirmed users* are users who have confirmed their attendance. *Pending users* are users who haven't yet decided to attend the event. *Declined users* are users who have declined to attend the event after they have been invited. Declinations are explicit; there is an invisible group of users who are in none of the above three types.

Attracting users to events or simply keeping them informed is a critical part of making this or any feature successful. To do so, we suggest events to users and display the suggested events in the user's landing page. The suggestion algorithm is simple, we just go through each of the user's friends and see which other events they have confirmed attending, and then suggest that event to the user.

Besides suggestions, the other means of discovering events are through the activity feeds (whenever an event is created, it is logged as an activity and published on the activity feed) and through user pages, where the list of a user's pages are also displayed. All events are public, as with content created within events like wall posts and pages.

Forming groups

Social networking services are made of people and people have a tendency to form groups or categories based on common characteristics or interests. The idea of groups in Colony is to facilitate such grouping of people with a simple set of features. Conceptually groups and events are very similar to each other, except that groups are not time-based like events, and don't have a concept of attendance. Groups have members, a wall, and can have specific pages created by the group.

Colony's capabilities to attract users to groups are slightly weaker than in events. Colony only suggests groups in the groups page rather than the landing page. However, groups also allow discovery through activity feeds and through user pages. Colony has only public groups and no restriction on who can join these public groups.

Commenting on and liking content

Two popular and common features in many consumer focused web applications are reviews and ratings. Reviews and ratings allow users to provide reviews (or comments) or ratings to editorial or user-generated content. The stereotypical review and ratings feature is Amazon.com's book review and rating, which allows users to provide book reviews as well as rate the book from one to five stars.

Colony's review feature is called **comments**. Comments are applicable to all user-generated content such as status updates, wall posts, photos, and pages. Comments provide a means for users to review the content and give critique or encouragement to the content creator.

Colony's rating feature is simple and follows Facebook's popular rating feature, called **likes**. While many rating features provide a range of one to five stars for the users to choose, Colony (and Facebook) asks the user to indicate if he likes the content. There is no dislike though, so the fewer number of likes a piece of content, the less popular it is.

Colony's comments and liking feature is applicable to all user-generated content such as statuses, photos, wall posts, activities, and pages.

Sharing photos

Photos are one of the most popular types of user-generated content shared online, with users uploading 3 billion photos a month on Facebook; it's an important feature to include in Colony. The photo-sharing feature in Colony is similar to the one in Photoclone.

The basic concept of photo sharing in Colony is that each user can have one or more albums and each album can have one or more photos. Photos can be commented, liked, and annotated. Unlike in Photoclone, photos in Colony cannot be edited.

Blogging with pages

Colony's pages are a means of allowing users to create their own full-page content, and attach it to their own accounts, a page, or a group. A user, event, or group can own one or more pages. Pages are meant to be user-generated content so the entire content of the page is written by the user. However in order to keep the look and feel consistent throughout the site, the page will be styled according to Colony's look and feel. To do this we only allow users to enter Markdown, a lightweight markup language that takes many cues from existing conventions for marking up plain text in e-mail. Markdown converts its marked-up text input to valid, well-formed XHTML. We use it here in Colony to let users write content easily without worrying about layout or creating a consistent look and feel.

Technologies and platforms used

We use a number of technologies in this chapter, mainly revolving around the Ruby programming language and its various libraries. Most of them have been described in Chapter 1. In addition to Ruby and its libraries we also use mashups, which are described next.

Mashups

As with previous chapters, while the main features in the applications are all implemented within the chapters itself, sometimes we still depend on other services provided by other providers. In this chapter we use four such external services—RPX for user web authentication, Gravatar for avatar services, Amazon Web Services S3 for photo storage, and Facebook Connect for reaching out to users on Facebook. RPX, Gravatar, and AWS S3 have been explained in previous chapters.

Facebook Connect

Facebook has a number of technologies and APIs used to interact and integrate with their platform, and Facebook Connect is one of them. Facebook Connect is a set of APIs that let users bring their identity and information into the application itself. We use Facebook Connect in this chapter to send out requests to a user's friends, inviting them to join our social network. The steps to integrate with Facebook Connect are detailed in Chapter 6, *Social Networking Services – Cloning Facebook 2*.

Note that for the user invitation feature, once a user has logged in through Facebook with RPX, he is considered to have logged into Facebook Connect and therefore can send invitations immediately without logging in again.

Building the clone

This is the largest clone built in the book and has many components. Unlike the previous chapters where all the source code are listed in the chapter itself, some of the less interesting parts of the code are not listed or described here. To get access to the full source code please go to `http://github.com/sausheong/Colony`

Configuring the clone

We use a few external APIs in Colony so we need to configure our access to these APIs. In a Colony all these API keys and settings are stored in a Ruby file called `config.rb`, shown as below:

```
S3_CONFIG = {}
S3_CONFIG['AWS_ACCESS_KEY'] = '<AWS ACCESS KEY>'
S3_CONFIG['AWS_SECRET_KEY'] = '<AWS SECRET KEY>'
RPX_API_KEY = '<RPX API KEY>'
```

Modeling the data

This is the chapter with the largest number of classes and relationships. A few major classes you see here are similar but not exactly the same as the ones in the previous chapters, so if you have gone through those chapters you would roughly know how it works.

The following diagram shows how the clone is modeled:

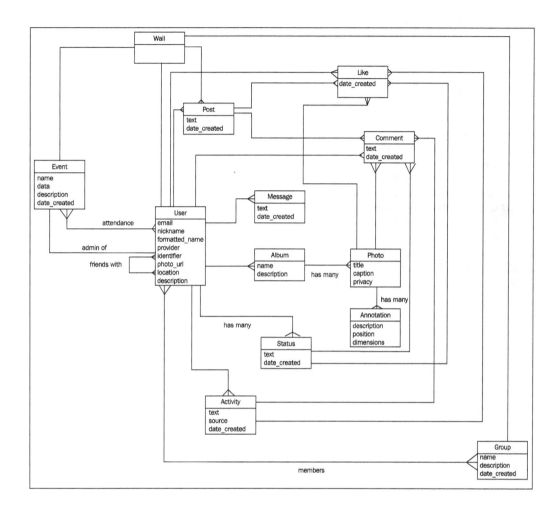

User

As before the first class we look at is the User class. If you have followed the previous chapters you will have realized that that this class is very similar to the ones before. However, the main differences are that there are more relationships with other classes and the relationship with other users follows that of a *friends* model rather than a *followers* model.

```
class User
  include DataMapper::Resource

  property :id,       Serial
  property :email,    String, :length => 255
```

```
property :nickname,    String, :length => 255
property :formatted_name, String, :length => 255
property :sex, String, :length => 6
property :relationship_status, String
property :provider,    String, :length => 255
property :identifier, String, :length => 255
property :photo_url,   String, :length => 255
property :location, String, :length => 255
property :description, String, :length => 255
property :interests, Text
property :education, Text
has n, :relationships
has n, :followers, :through => :relationships, :class_name =>
'User', :child_key => [:user_id]
has n, :follows, :through => :relationships, :class_name => 'User',
:remote_name => :user, :child_key -> [:follower_id]
has n, :statuses
belongs_to :wall
has n, :groups, :through => Resource
has n, :sent_messages, :class_name => 'Message', :child_key =>
[:user_id]
has n, :received_messages, :class_name => 'Message', :child_key =>
[:recipient_id]
has n, :confirms
has n, :confirmed_events, :through => :confirms, :class_name =>
'Event', :child_key => [:user_id], :date.gte => Date.today
has n, :pendings
has n, :pending_events, :through => :pendings, :class_name =>
'Event', :child_key => [:user_id], :date.gte => Date.today
has n, :requests
has n, :albums
has n, :photos, :through => :albums
has n, :comments
has n, :activities
has n, :pages

validates_is_unique :nickname, :message => "Someone else has taken
up this nickname, try something else!"
after :create, :create_s3_bucket
after :create, :create_wall

def add_friend(user)
  Relationship.create(:user => user, :follower => self)
end

def friends
  (followers + follows).uniq
end

def self.find(identifier)
  u = first(:identifier => identifier)
```

```
    u = new(:identifier => identifier) if u.nil?
    return u
  end

  def feed
    feed = [] + activities
    friends.each do |friend|
      feed += friend.activities
    end
    return feed.sort {|x,y| y.created_at <=> x.created_at}
  end

  def possessive_pronoun
    sex.downcase == 'male' ? 'his' : 'her'
  end

  def pronoun
    sex.downcase == 'male' ? 'he' : 'she'
  end

  def create_s3_bucket
    S3.create_bucket("fc.#{id}")
  end

  def create_wall
    self.wall = Wall.create
    self.save
  end

  def all_events
    confirmed_events + pending_events
  end

  def friend_events
    events = []
    friends.each do |friend|
      events += friend.confirmed_events
    end
    return events.sort {|x,y| y.time <=> x.time}
  end

  def friend_groups
    groups = []
    friends.each do |friend|
      groups += friend.groups
    end
    groups - self.groups
  end
end
```

As mentioned in the design section above, the data used in Colony is user-centric. All data in Colony eventually links up to a user. A user has the following relationships with other models:

- A user has none, one, or more status updates
- A user is associated with a wall
- A user belongs to none, one, or more groups
- A user has none, one, or more sent and received messages
- A user has none, one, or more confirmed and pending attendances at events
- A user has none, one, or more user invitations
- A user has none, one, or more albums and in each album there are none, one, or more photos
- A user makes none, one, or more comments
- A user has none, one, or more pages
- A user has none, one, or more activities
- Finally of course, a user has one or more friends.

Once a user is created, there are two actions we need to take. Firstly, we need to create an Amazon S3 bucket for this user, to store his photos.

```
after :create, :create_s3_bucket

def create_s3_bucket
  S3.create_bucket("fc.#{id}")
end
```

We also need to create a wall for the user where he or his friends can post to.

```
after :create, :create_wall
def create_wall
  self.wall = Wall.create
  self.save
end
```

Adding a friend means creating a relationship between the user and the friend.

```
def add_friend(user)
  Relationship.create(:user => user, :follower => self)
end
```

You might realize that this was a *follows* relationship in the previous chapters, so you might ask how could it go both ways? The answer to this question will be clearer once the discussion turns to sending a request to connect. In short, Colony treats both following and follows relationships as going both ways—they are both considered as a *friends* relationship. The only difference here is who will initiate the request to join. This is why when we ask the User object to give us its friends, it will add both followers and follows together and return a unique array representing all the user's friends.

```
def friends
   (followers + follows).uniq
end
```

The `Relationship` class is almost the same as the one used in the other chapters, except that each time a new relationship is created, an Activity object is also created to indicate that both users are now friends.

```
class Relationship
   include DataMapper::Resource

   property :user_id, Integer, :key => true
   property :follower_id, Integer, :key => true
   belongs_to :user, :child_key => [:user_id]
   belongs_to :follower, :class_name => 'User', :child_key =>
[:follower_id]
   after :save, :add_activity

   def add_activity
      Activity.create(:user => user, :activity_type => 'relationship',
:text => "<a href='/user/#{user.nickname}'>#{user.formatted_name}</a>
and <a href='/user/#{follower.nickname}'>#{follower.formatted_name}</
a> are now friends.")
   end
end
```

Finally we get the user's news feed by taking the user's activities and going through each of the user's friends, their activities as well.

```
def feed
   feed = [] + activities
   friends.each do |friend|
      feed += friend.activities
   end
   return feed.sort {|x,y| y.created_at <=> x.created_at}
end
```

Request

We use a simple mechanism for users to invite other users to be their friends. The mechanism goes like this:

1. Alice identifies another Bob whom she wants to befriend and sends him an invitation.

2. This creates a Request class which is then attached to Bob.

3. When Bob approves the request to be a friend, Alice is added as a friend (which is essentially making Alice follow Bob, since the definition of a friend in Colony is someone who is either a follower or follows another user).

```
class Request
  include DataMapper::Resource
  property :id, Serial
  property :text, Text
  property :created_at, DateTime

  belongs_to :from, :class_name => User, :child_key => [:from_id]
  belongs_to :user

  def approve
  self.user.add_friend(self.from)
  end
end
```

Message

Messages in Colony are private messages that are sent between users of Colony. As a result, messages sent or received are not tracked as activities in the user's activity feed.

```
class Message
  include DataMapper::Resource
  property :id, Serial
  property :subject, String
  property :text, Text
  property :created_at,  DateTime
  property :read, Boolean, :default => false
  property :thread, Integer

  belongs_to :sender, :class_name => 'User', :child_key => [:user_id]
  belongs_to :recipient, :class_name => 'User', :child_key =>
[:recipient_id]
end
```

A message must have a sender and a recipient, both of which are users.

```
has n, :sent_messages, :class_name => 'Message', :child_key => [:user_
id]
has n, :received_messages, :class_name => 'Message', :child_key =>
[:recipient_id]
```

The `read` property tells us if the message has been read by the recipient, while the thread property tells us how to group messages together for display.

Album

The photo sharing capabilities of Colony is transplanted from Photoclone in the previous chapter and therefore the various models involved in photo sharing are almost the same as the one in Photoclone. The main difference is that each time an album is created, an activity is logged.

```
class Album
  include DataMapper::Resource
  property :id,          Serial
  property :name,        String, :length => 255
  property :description, Text
  property :created_at, DateTime

  belongs_to :user
  has n, :photos
  belongs_to :cover_photo, :class_name => 'Photo', :child_key =>
[:cover_photo_id]
  after :save, :add_activity

  def add_activity
    Activity.create(:user => user, :activity_type => 'album', :text =>
"<a href='/user/#{user.nickname}'>#{user.formatted_name}</a> created a
new album <a href='/album/#{self.id}'>#{self.name}</a>")
  end
end
```

Photo

The `Photo` class is the main class in the photo-sharing feature of Colony. Just like the `Album` class, this is very similar to the one in Photoclone, except for some minor differences.

```
class Photo
  include DataMapper::Resource
  include Commentable
```

```
  attr_writer :tmpfile
  property :id,        Serial
  property :title,     String, :length => 255
  property :caption,   String, :length => 255
  property :privacy,   String, :default => 'public'

  property :format,    String
  property :created_at, DateTime

  belongs_to :album

  has n, :annotations
  has n, :comments
  has n, :likes

  after :save, :save_image_s3
  after :create, :add_activity
  after :destroy, :destroy_image_s3

  def filename_display; "#{id}.disp"; end
  def filename_thumbnail; "#{id}.thmb"; end

  def s3_url_thumbnail; S3.get_link(s3_bucket, filename_thumbnail,
Time.now.to_i + (24*60*60)); end
  def s3_url_display; S3.get_link(s3_bucket, filename_display, Time.
now.to_i + (24*60*60)); end

  def url_thumbnail
    s3_url_thumbnail
  end

  def url_display
    s3_url_display
  end

  def previous_in_album
    photos = album.photos
    index = photos.index self
    return nil unless index
    photos[index - 1] if index > 0
  end

  def next_in_album
```

```
    photos = album.photos
    index = photos.index self
    return nil unless index
    photos[index + 1] if index < album.photos.length
  end

  def save_image_s3
    return unless @tmpfile
    img = Magick::Image.from_blob(@tmpfile.open.read).first
    display = img.resize_to_fit(500, 500)
    S3.put(s3_bucket, filename_display, display.to_blob)

    t = img.resize_to_fit(150, 150)
    length = t.rows > t.columns ? t.columns : t.rows
    thumbnail =  t.crop(CenterGravity, length, length)
    S3.put(s3_bucket, filename_thumbnail, thumbnail.to_blob)
  end

  def destroy_image_s3
    S3.delete s3_bucket, filename_display
    S3.delete s3_bucket, filename_thumbnail
  end

  def s3_bucket
    "fc.#{album.user.id}"
  end

  def add_activity
    Activity.create(:user => album.user, :activity_type => 'photo',
:text => "<a href='/user/#{album.user.nickname}'>#{album.user.
formatted_name}</a> added a new photo - <a href='/photo/#{self.
id}'><img class='span-1' src='#{self.url_thumbnail}'/></a>")
  end
end
```

First of all, we removed the feature of storing temporary file caches on the filesystem of the server. The main reason is that of economy—we want to be able to deliver everything from Amazon S3 deploy on the Heroku cloud platform (which does not serve files). Of course this can be changed easily if you're planning to customize Colony.

Next, and related to the first difference, is that we no longer store the original photo. Instead, we only keep a reduced-size display photo and a thumbnail of the original photo. The rationale for this is the same as with Facebook. Colony is not a full-fledged photo-sharing site for photographers and is meant to share photos with friends only. Therefore storing large original files is unnecessary.

Photos can be commented on so it includes the `Commentable` module (explained later). Also each photo has none, one, or more comments and likes.

Finally as with many of the classes in Colony, creating a Photo is considered an activity and is logged for streaming on the activity feed. Note that we don't log an activity after a save, but only after we create an object `photo`. This is because `save` will be called each time the `photo` object is edited, annotated, or has its caption or description modified. This is not an activity we want to log in to the activity stream.

```
class Annotation
  include DataMapper::Resource
  property :id,          Serial
  property :description, Text
  property :x,           Integer
  property :y,           Integer
  property :height,      Integer
  property :width,       Integer
  property :created_at,  DateTime

  belongs_to :photo
  after :create, :add_activity

  def add_activity
    Activity.create(:user => self.photo.album.user, :activity_type
=> 'annotation', :text => "<a href='/user/#{self.photo.album.user.
nickname}'>#{self.photo.album.user.formatted_name}</a> annotated
a photo - <a href='/photo/#{self.photo.id}'><img class='span-1'
src='#{self.photo.url_thumbnail}'/></a> with '#{self.description}'")
  end
end
```

Annotation is another class, part of the photo-sharing feature that is transplanted from Photoclone, with activity logging added in. We will not go into this, if you want a refresher please read Chapter 4.

Status

Just as the `Album`, `Photo`, and `Annotation` classes are transplanted from Photoclone,
the `Status` and `Mention` classes are derived from Tweetclone.

```
class Status
  include DataMapper::Resource
  include Commentable

  property :id, Serial
  property :text, String, :length => 160
  property :created_at,  DateTime
  belongs_to :recipient, :class_name => "User", :child_key =>
[:recipient_id]
  belongs_to :user
  has n, :mentions
  has n, :mentioned_users, :through => :mentions, :class_name =>
'User', :child_key => [:user_id]
  has n, :comments
  has n, :likes

  before :save do
    @mentions = []
    process
  end

  after :save do
    unless @mentions.nil?
      @mentions.each {|m|
        m.status = self
        m.save
      }
    end
    Activity.create(:user => user, :activity_type => 'status', :text
=> self.text )
  end

  # general scrubbing
  def process
    # process url
    urls = self.text.scan(URL_REGEXP)
    urls.each { |url|
      tiny_url = RestClient.get "http://tinyurl.com/api-create.
php?url=#{url[0]}"
      self.text.sub!(url[0], "<a href='#{tiny_url}'>#{tiny_url}</a>")
```

```
    }
    # process @
    ats = self.text.scan(AT_REGEXP)
    ats.each { |at|
      user = User.first(:nickname => at[1,at.length])
      if user
        self.text.sub!(at, "<a href='/#{user.nickname}'>#{at}</a>")
        @mentions << Mention.new(:user => user, :status => self)
      end
    }
  end

  def starts_with?(prefix)
    prefix = prefix.to_s
    self.text[0, prefix.length] == prefix
  end

  def to_json(*a)
    {'id' => id, 'text' => text, 'created_at' => created_at, 'user' =>
user.nickname}.to_json(*a)
  end
end
```

As before, each time a user updates his status, an activity will be logged. Statuses can be commented upon and also liked. The `Mention` class is unchanged from Tweetclone. For an in-depth description of this class please refer to Chapter 3.

```
class Mention
  include DataMapper::Resource
  property :id,        Serial
  belongs_to :user
  belongs_to :status
end

URL_REGEXP = Regexp.new('\b ((https?|telnet|gopher|file|wais|ftp) :
[\w/#~:.?+=&%@!\-] +?) (?=[.:?\-] * (?: [^\w/#~:.?+=&%@!\-]| $ ))',
Regexp::EXTENDED)
AT_REGEXP = Regexp.new('@[\w.@_-]+', Regexp::EXTENDED)
```

Group

Each user can belong to none, one, or more groups. Each group that is created also belongs to a user and it's this user that the activity is logged to. Each group has a set of features:

- A group can have none, one, or more pages.

- A group has a wall where other users can post to. This wall is created right after the group is created.

```
class Group
    include DataMapper::Resource

    property :id, Serial
    property :name, String
    property :description, String

    has n, :pages
    has n, :members, :class_name => 'User', :through => Resource
    belongs_to :user
    belongs_to :wall

    after :create, :create_wall

    def create_wall
        self.wall = Wall.create
        self.save
    end

    after :create, :add_activity

    def add_activity
        Activity.create(:user => self.user, :activity_type => 'event',
    :text => "<a href='/user/#{self.user.nickname}'>#{self.user.
    formatted_name}</a> created a new group - <a href='/group/#{self.
    id}'>#{self.name}</a>.")
    end
end
```

Note that the `User-Group` relationship is a *many-to-many* relationship, and we use the `DataMapper::Resource` class as an anonymous class to represent the relationship. For convenience we also provide a method in the `User` object to retrieve all groups a user's friends belong to. This becomes useful for us later when suggesting groups for users to join.

```ruby
def friend_groups
  groups = []
  friends.each do |friend|
    groups += friend.groups
  end
  groups - self.groups
end
```

Event

Events are quite similar to Groups but with a twist. As before we log it as an activity each time the event is created. Each event has an administrative user who is the person who created the event.

```ruby
class Event
  include DataMapper::Resource

  property :id, Serial
  property :name, String
  property :description, String
  property :venue, String
  property :date, DateTime
  property :time, Time

  belongs_to :user
  has n, :pages
  has n, :confirms
  has n, :confirmed_users, :through => :confirms, :class_name =>
'User', :child_key => [:event_id], :mutable => true
  has n, :pendings
  has n, :pending_users, :through => :pendings, :class_name => 'User',
:child_key => [:event_id], :mutable => true
  has n, :declines
  has n, :declined_users, :through => :declines, :class_name =>
'User', :child_key => [:event_id], :mutable => true

  belongs_to :wall
```

```
  after :create, :create_wall

  def create_wall
    self.wall = Wall.create
    self.save
  end

  after :create, :add_activity

  def add_activity
    Activity.create(:user => self.user, :activity_type => 'event',
  :text => "<a href='/user/#{self.user.nickname}'>#{self.user.formatted_
  name}</a> created a new event - <a href='/event/#{self.id}'>#{self.
  name}</a>.")
  end
end
```

In addition, each event has three types of members depending on their current attendance status:

- Users confirmed to attend the event
- Users who are still undecided on attending the event
- Users who have declined to attend the event

For this implementation we use a separate class for each type of user, that is we have a `Confirm` class for confirmed users, a `Pending` class to indicate users who are undecided, and a `Decline` class to indicate users who have declined to attend the event.

```
class Pending
  include DataMapper::Resource
  property :id, Serial
  belongs_to :pending_user, :class_name => 'User', :child_key =>
[:user_id]
  belongs_to :pending_event, :class_name => 'Event', :child_key =>
[:event_id]
end

class Decline
  include DataMapper::Resource
  property :id, Serial
  belongs_to :declined_user, :class_name => 'User', :child_key =>
[:user_id]
  belongs_to :declined_event, :class_name => 'Event', :child_key =>
[:event_id]
```

```
end

class Confirm
  include DataMapper::Resource
  property :id, Serial
  belongs_to :confirmed_user, :class_name => 'User', :child_key =>
[:user_id]
  belongs_to :confirmed_event, :class_name => 'Event', :child_key =>
[:event_id]
end
```

As with `Group`, we have a convenient method in the `User` class to help us find the events the user's friends are attending. We only retrieve confirmed events for this list, which is then sorted according to ascending chronological order.

```
def friend_events
  events = []
  friends.each do |friend|
    events += friend.confirmed_events
  end
  return events.sort {|x,y| y.time <=> x.time}
end
```

Page

Pages are a simple means for users to publish their own web pages. A Page can be owned directly by a user, through a group, or through an event.

```
class Page
  include DataMapper::Resource
  include Commentable
  property :id, Serial
  property :title, String
  property :body, Text  property :created_at, DateTime
  has n, :comments
  has n, :likes
  belongs_to :user
  belongs_to :event
  belongs_to :group

  after :create, :add_activity

  def add_activity
    if self.event
      Activity.create(:user => self.user, :activity_type => 'event
page', :text => "<a href='/user/#{self.user.nickname}'>#{self.user.
formatted_name}</a> created a page - <a href='/event/page/#{self.
id}'>#{self.title}</a> for the event <a href='/event/#{self.event.
id}'>#{self.event.name}</a>.")
```

```
    elsif self.group
       Activity.create(:user => self.user, :activity_type => 'group
page', :text => "<a href='/user/#{self.user.nickname}'>#{self.user.
formatted_name}</a> created a page - <a href='/group/page/#{self.
id}'>#{self.title}</a> for the group <a href='/group/#{self.group.
id}'>#{self.group.name}</a>.")
    else
       Activity.create(:user => self.user, :activity_type => 'page',
:text => "<a href='/user/#{self.user.nickname}'>#{self.user.formatted_
name}</a> created a page - <a href='/page/#{self.id}'>#{self.title}</
a>.")
    end
  end
end
```

Page also logs activities according to whichever object that owns it.

Wall

A wall is a place where users can place their posts. A wall can belong to a user, event, or group. In fact each time a user, event, or group is created, we will automatically create a wall on its behalf.

```
class Wall
  include DataMapper::Resource
  property :id, Serial
  has n, :posts
end
```

The implementation of a wall by itself has no definite properties other than being a container for posts. A post is the actual content that a user will submit to a wall and it is something that can be commented and liked. A post on a wall can come from any user, so a post is also associated with the user who created the post.

```
class Post
  include DataMapper::Resource
  include Commentable
  property :id, Serial
  property :text, Text
  property :created_at, DateTime
  belongs_to :user
  belongs_to :wall
  has n, :comments
  has n, :likes
end
```

Activity

An activity is a log of a user's action in Colony that is streamed to the user's activity feed. Not all actions are logged as activities, for example messages are considered private and are therefore not logged.

```
class Activity
  include DataMapper::Resource
  include Commentable

  property :id, Serial
  property :activity_type, String
  property :text, Text
  property :created_at, DateTime
  has n, :comments
  has n, :likes
  belongs_to :user
end
```

Activities are commented and can be liked by other users.

Comment

Comments in Colony are stored and managed through the `Comment` class. All user-generated content including pages, posts, photo, and statuses can be commented by users in Colony. Activities can also be commented on.

```
class Comment
  include DataMapper::Resource

  property :id, Serial
  property :text, Text
  property :created_at, DateTime
  belongs_to :user
  belongs_to :page
  belongs_to :post
  belongs_to :photo
  belongs_to :activity
  belongs_to :status
end
```

Like

`Like` and `Comment` classes are very similar. The main difference between them is that the Like mechanism is binary (either you like the content or you don't) whereas you need to provide some content to comment.

```
class Like
  include DataMapper::Resource
  property :id, Serial
  belongs_to :user
  belongs_to :page
  belongs_to :post
  belongs_to :photo
  belongs_to :activity
  belongs_to :status
end
```

The implementation of the `Like` mechanism in Colony requires each class of objects that can be liked or commented on to include the `Commentable` module.

```
module Commentable
  def people_who_likes
    self.likes.collect { |l| "<a href='/user/#{l.user.nickname}'>#{l.
user.formatted_name}</a>"  }
  end
end
```

This allows you to retrieve an array of people of who likes the content, which are then formatted as HTML links for easy display.

This wraps up the data models that we will be using in Colony. In the next chapter we will cover Colony's application flow and deployment.

Summary

This is the second last chapter in this book and also the first one in a series of two chapters describing how we can clone a social networking service like Facebook. Social networking services are the next step in the evolution of Internet applications and Facebook is currently the most successful incarnation of this service. Cloning Facebook is not difficult though, as can be attested in this chapter and also in the many Facebook 'clones' out there on the Internet. Let's look at what we have covered in this chapter.

First, we went through a whirlwind tour of social networking services and their history, before discussing the most dominant service, Facebook. Next, we described some of its more essential features and we categorized the features into User, Community, and Content sharing features. After that, we went into a high level discussion on these various features and how we implement them in our Facebook clone, Colony. After that, we went briefly into the various technologies used in the clone.

After the technology discussion, we jumped straight into the implementation, starting with a detailed discussion of the data models used in this chapter. Our next chapter is the last chapter in this book. We will finish what we have started in this chapter with a detailed step-by-step description of Colony's application flow, followed with the deployment of Colony on the Heroku cloud platform.

6
Social Networking Services – Cloning Facebook 2

In the previous chapter we went through what social networking services are all about. We also designed a Facebook clone with a small list of essential features that a typical social networking service would have and talked through the design. We also started describing its implementation with a description of the data model used by Colony, our Facebook clone.

In this chapter we will continue with the clone we started previously. We will discuss the application flow of each chapter and finish up with our usual deployment to Heroku to a standalone server.

Let's start!

Building the application flow

While much of the application logic resides in the data model, the flow of the application determines how the user uses Colony. Let's begin with the overall structure of the application and then we'll inspect each feature for its flow.

Structure of the application and flow

Unlike the previous clones where we stored the entire flow in a single file, Colony is too big to fit into a single file, so we split the application along the lines of its features and use one file per feature. The main file is called `colony.rb`. It contains the main processing necessary to log in as well as the landing page.

```
require 'rubygems'
gem 'rest-client', '=1.0.3'
```

```
%w(config haml sinatra digest/md5 rack-flash json restclient models).
each { |lib| require lib}
set :sessions, true
set :show_exceptions, false
use Rack::Flash

get "/" do
  if session[:userid].nil? then
    @token = "http://#{env["HTTP_HOST"]}/after_login"
    haml :login
  else
    @all = @user.feed
    haml :landing
  end
end

get "/logout" do
  session[:userid] = nil
  redirect "/"
end

# called by RPX after the login completes
post "/after_login" do
  profile = get_user_profile_with params[:token]
  user = User.find(profile["identifier"])
  if user.new_record?
    photo = profile["photo"].nil? ? "http://www.gravatar.com/
avatar/#{Digest::MD5.hexdigest(profile["email"])}" : profile["photo"]
    unless user.update_attributes({:nickname => profile["identifier"].
hash.to_s(36), :email => profile["email"], :photo_url => photo,
:provider => profile["provider"]})
      flash[:error] = user.errors.values.join(",")
      redirect "/"
    end
    session[:userid] = user.id
    redirect "/user/profile/change"
  else
    session[:userid] = user.id
    redirect "/"
  end
end

%w(pages friends photos messages events groups comments user helpers).
each {|feature| load "#{feature}.rb"}
```

```
error NoMethodError do
  session[:userid] = nil
  redirect "/"
end

before do
  @token = "http://#{env["HTTP_HOST"]}/after_login"
  @user = User.get(session[:userid]) if session[:userid]
end
```

Let's jump into the code details of the main file. Note that we're using a specific gem version for RestClient. This is because as of writing the RightAWS gem we use for accessing S3 doesn't work with the latest version of RestClient.

```
gem 'rest-client', '=1.0.3'
```

As mentioned earlier, each feature is contained in a file and we load each feature by file.

```
%w(pages friends photos messages events groups comments user helpers).
each {|feature| load "#{feature}.rb"}
```

The one piece of data that we will always get for each route is the currently logged in user's ID, which we store in the session.

```
before do
  @user = User.get(session[:userid]) if session[:userid]
end
```

The `before` filter is run before each request to Colony and returns `User` object, which is used in most of the routes. It also becomes a means of securing pages because if the user has not logged in, we will not be able to retrieve the `User` object. This will result in an error which clears the session and sends the user back to the login page.

```
error NoMethodError do
  session[:userid] = nil
  redirect "/"
end
```

Authenticating and managing users

As with the other clones in this book we use RPX for Colony to reduce the amount of work needed to build an authentication system. Let's describe what will happen. The first and the most basic route is the *index route*. If the user is already logged in and has a session, we will redirect him to the landing page described previously.

```
get "/" do
  if session[:userid].nil? then
    haml :login
  else
    @all = @user.feed
    haml :landing
  end
end
```

We use Haml for the view pages. As we did earlier, we define a separate layout Haml page that will be used in all the subsequent pages.

```
!!! 1.1
%html{:xmlns => "http://www.w3.org/1999/xhtml", :'xmlns:fb' =>
"http://www.facebook.com/2008/fbml"}
  %head
    %title Colony
    %link{:rel => 'stylesheet', :href => '/css/blueprint/screen.css',
:type => 'text/css'}
    %link{:rel => 'stylesheet', :href => '/css/blueprint/plugins/
fancy-type/screen.css', :type => 'text/css'}
    %link{:rel => 'stylesheet', :href => '/css/additional.css', :type
=> 'text/css'}
    %link{:href => '/css/datepicker.css', :rel => 'stylesheet', :type
=> 'text/css'}
    %script{:src => '/js/jquery.min.js', :type => 'text/javascript'}
    %script{:src => '/js/select.js', :type => 'text/javascript'}
    %script{:src => '/js/notes.js', :type => 'text/javascript'}
    %script{:src => '/js/datepicker.js', :type => 'text/javascript'}
    %script{:src => '/js/timepicker.js', :type => 'text/javascript'}

  %body
    %script{:type => "text/javascript", :src  => "http://static.
ak.connect.facebook.com/js/api_lib/v0.4/FeatureLoader.js.php"}
    .container
      = yield
      %hr.space
      .span-24.last
        .small.span-5.prepend-19
          copyright &copy
          %a{:href => 'http://www.saush.com'} Chang Sau Sheong
          2010
```

Like Tweetclone, but unlike Photoclone, we only place the RPX code in the login page. Sinatra looks for all view templates in a folder called `views` by default. Our login page, called `login.haml`, is found at the same place.

```
.span-24
  .span-11
    %img.span-12.prepend-6{:src => '/images/colony_login.png'}
    .span-10.prepend-7
      %h2{:style => 'font-size:2em;margin-bottom:0.75em;margin-top:0;
padding-top: 0;'} Connect with friends, share your life
        .subtitle You don't need to register any accounts, just use an
existing account from your favorite Internet provider!
    .span-3.prepend-9
      %a.rpxnow{:onclick => "return false;", :href => "https://colony.
rpxnow.com/openid/v2/signin?token_url=#{@token}" }
        %h2{:style => "font-size:2em;margin-bottom:0.75em;"} Sign In

%script{:type => 'text/javascript'}
  var rpxJsHost = (("https:" == document.location.protocol) ?
"https://" : "http://static."); document.write(unescape("%3Cscript
src='" + rpxJsHost + "rpxnow.com/js/lib/rpx.js' type='text/
javascript'%3E%3C/script%3E"));
%script{:type => "text/javascript"}
  RPXNOW.overlay = true;
  RPXNOW.language_preference = 'en';
```

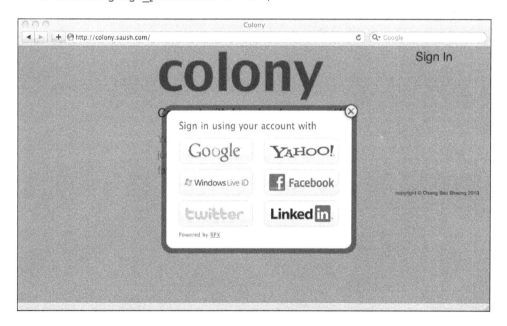

To allow login, we add an HTML anchor link that redirects us to RPX, passing in the token.

```
%a.rpxnow{:onclick => "return false;", :href => "https://colony.
rpxnow.com/openid/v2/signin?token_url=#{@token}" }
  %h2{:style => "font-size:2em;margin-bottom:0.75em;"} Sign In
```

This will redirect the user to the RPX site, which in turn redirects the user to the appropriate provider. On completion of the authentication, RPX will call on Colony at the URL (`after_login`) which was provided earlier. RPX passes a `token` parameter to us in this call, which we will use to retrieve the user's profile.

We will define a separate helper method to do the work of retrieving the user's profile. All such methods are placed in the `helpers.rb` file:

```
def get_user_profile_with(token)
   response = RestClient.post 'https://rpxnow.com/api/v2/auth_info',
'token' => token, 'apiKey' => '<RPX API key>', 'format' => 'json',
'extended' => 'true'
   json = JSON.parse(response)
   return json['profile'] if json['stat'] == 'ok'
   raise LoginFailedError, 'Cannot log in. Try another account!'
end
```

We use the Rest-Client library again to send the POST request to RPX, passing in the token and requesting the information back in JSON format. If successful, RPX will return some information on the users, which we will use the Ruby JSON library to parse and return. Let's look at the *after_login* route next.

```
post '/after_login' do
  profile = get_user_profile_with params[:token]
  user = User.find(profile['identifier'])
  if user.new_record?
    photo = profile ['email'] ? "http://www.gravatar.com/
avatar/#{Digest::MD5.hexdigest(profile['email'])}" : profile['photo']
    unless user.update_attributes({:nickname => profile['identifier'].
hash.to_s(36), :email => profile['email'], :photo_url => photo,
:provider => profile['provider']})
      flash[:error] = user.errors.values.join(',')
      redirect "/"
    end
    session[:userid] = user.id
    redirect '/user/profile/change'
  else
    session[:userid] = user.id
    redirect "/"
  end
end
```

After getting the user's profile from the authentication provider through RPX, we try to retrieve the user's record from our database, using the unique identifier. If the user's record does not exist, we'll create a new record. If it's a new record, we will update the rest of the attributes from his/her profile. This includes a photo link from Gravatar.

Gravatar uses e-mail addresses that are hashed using MD5 to uniquely identify a user's avatar. Since a user can have multiple e-mail addresses, he can have multiple avatars:

```
photo = profile ['email'] ? "http://www.gravatar.com/
avatar/#{Digest::MD5.hexdigest(profile['email'])}" : profile['photo']
```

We can optionally take the URL to an avatar photo from the photo link, if it is provided in the profile, though Gmail doesn't provide that as of date. As done before, if the user is not a Gravatar user, Gravatar returns a default avatar.

As in Photoclone we set the nickname here as well. We hash the identifier returned by the authentication provider and convert it into an alphanumeric string, which we use as the nickname. This means if a user doesn't change his nickname later, this will become his nickname. Finally we set `session[:userid]` with the user ID and redirect the user to change his profile.

The *user profile* and *change profile* routes do very little, other than redirecting to their respective views.

```
get "/user/profile" do
   haml :profile
end

get "/user/profile/change" do
   haml :change_profile
end
```

The *change profile* route does the actual work of saving any changes on the user profile. There is more to store here than there was with Photoclone.

```
post "/user/profile" do
   unless @user.update_attributes(:nickname => params[:nickname],
                                   :formatted_name => params[:formatted_
name],
                                   :location => params[:location],
                                   :description => params[:description],
                                   :sex => params[:sex],
                                   :relationship_status =>
params[:relationship_status],
```

```
                                       :interests => params[:interests],
                                       :education => params[:education])
    flash[:error] = @user.errors.values.join(",")
    redirect "/user/profile/change"
  end
  redirect "/"
end
```

Finally, the *logout* route simply resets `session[:userid]` and redirects the user back to the *index* route. Without the user ID, the *index* route shows the login page.

```
get '/logout' do
  session[:userid] = nil
  redirect '/'
end
```

This wraps up authentication and user management.

Landing page, news feed, and statuses

The landing page is the first page that the user sees when he logs in. It contains summary information for the user and is probably the most frequently used page. The centerpiece of the landing page is the user's news feed.

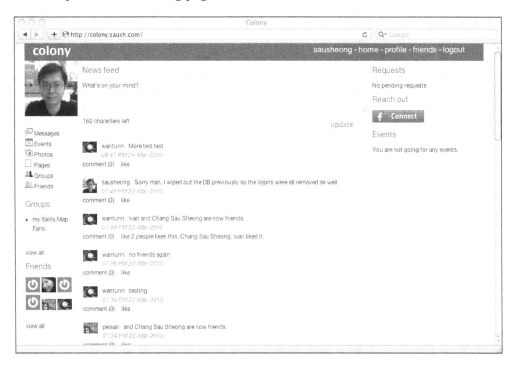

The *main* route will redirect the user to the login page, if he hasn't logged in yet, and to the landing page, if he has.

```
get "/" do
  if session[:userid].nil? then
    haml :login
  else
    @all = @user.feed
    haml :landing
  end
end
```

The news feed is processed in the landing page, which is nothing more than a collection of snippets. As explained in the previous chapters, a snippet is a small piece of template code that we re-use in various view templates. We use snippets extensively in Colony.

```
=snippet :'/snippets/top'

.span-24.last
  .span-3
    %img.span-3{:src => "#{@user.photo_url}"}
    =snippet :'/snippets/links'

    %h3 Groups
    =snippet :'/snippets/mini_groups'
    %h3 Friends
    =snippet :'/snippets/mini_friends', :locals => {:user => @user}
  .span-15

    %h3 News feed
    =snippet :'/snippets/update_box'
    %hr.space
    =snippet :'/snippets/feeds'

  .span-6.last
    %h3 Requests
    =snippet :'/snippets/mini_requests'
    %h3 Reach out
    =snippet :'/snippets/mini_invite'
    %h3 Events
    =snippet :'/snippets/mini_events'
%hr.space
```

In particular, the news feed is used in the *feeds* snippet, in the `feeds.haml` file. The feeds snippet shows a list of feed items, given that we use the `@all` instance variable.

```
.feeds
  -@all.each do |item|
    .span-1
      %img.span-1{:src => "#{item.user.photo_url}"}
    .span-13.last
      %a{:href => "/user/#{item.user.nickname}"}
        =item.user.nickname
       
      =item.text

    .span-8.last
      %em.quiet
        =time_ago_in_words(item.created_at.to_time)

      =snippet :'/snippets/comment_and_like', {:locals => {:item =>
item}}
```

We iterate through the news feed and display each one of the news feed items. Remember news feeds are basically activities, but a user's activity feed includes his activities and posts. We pass each item into the *comment and like* snippet as a variable to be used to display the comments and list of likes.

```
.span-15.last
  .span-2
    %a{:href =>"#", :onclick => "$('#comment_box_#{item.class.
to_s}_#{item.id}').toggle();$('#comment_box_#{item.class.to_s}_#{item.
id}').focus();"} comment (#{item.comments.size})

  .span-13.last
    %form{:method => 'post', :action => "/like/#{item.class.
to_s.downcase}/#{item.id}", :id => "form_like_#{item.class.to_s.
downcase}_#{item.id}"}
      %input{:type => 'hidden', :name => 'return_url', :value =>
request.url.to_s}
      %input{:type => 'hidden', :name => '_method', :value => 'put'}
    %a{:href =>"#", :onclick => "$('#form_like_#{item.class.to_s.
downcase}_#{item.id}').submit();"} like
    - unless item.likes.empty?
      #{item.likes.size} people likes this. #{item.people_who_likes.
join(', ')} liked it.

  .span-13.hide.last{:id => "comment_box_#{item.class.to_s}_#{item.id}"}
```

```
%form{:method => 'post', :action => "/comment/#{item.class.to_s.
downcase}/#{item.id}"}
    %textarea.span-10{:name => 'text', :style => 'height: 30px;'}
    %input{:type => 'hidden', :name => 'return_url', :value =>
request.url.to_s}
    %input{:type => 'hidden', :name => '_method', :value => 'put'}
    %br
    %input{:type => 'submit', :value => 'comment'}

%hr.space

- unless item.comments.empty?
  .span-14.push-1.last
    - item.comments.each do |comment|
      .span-1
        %a{:href => "/user/#{comment.user.nickname}"}
          %img.span-1{:src => "#{comment.user.photo_url}"}
      .span-12.last.comment_box
        #{comment.text}
        %br
        %em.quiet
          =time_ago_in_words(comment.created_at.to_time)
```

The *comment and like* snippet is split into three sections. The first section deals with the likes, allowing the user to like the item as well as listing the people who like this item.

```
%form{:method => 'post', :action => "/like/#{item.class.to_s.
downcase}/#{item.id}", :id => "form_like_#{item.class.to_s.
downcase}_#{item.id}"}
    %input{:type => 'hidden', :name => 'return_url', :value =>
request.url.to_s}
    %input{:type => 'hidden', :name => '_method', :value => 'put'}
  %a{:href =>"#", :onclick => "$('#form_like_#{item.class.to_s.
downcase}_#{item.id}').submit();"} like
    - unless item.likes.empty?
      #{item.likes.size} people likes this. #{item.people_who_likes.
join(', ')} liked it.
```

The second section allows users to add comments to the item using a form.

```
.span-13.hide.last{:id => "comment_box_#{item.class.to_s}_#{item.id}"}
  %form{:method => 'post', :action => "/comment/#{item.class.to_s.
downcase}/#{item.id}"}
    %textarea.span-10{:name => 'text', :style => 'height: 30px;'}
```

```
    %input{:type => 'hidden', :name => 'return_url', :value =>
request.url.to_s}
    %input{:type => 'hidden', :name => '_method', :value => 'put'}
    %br
    %input{:type => 'submit', :value => 'comment'}
```

The final section displays all the comments on the item.

```
- unless item.comments.empty?
  .span-14.push-1.last
    - item.comments.each do |comment|
      .span-1
        %a{:href => "/user/#{comment.user.nickname}"}
          %img.span-1{:src => "#{comment.user.photo_url}"}
      .span-12.last.comment_box
        #{comment.text}
        %br
        %em.quiet
          =time_ago_in_words(comment.created_at.to_time)
```

With that we have our news feed. Let's go back a little bit and discuss the common snippets. The *top* snippet provides us with the top bar.

```
.span-24
  .span-2
    %a{:href => '/'}
      %img{:src => '/images/colony_header.png'}
  - if @user
    .span-9.prepend-13.last
      %a.topbar{:href =>"/user/#{@user.nickname}"} #{@user.nickname} -
      %a.topbar{:href => '/'} home -
      %a.topbar{:href => '/user/profile'}  profile -
      %a.topbar{:href => '/friends'}  friends -
      %a.topbar{:href => '/logout'}  logout
  - else
    .span-2.prepend-20.last
      %a.topbar.rpxnow{:onclick => "return false;", :href => "https://
colony.rpxnow.com/openid/v2/signin?token_url=#{@token}" } sign in
```

The *links* snippet provides us with a simple left navigation sidebar.

```
%hr.space
.span-3
  .icons.icons_messages
  - num_unread_msgs =  @user.received_messages.all(:read => false).
size
  %a{:href => '/messages/inbox'} Messages
  - if num_unread_msgs > 0
    (#{num_unread_msgs})

.span-3
  .icons.icons_event
  %a{:href => '/events'} Events
.span-3
  .icons.icons_photo
  %a{:href => '/albums'} Photos
.span-3
  .icons.icons_pages
  %a{:href => '/user/pages'} Pages
.span-3
  .icons.icons_group
  %a{:href => '/groups'} Groups
.span-3
  .icons.icons_friends
  %a{:href => '/friends'} Friends
%hr.space
```

The other snippets in the landing page will be described in their respective features. A user updates his status (as in Tweetclone) through the *update box* snippet in a file named `update_box.haml`. This snippet is like the one in Tweetclone, using a text limiter Javascript and posting the status content to the `user status` route.

```
post '/user/status' do
  Status.create(:text => params[:status], :user => @user)
  redirect "/"
end
```

The *user status* route simply creates the status update and redirects the user back to the landing page. The *update box* snippet is only used in the landing page.

Inviting friends and friends list

The *invite friends* and *friends* list features are implemented with a file named
`friends.rb`. Let's look at the friends list first.

```
get '/friends' do
  if params[:query]
    results = User.all(:nickname.like => params[:query] + '%') + User.
all(:formatted_name.like => '%' + params[:query] + '%')
    @search_results = results.uniq[0..24]
  end
  haml :'/friends/friends', :locals => {:show_search => true, :user =>
@user}
end
```

The *friends* route performs two tasks. Firstly, it performs a simple search on all users
in the application, based on either the user's nickname or formatted name, and
returns the first 25 results found. Secondly, it tells the *view* page to show the search
for friends form and passes the user to the page. We do this to reuse the same page to
show the friends of a specific user and not your own friends.

All the views are in a folder named `friends`. The first page we will be looking at is
the `friends.haml` page.

```
=snippet :'/snippets/top'

.span-24.last
  .span-3
    %img.span-3{:src => "#{user.photo_url}"}
    =snippet :'/snippets/links'
  .span-15
    - if show_search
      %h3 Find your friends
      %form{:method => 'get'}
        Look for friends here -
        %input.span-8{:type => 'text', :name => 'query'}
        %input{:type => 'submit', :value => 'search people'}

      - if @search_results
        %hr.space
        - @search_results.each do |res|
          .span-1
            %img.span-1{:src => "#{res.photo_url}"}
          .span-12
            - unless res == @user
```

```
              %a{:href => "/user/#{res.nickname}"} #{res.formatted_
name} (#{res.nickname})
                  from #{res.location}
                  %br
                  - if @user.friends.include? res
                    #{res.pronoun.capitalize} is your friend.
                  - else
                    %a{:href => "/request/#{res.id}"} add as friend
                - else
                  This is me!
              %hr.space

      %h3 Friends
      - user.friends.each do |friend|
        .span-2
          %img.span-2{:src => "#{friend.photo_url}"}
        .span-12
          %a{:href => "/user/#{friend.nickname}"} #{friend.formatted_
name}
          %br
          #{friend.location}
        .span-1.last
          %form{:id => "form_friend_#{friend.id}", :method => 'post',
:action => "/friend/#{friend.id}"}
            %input{:type => 'hidden', :name => '_method', :value =>
'delete'}
            %a{:href => '#', :onclick => '$("#form_friend_' + "#{friend.
id}" + '").submit();', :class => 'remove_link'}
```

Notice the simple use of pronouns to make the experience friendlier. We also allow
the user to add people he has found as friends using a link to the *create request* route.

```
- if @user.friends.include? res
  #{res.pronoun.capitalize} is your friend.
- else
  %a{:href => "/request/#{res.id}"} add as friend
```

Below the search form and the search results we show a list of friends the user has.
For each friend displayed, we allow the friend to be viewed using a link to the *view
user* route, and also to be removed from the **Friends** list.

```
%h3 Friends
    - user.friends.each do |friend|
      .span-2
        %img.span-2{:src => "#{friend.photo_url}"}
      .span-12
```

```
      %a{:href => "/user/#{friend.nickname}"} #{friend.formatted_
name}
      %br
      #{friend.location}
    .span-1.last
      %form{:id => "form_friend_#{friend.id}", :method => 'post',
:action => "/friend/#{friend.id}"}
        %input{:type => 'hidden', :name => '_method', :value => 'de-
lete'}
        %a{:href => '#', :onclick => '$("#form_friend_' + "#{friend.
id}" + '").submit();', :class => 'remove_link'}
```

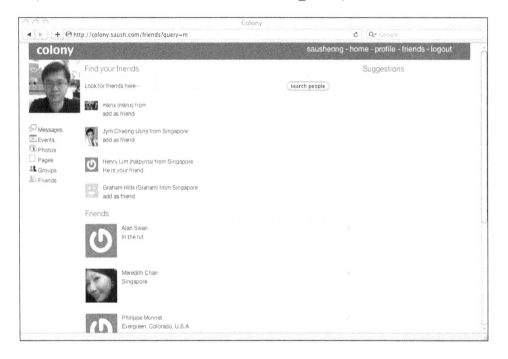

To add a friend, we need to create a `request` object, and attach it to the user that we want as a friend. This is initiated with the *create request* route.

```
get '/request/:userid' do
  @friend = User.get(params[:userid])
  haml :'/friends/request'
end
```

This retrieves the user we want to befriend, and shows us the *request creation* page.

```
=snippet :'/snippets/top'
.span-3
  %img.span-3{:src => "#{@user.photo_url}"}
  =snippet :'/snippets/links'
.span-20.last
  %h3 Add #{@friend.formatted_name} as a friend?
  %h4 #{@friend.formatted_name} will have to confirm that you are
friends.

  %form{:action => '/request', :method => 'post'}
    .span-20 Add a personalized message (optional)
    .span-20
      %textarea.span-10{:name => 'text'}
    %input{:type => 'hidden', :name => '_method', :value => 'put'}
    %input{:type => 'hidden', :name => 'receiverid', :value => "#{@
friend.id}"}

    %input{:type => 'submit', :value => 'send request'}
```

The *request creation* page allows us to add an optional personalized message which is sent along the request.

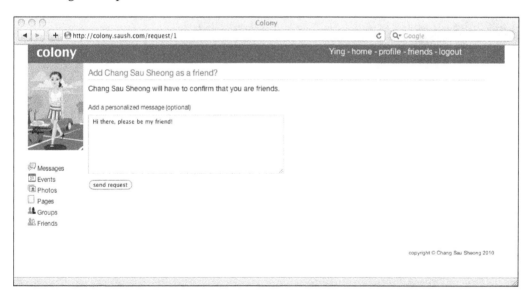

The form submits to the *put request* route, which creates a request that sets `from` to the requesting user and the `user` to the person he wishes to befriend.

```
put '/request' do
  Request.create(:text => params[:text], :from => @user, :user =>
User.get(params[:receiverid]))
  redirect '/friends'
end
```

Once the user receives the request, he or she will see a new request on the landing page, displayed using the *mini request* snippet.

```
- unless @user.requests.empty?
  .icons.icons_add_friend
  %a{:href => '/requests/pending'}
    You have #{@user.requests.size} friend request(s).
- else
  No pending requests
```

Clicking on the request link will allow the user to see a list of pending requests, which he may approve or ignore. This is done in the *request pending* route.

```
get '/requests/pending' do
  haml :'/friends/pending_requests'
end
```

This goes to the *request pending* page.

```
=snippet :'/snippets/top'
.span-3
  %img.span-3{:src => "#{@user.photo_url}"}
  =snippet :'/snippets/links'
.span-21.last
  %h3 Pending requests
  - if @user.requests.empty?
    You have no pending requests.
  - @user.requests.each do |req|
    .span-13
      .span-2
        %img.span-2{:src => "#{req.from.photo_url}"}
      .span-10
      #{req.text}
      %br
      %form{:id => "form_approve_#{req.id}", :method => 'post',
:action => "/friend/#{req.id}"}
        %input{:type => 'hidden', :name => '_method', :value => 'put'}
        %a{:href => '#', :onclick => '$("#form_approve_' + "#{req.id}"
+ '").submit();'} approve
          \.
        %a{:href => "/friend/ignore/#{req.id}"} ignore

    %hr.space
```

To approve the friendship, the user clicks on the **approve** link which goes to the *approve request* route. This retrieves the request and approves it if it really belongs to the current logged in user (we don't want just anyone to come in to approve the request).

```
put '/friend/:requestid' do
  req = Request.get(params[:requestid])
if @user.requests.include? req
  req.approve
  req.destroy
end
  redirect '/requests/pending'
end
```

Approving the request simply means that the user is added as a friend to the current user.

```
def approve
  self.user.add_friend(self.from)
end
```

Similarly to ignore the request the user clicks on the **ignore** link which goes to the *ignore request* route. This will destroy the request if the user is the correct one.

```
get '/friend/ignore/:requestid' do
  req = Request.get(params[:requestid])
req.destroy if @user.requests.include? req
redirect '/requests/pending'
end
```

In the landing page, there is a *mini friends* snippet from a file named `mini_friends.haml` that displays a minified image of the friends the user has (up to 12 friends at once).

```
- if user.friends.empty?
  You don't have any friends in Colony! Start adding friends today!
- else
  - user.friends[0..11].each do |f|
    %a{:href => "/user/#{f.nickname}"}
      %img.span-1{:src => "#{f.photo_url}"}

%hr.space
- if user == @user
  %a{:href => "/friends"} view all
- else
  %a{:href => "/friends/#{user.id}"} view all
```

If this snippet is used in the user page instead of the landing page, this will show the viewed user's friends, via the *user friends* route.

```
get '/friends/:id' do
  viewed_user = User.get params[:id]
  haml :'/friends/friends', :locals => {:show_search => false, :user
=> viewed_user}
end
```

That's all for the friends list. Let's take a look at how we can invite friends to join us in Colony. The design of the feature of inviting friends is based on Facebook Connect. We use Facebook Connect to allow a user to log in to his Facebook account, and then using this account, send invitations to his friends through Facebook.

When a user logs in, there is a button to the right of the landing page that invites the user to log in to Facebook Connect, if he wasn't logged in to Facebook. Clicking on that will request the user to log in to his Facebook account. Note that if you have used the Facebook account to log in to Colony in the first place (through RPX) you would have automatically logged in to Facebook Connect already.

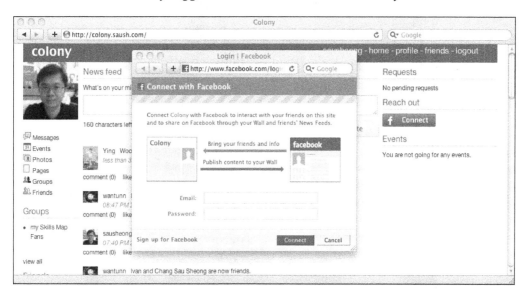

Let's look at how we use Facebook Connect in Colony. There are three basic steps to enable Facebook Connect for a web application.

1. Register the application with Facebook by creating a Facebook application. This will also give you the application key.

2. Create a cross-domain communication channel file called xd_receiver.htm and place it in a directory relative to the Connect URL specified in the first step.

3. Write the necessary Javascript and FBML.

Registering a Facebook application

Without going through every detail, here are the essential steps to create a Facebook application for Colony's Facebook Connect integration:

1. Go to http://www.facebook.com/developers/createapp.php to create a new application.

2. Go to http://www.facebook.com/developers/createapp.php to create a new application.

3. Enter 'Colony' in the **Application Name** field and save to proceed.

4. Take note of the API Key, as we'll need this shortly.

5. Click on the **Connect** tab. Set Connect URL to http://colony.saush.com.

Creating a cross-domain communication channel file

The Facebook JavaScript Client Library uses a cross-domain communications library to establish communication between external web pages and Facebook pages, and services inside a browser. To reference the library, we need to create a cross-domain communications channel file named `xd_receiver.htm` with the following information:

```
<!DOCTYPE html PUBLIC "-//W3C//DTD XHTML 1.0 Strict//EN" "http://www.
w3.org/TR/xhtml1/DTD/xhtml1-strict.dtd">
<html xmlns="http://www.w3.org/1999/xhtml">
  <head>
    <title>xd</title>
  </head>
  <body>
    <script src="http://static.ak.facebook.com/js/api_lib/v0.4/
XdCommReceiver.js" type="text/javascript"></script>
  </body>
</html>
```

We then place this file in the public folder.

Writing the code

Our Facebook Connect code is in a snippet called *mini invite* in the file `mini_invite.haml`.

```
=snippet :'/snippets/fbinit'
%div#fblogin
  %fb:login-button{:onlogin => "$('#fblogin').hide();$('#fbuser').
show();"}
    %fb:intl
      Connect with Facebook
%div#fbuser.hide
  %fb:profile-pic{:uid => "loggedinuser", :'facebook-logo' =>"true",
:linked => "true"}
  %br
  %a{:href => '/invite'}
    Invite your Facebook friends!

:javascript
  FB.ensureInit(function() {
    FB.Connect.get_status().waitUntilReady( function( status ) {
      switch ( status ) {
```

```
        case FB.ConnectState.connected:
          loggedIn = true;
        break;
        case FB.ConnectState.appNotAuthorized:
        case FB.ConnectState.userNotLoggedIn:
          loggedIn = false;
        }
      });
    });
    if (loggedIn) {
      $("#fblogin").hide();
      $("#fbuser").show();
    }
    else {
      $("#fblogin").show();
      $("#fbuser").hide();
    }
```

Notice that the code here is all JavaScript from the Facebook JavaScript libraries and FBML. The first line inserts a snippet named `fbinit.haml` that initializes Facebook with the application key and `xd_receiver.htm`.

```
:javascript
  FB.init("<FB APP KEY>", "xd_receiver.htm");
```

Why not just insert this line into the code? It's because there is another location where we are using the Facebook JavaScript libraries and we will need to reuse `fbinit.haml`.

Creating FBML with Haml is easy; remember that Haml can create any XML-like markup language.

```
%fb:login-button{:onlogin => "$('#fblogin').hide();$('#fbuser').
show();"}
    %fb:intl
      Connect with Facebook
%div#fbuser.hide
  %fb:profile-pic{:uid => "loggedinuser", :'facebook-logo' =>"true",
:linked => "true"}
```

We tell the FBML login button that whenever the login button is clicked, we need to hide that button and show the `fbuser` element. This element contains the profile picture FBML, which forms the necessary HTML tags for us to display the image.

As for the Javascript, the first thing we need to do is to initialize the library with the application key and tell it where to look for the `xd_receiver.htm` file we created earlier in step 2.

After logging in, the Facebook Connect button is replaced by the user's Facebook profile photo as well as a link to get the user invite his Facebook friends. The rest of the JavaScript simply detects if the user has logged in, and toggles the display of the button or the profile picture and link accordingly.

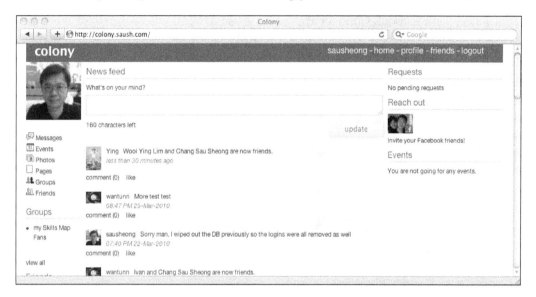

When the user clicks on the link, he will be directed to a new page, with a list of his Facebook friends who he can send the invitation to join. This link goes to the *invite* route.

```
get '/invite' do
  haml :'/friends/invite'
end
```

The route just redirects to the *invite* page.

```
=snippet :'/snippets/top'
%script{:src => "http://static.ak.connect.facebook.com/js/api_lib/
v0.4/FeatureLoader.js.php",  :type=>"text/javascript"}
%fb:serverfbml
  %script{:type=>"text/fbml"}
    %fb:fbml
      %fb:request-form{:action => "http://colony.saush.com/", :method
=> "GET", :invite => "true", :type => "Colony", :content => "I am a
member of Colony and would like to invite you share the experience.
To visit the Colony, simply click on the Visit button below.<fb:req-
choice url='http://colony.saush.com/' label='Visit' />"}
        %fb:multi-friend-selector{:showborder => "false", :actiontext
=> "Invite your Facebook Friends to use Colony"}
=snippet :'/snippets/fbinit'
```

This is a whole bunch of FBML. We start off by adding the Facebook Javascript libraries, followed by the FBML tag `<fb:serverfbml>`. This tag enables us to place FBML tags inside a Facebook iframe, which means everything else nested in this tag is actually inside a Facebook iframe. Why is this?

This is because Facebook Connect applications use XFBML whereas usual Facebook applications use FBML. If we want to use any FBML tag inside a Facebook Connect, we need to wrap it around a ServerFBML tag.

Next, we have the usual `<fb:fbml>` tag, which indicates that we're using FBML now, followed by the `<fb:request-form>` tag, which creates a form to send invitations to users. Finally, nested within the request form, we use the `<fb:multi-friend-selector>` tag. This tag provides us with a list of the user's friends which he can select to send invitations with, using the request form. Right at the end of the template we re-use the `fbinit` snippet to initialize the libraries.

Clicking on the **Send** button will send an invitation to the user(s), and it will appear in Facebook's list of requests.

User page and activity feeds

Next, we look at user pages and the activity feeds in the user pages. The *user* route is found in the `user.rb` file.

```
get "/user/:nickname" do
  @myself = @user
  @viewed_user = User.first(:nickname => params[:nickname])
  @viewing_self = (@viewed_user == @myself)
  all = [] + @viewed_user.activities + @viewed_user.wall.posts + @
viewed_user.statuses
  @all = all.sort {|x,y| y.created_at <=> x.created_at}
  haml :user
end
```

If you are observant, you might notice that this route (like all other routes with variables in its definition) is placed at the last in the file. This is to prevent confusion by Sinatra when it is called. For example, in the same `user.rb` file we have the *user profile* (user/profile) and *user status* (user/status) routes. If we placed the *user* route (user/:nickname) definition before these two route definitions, when the *user profile* route is called Sinatra will be misinformed that it is called with a user named 'profile'!

The *user* route has two user objects, the currently logged in user and the user that is being viewed. These two users can be the same (if the logged in user is viewing his own page), and if this is the case then we set the `@viewing_self` variable to be true. We also extract all the viewed user's activities, wall posts, and statuses and sort them by reverse chronological order.

The route goes to the user page, called `user.haml`. This page, like the landing page, contains a number of snippets.

```
=snippet :'/snippets/top'

.span-24.last
  .span-3
    %img.span-3{:src => "#{@viewed_user.photo_url}"}
    =snippet :'/snippets/links'
    %h3 Friends
    =snippet :'/snippets/mini_friends', :locals => {:user => @viewed_
user}
  .span-15

    %h3 Wall
    =snippet :'/snippets/wall_box'
    %hr.space
    =snippet :'/snippets/feeds'

  .span-6.last
    %h3 Information
    .span-5 Name : #{@viewed_user.formatted_name}
    .span-5 Location : #{@viewed_user.location}
    .span-5 #{@viewed_user.description}
    %hr.space

    %h3 Photos
    =snippet :'/snippets/mini_album'

    %h3 Pages
    =snippet :'/snippets/mini_pages', {:locals => {:owner => @viewed_
user, :owner_name => 'user'}}
```

Notice that we have re-used a number of snippets (this is the reason why we started using snippets). The activity feed is used by the *feeds* snippet.

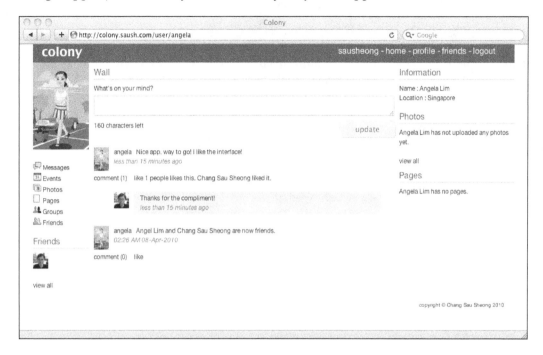

Posting to a wall

A wall is the place where users can post their views on. Walls belong to users, events, and groups, and each one of these can only have one wall. A post is content generated by the user placed on a wall.

The implementation of the wall is done at the various owning object's route files. Let's look at the user wall first. The wall posting form is in the *wall box* snippet, in a file named `wall_box.haml`. This snippet is found in the user page.

```
=snippet :'/snippets/text_limiter_js'
What's on your mind?
%form{:method => 'post', :action => '/user/wall'}
  %textarea.update.span-15#update{:name => 'status', :rows => 2,
:onKeyDown => "text_limiter($('#update'), $('#counter'))"}
    .span-6
      %span#counter
        160
      characters left
    .prepend-12
```

```
    %input{:type => 'hidden', :name => 'wallid', :value => "#{@viewed_
user.wall.id}"}
    %input{:type => 'hidden', :name => 'nickname', :value => "#{@
viewed_user.nickname}"}
    %input#button{:type => 'submit', :value => 'update'}
```

This snippet is very similar to the *status update* snippet, except we need to pass in the wall ID as well as the nickname of the user whom the wall belongs to. The form posts to the user wall route, which is found in the `user.rb` file.

```
post '/user/wall' do
   Post.create(:text => params[:status], :user => @user, :wall_id =>
params[:wallid])
   redirect "/user/#{params[:nickname]}"
end
```

This creates a post from a user to a wall. To view the posts, we re-use the *feeds* snippet we described earlier, which is also in the user page. We used this snippet to view the user's news feed, but we can also use it to view the activity for the viewed user.

```
.feeds
  -@all.each do |item|
    .span-1
      %img.span-1{:src => "#{item.user.photo_url}"}
    .span-13.last
      %a{:href => "/user/#{item.user.nickname}"}
        =item.user.nickname
       
      =item.text

    .span-8.last
      %em.quiet
        =time_ago_in_words(item.created_at.to_time)

    =snippet :'/snippets/comment_and_like', {:locals => {:item =>
item}}
```

Next we look at a wall belonging to a group. The form is in the *group wall* snippet in a file named `group_wall_box.haml`.

```
=snippet :'/snippets/text_limiter_js'
What's on your mind?
%form{:method => 'post', :action => '/group/wall'}
   %textarea.update.span-15#update{:name => 'status', :rows => 2,
:onKeyDown => "text_limiter($('#update'), $('#counter'))"}
   .span-6
     %span#counter
```

```
    160
  characters left
 .prepend-12
    %input{:type => 'hidden', :name => 'wallid', :value => "#{@group.
wall.id}"}
    %input{:type => 'hidden', :name => 'group', :value => "#{@group.
id}"}
    %input#button{:type => 'submit', :value => 'update'}
```

This snippet allows the user to post to the group wall and it is found in the group page (discussed in a later section).

```
%h3 Wall
  =snippet :'/snippets/group_wall_box'

  %hr.space

  -@group.wall.posts.each do |post|
    .span-2
      %img.span-2{:src => "#{post.user.photo_url}"}
    .span-4
      #{post.user.formatted_name}
      %br
      #{post.created_at.strftime "%d %b %Y"}
      %br
      #{post.created_at.strftime "%I:%M %P"}
    .span-8
      #{post.text}
    %hr
```

For this wall, instead of using a snippet to view all the wall posts for this group, we add it in directly on the page. The route to create the group wall posts is also very similar to the one used for creating user wall posts.

```
post '/group/wall' do
  Post.create(:text => params[:status], :user => @user, :wall_id =>
params[:wallid])
  redirect "/group/#{params[:group]}"
end
```

Similarly for the event wall, we have an *event wall* snippet in a file named `event_wall_box.haml`.

```
=snippet :'/snippets/text_limiter_js'
What's on your mind?
%form{:method => 'post', :action => '/event/wall'}
  %textarea.update.span-15#update{:name => 'status', :rows => 2,
:onKeyDown => "text_limiter($('#update'), $('#counter'))"}
  .span-6
    %span#counter
      160
    characters left
  .prepend-12
    %input{:type => 'hidden', :name => 'wallid', :value => "#{@event.
wall.id}"}
    %input{:type => 'hidden', :name => 'event', :value => "#{@event.
id}"}
    %input#button{:type => 'submit', :value => 'update'}
```

Correspondingly, we also have the event wall on the event page, which we will look at later.

```
%h3 Wall
  =snippet :'/snippets/event_wall_box'

  %hr.space

  -@event.wall.posts.each do |post|
    .span-2
      %img.span-2{:src => "#{post.user.photo_url}"}
    .span-4
      #{post.user.formatted_name}
      %br
      #{post.created_at.strftime "%d %b %Y"}
      %br
      #{post.created_at.strftime "%I:%M %P"}
    .span-8
      #{post.text}
    %hr
```

The route to create the wall posts for an event is also quite similar.

```
post '/event/wall' do
  Post.create(:text => params[:status], :user => @user, :wall_id =>
params[:wallid])
  redirect "/event/#{params[:event]}"
end
```

Sharing photos

Let's continue with more user-generated content, this time with photos. The photo-sharing feature in Colony is transplanted from Photoclone and share many similarities in design and code. The basic model for the photo-sharing feature is that of albums as containers to photos. Each user can have one or more albums, and each album has one or more photos in them. For the implementation we will look into the albums first, then move on to uploading photos then annotating them.

Managing albums

Albums are relatively simple to implement. The *albums* route shows a list of albums belonging to the currently logged in user.

```
get "/albums" do
  @myself = @user = User.get(session[:userid])
  haml :"albums/manage"
end
```

For the viewed user, we use the *user albums* route, which retrieves the albums belonging to that user we are viewing.

```
get "/albums/:user_id" do
  @myself = User.get(session[:userid])
  @user = User.get(params[:user_id])
  haml :"albums/manage"
end
```

Both routes go to the *manage album* page.

```
=snippet :'/snippets/top'
.span-24
  .span-3
    %img.span-3{:src => "#{@user.photo_url}"}
    =snippet :'/snippets/links'
  .span-21.last
    %hr.space
    .span-17
      %div.icons.icons_photo
      %strong{:style => 'vertical-align:bottom;font-size:18px;'}
        #{@user == @myself ? 'Your' : "#{@user.formatted_name}'s"}
albums
    - if @user == @myself
      .span-4.last.right
        %a.button{:href => '/album/add'} new album

    - if @user != @myself
      - if @myself.friends.include? @user
        .span-17.last You and #{@user.formatted_name} are friends.
      - else
        .span-17.last
          #{@user.formatted_name} and you are not connected in Colony.

    %hr.space

    -@user.albums.each do |album|
      %hr.space
      .span-3
        - if album.cover_photo
          %img.span-3{:src => "#{album.cover_photo.url_thumbnail}"}
        - elsif !album.photos.empty?
          %img.span-3{:src => "#{album.photos.first.url_thumbnail}"}
        - else
          %img.span-2{:src => "/images/album_icon.png"}

      .span-18.last
        %h4{:style => 'margin-bottom:5px;'}
          %a{:href => "/album/#{album.id}"} #{album.name}
        #{album.description}
        %hr.space
        - unless album.photos.empty?
```

```
%div{:style => 'font-style: italic;'} (#{album.photos.size}
photos in this album, last photo uploaded on #{album.photos.last.
created_at.strftime('%d-%b-%Y')})
```

```
- if @user == @myself
  - if album.photos.empty?
    %div{:style => "width: 50px;float: left;"}
      %form{:id => "form_#{album.id}", :method => 'post',
:action => "/album/#{album.id}"}
        %input{:type => 'hidden', :name => '_method', :value
=> 'delete'}
        %a{:href => '#', :onclick => '$("#form_' + "#{album.
id}" + '").submit();'} remove
      .span-2
        %a{:href => "/album/#{album.id}/upload"} upload
```

The *manage album* page uses two instance variables for this—`@myself` indicates the logged in user and `@user` indicates the user whose list of albums are being viewed. We use these two instance variables to format the view accordingly and display the appropriate messages.

We also display a cover photo. If there is a given cover photo (the user has explicitly set one of the photos as the cover photo) we will show that, otherwise we'll show the first photo in the list or a default album icon, if the album is empty.

```
- if album.cover_photo
  %img.span-3{:src => "#{album.cover_photo.url_display}"}
- elsif !album.photos.empty?
  %img.span-3{:src => "#{album.photos.first.url_display}"}
- else
  %img.span-3{:src => "/images/album_icon.png"}
```

Lastly, we'll only allow some actions if the current user is managing his own albums, and only allow the album to be deleted if the album is empty.

```
- if @user == @myself
  - if album.photos.empty?
    %div{:style => "width: 50px;float: left;"}
    %form{:id => "form_#{album.id}", :method => 'post', :action => "/
album/#{album.id}"}
      %input{:type => 'hidden', :name => '_method', :value =>
'delete'}
      %a{:href => '#', :onclick => '$("#form_' + "#{album.id}" + '").
submit();'} remove
    .span-2
      %a{:href => "/album/#{album.id}/upload"} upload
```

Note that delete uses the DELETE method and we are using the form submit hack to get around the problem of browsers not supporting any other HTTP methods other than GET and POST. Here is the *delete album* route.

```
delete "/album/:id" do
  album = Album.get(params[:id])
  user = User.get(session[:userid])
  if album.user == user
    if album.destroy
      redirect "/albums"
    else
      throw "Cannot delete this album!"
    end
  else
    throw "This is not your album, you cannot delete it!"
  end
end
```

Viewing someone else's albums uses the same view. The only difference is that the @myself variable points to the logged in user and the @user variable points to the viewed user. The view *user album* route is as follows:

```
get "/albums/:user_id" do
  @myself = User.get(session[:userid])
  @user = User.get(params[:user_id])
  haml :"albums/manage"
end
```

Creating an album is easy as well.

```
get "/album/add" do
  haml :"/albums/add"
end
```

The *add album* page provides the user a form to add the album, which submits to a *create album* route as below. After creating the album, the user is redirected to the *main albums* page.

```
post "/album/create" do
  album = Album.new
  album.attributes = {:name => params[:name], :description =>
params[:description]}
  album.user = @user
  album.save
  redirect "/albums"
end
```

Next, we display the album with the *view album* route.

```
get "/album/:id" do
  @album = Album.get params[:id]
  haml :"/albums/view"
end
```

Displaying the album is done with the *view album* page in a file named `view.haml`.

```
=snippet :'/snippets/top'
=snippet :'/snippets/album_inline_js'
.span-24.last
  .span-3
    %img.span-3{:src => "#{@album.user.photo_url}"}
    =snippet :'/snippets/links'
  .span-15.last
    - if @user == @album.user
      %h3.edit_name{:style => 'margin-bottom: 0;'} #{@album.name}
      %h4.edit_area #{@album.description}
    - else
      %h3{:style => 'margin-bottom: 0;'} #{@album.name}
      %h4 #{@album.description}

    - if @user == @album.user
      %a{:href => "/album/#{@album.id}/upload"} Upload photos
    - if @user
      \-
      %a{:href => "/albums/#{@album.user.id}"} Back to albums
    - else
      \-
      %a{:href => "/user/#{@album.user.nickname}"} Back to albums

    %hr.space

    - if @user
      - if @album.photos.empty?
        %h4
          There are no photos in this album.
          %a{:href => "/album/#{@album.id}/upload"} Upload some
photos?

        - @album.photos.each  do |photo|
          %a{:href => "/photo/#{photo.id}"}
            %img.span-2{:src => "#{photo.url_thumbnail}"}
```

The *view album* page allows you to edit the name and the description of the album inline through Javascript. The *inline album* snippet in the file name `album_inline_js.haml` provides the code for us to do this. You would have seen this in Photoclone.

As in Chapter 4, modifying the name or description properties will use AJAX to call the *edit album properties* route.

```
post "/album/:property/:photo_id" do
  album = Album.get params[:photo_id]
  if %w(name description).include? params[:property]
    album.send(params[:property] + '=', params[:value])
    album.save
  end
  album.send(params[:property])
end
```

This allows us to change the necessary album properties, in our case the name and a description of the album. Notice that we don't allow changing other properties besides `name` and `description`. The details of this mechanism are described in full in Chapter 4.

Next, if the owner of the album is the currently logged in user, we will allow uploading new photos. Otherwise we will only allow returning back to the albums list.

```
- if @user == @album.user
    %h3.edit_name{:style => 'margin-bottom: 0;'} #{@album.name}
    %h4.edit_area #{@album.description}
  - else
    %h3{:style => 'margin-bottom: 0;'} #{@album.name}
    %h4 #{@album.description}

  - if @user == @album.user
    %a{:href => "/album/#{@album.id}/upload"} Upload photos
  - if @user
    \-
    %a{:href => "/albums/#{@album.user.id}"} Back to albums
  - else
    \-
    %a{:href => "/user/#{@album.user.nickname}"} Back to albums
```

Finally, we show a list of photos in this album.

```
- if @user
    - if @album.photos.empty?
        %h4
            There are no photos in this album.
            %a{:href => "/album/#{@album.id}/upload"} Upload some
photos?

    - @album.photos.each  do |photo|
        %a{:href => "/photo/#{photo.id}"}
            %img.span-2{:src => "#{photo.url_thumbnail}"}
```

Uploading photos

Let's turn to uploading photos next. The *upload photo* route is in the same
`photos.rb` file.

```
get "/upload" do
  @albums = @user.albums
  haml :upload
end
```

This allows us to show all albums that belong to the logged in user and allow him to
choose which album he wants to upload in. However, when we want to choose the
album we must upload to we use this route instead:

```
get "/album/:id/upload" do
  @albums = [@user.albums.get(params[:id])]
  haml :upload
end
```

Either route provides the albums for the *upload photos* page.

```
=snippet :'/snippets/top'
.span-3
  %img.span-3{:src => "#{@user.photo_url}"}
  =snippet :'/snippets/links'
.span-21.last
  %h3 Upload photos to an album
  - unless @albums.empty?
    .span-24.last
      %form{:method => 'post', :action => '/upload',
:enctype=>"multipart/form-data"}
        Upload photos to this album -
        %select.span-8{:name => 'album_id'}
```

```
        - @albums.each do |album|
          %option{:value => "#{album.id}"} #{album.name}
      %hr.space
      .span-23.push-1
        %ol
          %li
            %input{:type => 'file', :name => 'file1', :size => 60}
          %li
            %input{:type => 'file', :name => 'file2', :size => 60}
          %li
            %input{:type => 'file', :name => 'file3', :size => 60}
          %li
            %input{:type => 'file', :name => 'file4', :size => 60}
          %li
            %input{:type => 'file', :name => 'file5', :size => 60}
          %li
            %input{:type => 'file', :name => 'file6', :size => 60}

      %input{:type => 'submit', :value => 'upload'}
  - else
    %h3
      Looks like you don't have any albums yet.
      %a{:href => "/album/add"} Create one
      before uploading photos!
```

Most of the work is done by the model, but the *upload photo* route for uploading does some basic manipulation to get the pieces of data in place.

```
post "/upload" do
  album = Album.get params[:album_id]
  (1..6).each do |i|
    if params["file#{i}"] && (tmpfile = params["file#{i}"][:tempfile])
&& (name = params["file#{i}"][:filename])
      Photo.new(:title => name, :album => album, :tmpfile => tmpfile).
save
    end
  end
  redirect "/album/#{album.id}"
end
```

The parameters provided by most browsers are nested such that a parameter nested in the parameter (in this case it is file1, file2, and so on) named tempfile will contain the binary data and one named filename will contain the name of the file that is uploaded. Extracting the data and passing it to the Photo object will persist the data, as described in the Photo class used earlier.

Displaying photos

To explain how Colony displays photos properly we will break up the description into several parts.

- Displaying the photo including the title and caption, both of which can be edited inline
- Displaying photo metadata
- Navigation in the album to the next and previous photos
- Annotating the photo

Let's start with the *view photo* route.

```
get "/photo/:id" do
  @photo = Photo.get params[:id]

  notes = @photo.annotations.collect do |n|
    '{"x1": "' + n.x.to_s + '", "y1": "' + n.y.to_s +
    '", "height": "' + n.height.to_s + '", "width": "' + n.width.to_s
+
    '","note": "' + n.description + '"}'
  end
  @notes = notes.join(',')
  @prev_in_album = @photo.previous_in_album
  @next_in_album = @photo.next_in_album
  haml :'/photos/photo'
end
```

We retrieve the annotations from the photo as well as find the next and previous photos in the same album then show the *view photo* page. This page is one of the longest in Colony and is stuffed with features. Let's look at them one at a time.

```
=snippet :'/snippets/top'
=snippet :'/snippets/annotations_js'
=snippet :'/snippets/photo_inline_js'

.span-24
  .span-3
    %img.span-3{:src => "#{@user.photo_url}"}
    =snippet :'/snippets/links'
  .span-15

    - if @user === @photo.album.user
      %h2.edit_title #{@photo.title}
    - else
```

```
        %h2 #{@photo.title}
      %img{:id => 'photo', :src => "#{@photo.url_display}"}
      - if @user === @photo.album.user
        %h4.edit_area #{@photo.caption}
      - else
        %h4 #{@photo.caption}


    .span-3
      %a{:href => "/album/#{@photo.album.id}"} Back to album
    - if @user == @photo.album.user
      .span-3
        %a{:href => '#', :id => 'add_annotation' } annotate photo
      .span-3
        %form{:id => "form_cover_photo", :method => 'post', :action =>
"/album/cover/#{@photo.id}"}
          %a{:href => '#', :onclick => '$("#form_cover_photo").
submit();'} set album cover
      .span-3.last
        %form{:id => "form_photo_#{@photo.id}", :method => 'post',
:action => "/photo/#{@photo.id}"}
          %input{:type => 'hidden', :name => '_method', :value =>
'delete'}
          %a{:href => '#', :onclick => '$("#form_photo_' + "#{@photo.
id}" + '").submit();'} delete photo


    =snippet :'/snippets/comment_and_like', {:locals => {:item => @
photo}}


  .span-6.last
    %img.span-1{:src => "#{@photo.album.user.photo_url}"}
    Uploaded on #{@photo.created_at.strftime("%d %b %Y")} by
    - if @user
      %form{:id => "form_create_#{@photo.album.user.id}", :method =>
'post', :action => "/follow/#{@photo.album.user.id}"}
        %input{:type => 'hidden', :name => '_method', :value => 'put'}
        %a{:href => '#', :onclick => '$("#form_create_' + "#{@photo.
album.user.id}" + '").submit();'}
          =@photo.album.user.formatted_name
    - else
      =@photo.album.user.formatted_name
    %h4
      This photo is
      - if @user === @photo.album.user
        %b.edit_privacy #{@photo.privacy}
      - else
```

```
        %b #{@photo.privacy}
    - if @user === @photo.album.user
      %h3 Annotations
      - if @photo.annotations.empty?
        %h4 No annotations on this photo.
      - else
        - @photo.annotations.each do |note|
          .span-6
            =note.description
          .span-3
            %form{:id => "form_#{note.id}", :method => 'post', :action
=> "/annotation/#{note.id}"}
              %input{:type => 'hidden', :name => '_method', :value =>
'delete'}
              %a{:href => '#', :onclick => '$("#form_' + "#{note.id}"
+ '")').submit();'} [remove]
        %hr.space


    %h3 #{@photo.album.name}

    - if @prev_in_album
      %a{:href => "/photo/#{@prev_in_album.id}"}
        %img.span-2{:src => "#{@prev_in_album.url_thumbnail}"}
    - else
      %img.span-2{:src => '/images/spacer.gif'}
    - if @next_in_album
      %a{:href => "/photo/#{@next_in_album.id}"}
        %img.span-2{:src => "#{@next_in_album.url_thumbnail}"}
    - else
      %img.span-2{:src => '/images/spacer.gif'}
    %br
    - if @prev_in_album
      %a{:href => "/photo/#{@prev_in_album.id}"}
        %img.span-2{:src => "/images/left_arrow.gif"}
    %a{:href => "/album/#{@photo.album.id}"}
      %img.span-2{:src => "/images/browse.gif"}
    - if @next_in_album
      %a{:href => "/photo/#{@next_in_album.id}"}
        %img.span-2{:src => "/images/right_arrow.gif"}

%hr.space

.span-24
  #annotation_form
```

```
    %form{:id => 'annotation_add_form', :method => 'post', :action =>
"/annotation/#{@photo.id}"}
      %fieldset
        %legend
        %input{:name => 'annotation[x1]', :type => 'hidden', :id =>
'annotation_x1'}
        %input{:name => 'annotation[y1]', :type => 'hidden', :id =>
'annotation_y1'}
        %input{:name => 'annotation[height]', :type => 'hidden', :id
=> 'annotation_height'}
        %input{:name => 'annotation[width]', :type => 'hidden', :id =>
'annotation_width'}
        %textarea{:name => 'annotation[text]', :id => 'annotation_
text'}
      .submit
        %input{:type => 'submit', :value => 'add'}
        %input{:type => 'button', :value => 'cancel', :id => 'cancel_
note'}
```

First let's look at the action menubar, which is placed right below the displayed photo. This menubar contains all the actions that can be done on the photo. Most of the actions are only available to the owner of the photo. Notice that unlike in Photoclone, we don't allow the photos to be edited.

```
.span-3
    %a{:href => "/album/#{@photo.album.id}"} Back to album
  - if @user == @photo.album.user
    .span-3
        %a{:href => '#', :id => 'add_annotation' } annotate photo
    .span-3
        %form{:id => "form_cover_photo", :method => 'post', :action =>
"/album/cover/#{@photo.id}"}
            %a{:href => '#', :onclick => '$("#form_cover_photo").
submit();'} set album cover
    .span-3.last
        %form{:id => "form_photo_#{@photo.id}", :method => 'post',
:action => "/photo/#{@photo.id}"}
            %input{:type => 'hidden', :name => '_method', :value =>
'delete'}
            %a{:href => '#', :onclick => '$("#form_photo_' + "#{@photo.
id}" + '").submit();'} delete photo
```

Next, we look at displaying the photo and doing inline editing of the title and caption.

```
- if @user === @photo.album.user
    %h2.edit_title #{@photo.title}
  - else
    %h2 #{@photo.title}
  %img{:id => 'photo', :src => "#{@photo.url_display}"}
  - if @user === @photo.album.user
    %h4.edit_area #{@photo.caption}
  - else
    %h4 #{@photo.caption}
```

As with editing the album title and description earlier, we use a similar snippet called `photo_inline_js.rb` to add in the necessary JavaScript, and an *edit photo properties* route to do the actual modification of the properties. The *edit photo properties* route is as below:

```
post "/photo/:property/:photo_id" do
  photo = Photo.get params[:photo_id]
  if %w(title caption).include? params[:property]
    photo.send(params[:property] + '=', params[:value])
    photo.save
  end
  photo.send(params[:property])
end
```

Just as in Photoclone, we show a list of annotations on the photo and below that is the navigation amongst photos in the same album. Remember we got these two variables in the route:

```
@prev_in_album = @photo.previous_in_album(@user)
@next_in_album = @photo.next_in_album(@user)
```

These two variables are used to determine the next and previous photos to view. The logic to retrieve the correct photo is in the Photo class but the layout is determined here.

```
%h3 #{@photo.album.name}

    - if @prev_in_album
      %a{:href => "/photo/#{@prev_in_album.id}"}
        %img.span-2{:src => "#{@prev_in_album.url_thumbnail}"}
    - else
      %img.span-2{:src => '/images/spacer.gif'}
    - if @next_in_album
      %a{:href => "/photo/#{@next_in_album.id}"}
        %img.span-2{:src => "#{@next_in_album.url_thumbnail}"}
    - else
      %img.span-2{:src => '/images/spacer.gif'}
    %br
    - if @prev_in_album
      %a{:href => "/photo/#{@prev_in_album.id}"}
        %img.span-2{:src => "/images/left_arrow.gif"}
    %a{:href => "/album/#{@photo.album.id}"}
      %img.span-2{:src => "/images/browse.gif"}
    - if @next_in_album
      %a{:href => "/photo/#{@next_in_album.id}"}
        %img.span-2{:src => "/images/right_arrow.gif"}
```

Note that the previous and next photos in the list shows a last-in-first-out (LIFO) structure. The last uploaded photo is considered the first photo to view while the next photo goes to the second to last.

Annotating photos

Annotating a photo involves placing a bounding box around an area and attaching some text to this area. To annotate on a photo in Colony, we place a JavaScript layer on top of the photo and draw a white box around the item that the user marked. This is the same technique we used in Photoclone.

First, we use two JavaScript libraries, both of which are initalized in the `layout.rb` file.

```
%script{:src => '/js/select.js', :type => 'text/javascript'}
%script{:src => '/js/notes.js', :type => 'text/javascript'}
```

The two important functions in the two files of note are `img_annotations` in the `notes.js` file and `imgAreaSelect` in the `select.js` file. To add the annotation feature, we include an annotations snippet in a file called `annotations_js.haml` in the *view photo* page.

```
=snippet :'/snippets/annotations_js'
```

This snippet allows us to provide annotations to photo.

```
:javascript
notes = [ #{@notes} ];

$(window).load(function () {
$('#photo').img_annotations();

$('#cancel_note').click(function(){
$('#photo').imgAreaSelect({ hide: true });
$('#annotation_form').hide();
});

$('#add_annotation').click(function(){
$('#photo').imgAreaSelect({ onSelectChange: show_add_annotation, x1:
120, y1: 90, x2: 280, y2: 210 });
return false;
});
});

function show_add_annotation (img, area) {
  imgOffset = $(img).offset();
  form_left  = parseInt(imgOffset.left) + parseInt(area.x1);
  form_top   = parseInt(imgOffset.top) + parseInt(area.y1) +
parseInt(area.height)+5;

  $('#annotation_form').css({ left: form_left + 'px', top: form_top +
'px'});
```

```
$('#annotation_form').show();
$('#annotation_form').css("z-index", 10000);
$('#annotation_x1').val(area.x1);
$('#annotation_y1').val(area.y1);
$('#annotation_height').val(area.height);
$('#annotation_width').val(area.width);
}
```

notes is a JavaScript variable used to store a list of notes added to the photo.

```
notes = [ #{@notes} ];
```

The data is something like this:

```
notes = [ {"x1": "63", "y1": "39", "height": "239", "width":
"384","note": "School trip to the zoo!!"},{"x1": "325", "y1": "8",
"height": "74", "width": "146","note": "This is me!"} ];
```

x1 and y1 are the coordinates of the upper left corner of the white box while height and width defines the height and width of the box. The note field is the actual text to be displayed. We indicate the image to be annotated to be the element that has a class ID photo.

```
$('#photo').img_annotations();
```

Remember the function img_annotations, which we are using here. When we click on an element that has the class ID add_annotation, we use the imgAreaSelect function to draw the white select box and at the same time, call the show_add_annotation function.

```
$('#add_annotation').click(function(){
$('#photo').imgAreaSelect({ onSelectChange: show_add_annotation, x1:
120, y1: 90, x2: 280, y2: 210 });
return false;
});
});
```

The show_add_annotation function in turn shows a form just below the white box, and pre-populates certain dimensions data into that form.

```
function show_add_annotation (img, area) {
  imgOffset = $(img).offset();
  form_left  = parseInt(imgOffset.left) + parseInt(area.x1);
  form_top   = parseInt(imgOffset.top) + parseInt(area.y1) +
parseInt(area.height)+5;
```

```
    $('#annotation_form').css({ left: form_left + 'px', top: form_top +
'px'});
    $('#annotation_form').show();
    $('#annotation_form').css("z-index", 10000);
    $('#annotation_x1').val(area.x1);
    $('#annotation_y1').val(area.y1);
    $('#annotation_height').val(area.height);
    $('#annotation_width').val(area.width);
}
```

The annotation form is a simple HTML form that allows the user to create
the annotation.

```
#annotation_form
    %form{:id => 'annotation_add_form', :method => 'post', :action => "/
annotation/#{@photo.id}"}
    %fieldset
      %legend
      %input{:name => 'annotation[x1]', :type => 'hidden', :id =>
'annotation_x1'}
      %input{:name => 'annotation[y1]', :type => 'hidden', :id =>
'annotation_y1'}
      %input{:name => 'annotation[height]', :type => 'hidden', :id =>
'annotation_height'}
      %input{:name => 'annotation[width]', :type => 'hidden', :id =>
'annotation_width'}
      %textarea{:name => 'annotation[text]', :id => 'annotation_text'}
    .submit
      %input{:type => 'submit', :value => 'add'}
      %input{:type => 'button', :value => 'cancel', :id => 'cancel_
note'}
```
The cancel button calls the cancel_note function to hide the form once
more.

```
$('#cancel_note').click(function(){
$('#photo').imgAreaSelect({ hide: true });
$('#annotation_form').hide();
});
```

The *add anotation* route creates a note whenever the form posts to it, given the photo ID.

```
post "/annotation/:photo_id" do
  photo = Photo.get params[:photo_id]
  note = Annotation.create(:x => params["annotation"]["x1"],
                           :y => params["annotation"]["y1"],
                           :height => params["annotation"]["height"],
                           :width => params["annotation"]["width"],
                           :description => params["annotation"]
["text"])
  photo.annotations << note
  photo.save
  redirect "/photo/#{params[:photo_id]}"
end
```

The annotation is created and added to the photo and the user is redirected back to the *view photo* route. To remove the annotation, the user can click on the remove link at the list of annotations to the right.

```
%h3 Annotations
  - if @photo.annotations.empty?
    %h4 No annotations on this photo.
  - else
    - @photo.annotations.each do |note|
      .span-6
        =note.description
      .span-3
        %form{:id => "form_#{note.id}", :method => 'post', :action =>
"/annotation/#{note.id}"}
          %input{:type => 'hidden', :name => '_method', :value =>
'delete'}
          %a{:href => '#', :onclick => '$("#form_' + "#{note.id}" +
'").submit();'} [remove]
```

This will simply remove the annotation and reload the same page.

```
delete "/annotation/:id" do
  note = Annotation.get(params[:id])
  photo = note.photo
  if note.destroy
    redirect "/photo/#{photo.id}"
  else
      throw "Cannot delete this annotation!"
  end
end
```

Viewing friends' photos

While viewing a friend's albums and photos is implemented the same way as viewing the users's albums and photos, there are few ways of attracting other users to view your photos. First, viewing a user's page will also show a list of photos the viewed user has. This is done with the the *mini album* snippet, which shows the most recent 16 photos belonging to that user.

```
- if @viewed_user.photos.empty?
  #{@viewed_user.formatted_name} has not uploaded any photos yet.
- @viewed_user.photos[0..15].each do |photo|
  %a{:href => "/photo/#{photo.id}"}
    %img.span-1{:src => photo.url_thumbnail }
%hr.space
%a{:href => "/albums/#{@viewed_user.id}"} view all
```

Clicking on an individual photo will show that photo while clicking on **view all** will show all photos in that album.

Also, each time a photo is uploaded, the activity of uploading that photo is logged and shown in the user's news and activity feeds. Also when the photo is annotated, the action is also logged as an activity and appears in the news and activity feeds.

Sending messages

Sending messages is yet another feature transplanted from Tweetclone. However, the implementation of sending messages in Colony is different. Importantly, the main class used in this feature in Colony is the Message class, while in Tweetclone we use the Status class for both public statuses and private messages.

The routing logic for this feature is in the `messages.rb` file. Let's look at viewing all messages first. The same route is used to view both sent and received messages.

```
get '/messages/:type' do
  @friends = @user.friends
  case params[:type]
  when 'inbox'   then @messages = Message.all(:recipient_id => @user.
id, :order => [ :created_at.desc ]); @label = 'Inbox'
  when 'sent_box' then @messages = Message.all(:user_id => @user.id,
:order => [ :created_at.desc ]); @label = 'Sent'
  end
  haml :'/messages/messages'
end
```

The `type` parameter in this route is used to differentiate between sent (sent box)/ received (inbox) messages, and the retrieved messages are passed to the messages page.

```
=snippet :'/snippets/top'
.span-24
  .span-3
    %img.span-3{:src => "#{@user.photo_url}"}
    =snippet :'/snippets/links'

  .span-21.last
    %hr.space
    .span-4
      %div.icons.icons_messages
      %strong{:style => 'vertical-align:bottom;font-size:18px;'} #{@
label}
    .span-12  
    .span-5.last.right
      %a.button{:href =>'/messages/inbox'} inbox
      %a.button{:href =>'/messages/sent_box'} sent
      %a.button{:href =>'#', :onclick => "$('#compose_box').
toggle();"} + new message
    %hr.space

    #compose_box.span-21.last.hide
      %form{:action => "/message/send", :method => 'post'}
        Subject
        %br
        %input.span-15{:type => 'text', :name => 'subject'}
        %br
```

```
      Recipient (please enter nickname)
      %br
      %input.span-15{:type => 'text', :name => 'recipient'}
      %br
      Message
      %br
      %textarea.span-15{:name => 'text'}
      %br
      %input{:type => 'submit', :value => 'send'}
    %hr.space

  #messages_list

  - @messages.each do |msg|
    - usr = params[:type] == 'inbox' ? msg.sender : msg.recipient
    .span-3
      %img.span-2{:src => "#{usr.photo_url}"}
    .span-4
      %a{:href => "/user/#{usr.nickname}"} #{usr.formatted_name}
      .quiet #{msg.created_at.strftime '%b %d at %I:%M %p'}
    .span-13
      .loud
        %a{:href => "/message/#{msg.id}"}
          - if msg.read?
            #{msg.subject}
          -else
            %strong #{msg.subject}
      #{msg.text[0,150]} ...
    .span-1.last
      %form{:id => "form_msg_#{msg.id}", :method => 'post',
:action => "/message/#{msg.id}"}
        %input{:type => 'hidden', :name => '_method', :value =>
'delete'}
        %a{:href => '#', :onclick => '$("#form_msg_' + "#{msg.id}"
+ '").submit();', :class => 'remove_link'}
    %hr
```

We toggle a compose message form to allow the user to click to write messages.

```
#compose_box.span-21.last.hide
    %form{:action => "/message/send", :method => 'post'}
    Subject
    %br
    %input.span-15{:type => 'text', :name => 'subject'}
    %br
```

```
Recipient (please enter nickname)
%br
%input.span-15{:type => 'text', :name => 'recipient'}
%br
Message
%br
%textarea.span-15{:name => 'text'}
%br
%input{:type => 'submit', :value => 'send'}
```

This submits a request to the *send message* route, which saves the message.

```
post '/message/send' do
  recipient = User.first(:nickname => params[:recipient])
  m = Message.create(:subject => params[:subject], :text =>
params[:text], :sender => @user, :recipient => recipient)
  if params[:thread].nil?
    m.thread =  m.id
  else
    m.thread = params[:thread].to_i
  end
  m.save
  redirect '/messages/sent_box'
end
```

Notice the thread property of a message. We will be using this later to filter messages of the same thread. At this point, we only capture the thread number if the message has a thread; if not it will use the message ID as the starting thread number.

We also list the messages provided, and truncate each message to 150 characters only.

```
@messages.each do |msg|
            - usr = params[:type] == 'inbox' ? msg.sender : msg.recipient
          .span-3
            %img.span-2{:src => "#{usr.photo_url}"}
          .span-4
            %a{:href => "/user/#{usr.nickname}"} #{usr.formatted_name}
            .quiet #{msg.created_at.strftime '%b %d at %I:%M %p'}
          .span-13
            .loud
              %a{:href => "/message/#{msg.id}"}
                - if msg.read?
                  #{msg.subject}
                -else
                  %strong #{msg.subject}
          #{msg.text[0,150]} ...
```

Finally, we let the users delete messages in their inbox as well as from their sent box.

```
%form{:id => "form_msg_#{msg.id}", :method => 'post', :action => "/
message/#{msg.id}"}
  %input{:type => 'hidden', :name => '_method', :value => 'delete'}
  %a{:href => '#', :onclick => '$("#form_msg_' + "#{msg.id}" + '").
submit();', :class => 'remove_link'}
```

Let's look at viewing the messages next, starting with the *view message* route.

```
get '/message/:id' do
  @message = Message.get(params[:id])
  @message.read = true
  @message.save
  @messages = Message.all(:thread => @message.thread).sort{|m1, m2|
m1.created_at <=> m2.created_at}
  haml :'/messages/message'
end
```

This is simply getting the message and then all messages with the same thread number, but sorted according to their reverse chronological date of creation. The messages are then displayed in the *view message* page in a file named `message.haml`. Note that we also set the `read` property to true, to indicate that the message has been read.

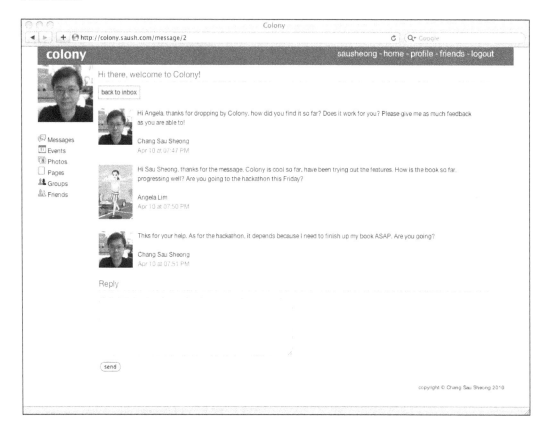

```
=snippet :'/snippets/top'
.span-24
  .span-3
    %img.span-3{:src => "#{@user.photo_url}"}
    =snippet :'/snippets/links'

  .span-20
    %h3 #{@message.subject}
    %a.button{:href =>'/messages/inbox'} back to inbox
    %hr.space

    - @messages.each do |msg|
      .span-2
        %img.span-2{:src => "#{msg.sender.photo_url}"}
```

```
.span-17
  #{msg.text}
  %hr.space
  #{msg.sender.formatted_name}
    .quiet #{msg.created_at.strftime '%b %d at %I:%M %p'}
  %hr.space

%h3 Reply
%form{:action => "/message/send", :method => 'post'}
  %input{:type => 'hidden', :name => 'subject', :value => "#{@
message.subject}"}
  %input{:type => 'hidden', :name => 'recipient', :value => "#{@
message.sender.nickname}"}
  %input{:type => 'hidden', :name => 'thread', :value => "#{@
message.thread}"}
  %textarea.span-10{:name => 'text'}
  %br
  %input{:type => 'submit', :value => 'send'}
```

We display the main message, followed by each message in the same message thread, then provide a reply form to reply this message.

Finally, let's see how we delete a message with the *delete message* route.

```
delete '/message/:id' do
  message = Message.get(params[:id])
  if message.sender == @user
    message.sender = nil
  elsif message.recipient == @user
    message.recipient = nil
  end
  message.save
  redirect '/messages/inbox'
end
```

Notice we don't actually delete the message, only de-link it from the various users. This is useful to keep track of messages for auditing purposes.

Now that we are able to send, view, and delete messages put in the finishing touch to let the user know about these messages. We place a number after the messages link at the left navigation bar to indicate the number of unread messages a user has. In the *links* snippet, we have the following code:

```
.icons.icons_messages
  - num_unread_msgs =  @user.received_messages.all(:read => false).
size
  %a{:href => '/messages/inbox'} Messages
  - if num_unread_msgs > 0
    (#{num_unread_msgs})
```

Creating events

Events can be thought of as locations in time where people can come together for an activity. To recap, in Colony's implementation of events, an event can have a wall, pages, and three types of users according to their attendance status. The first type is the confirmed user (those who have confirmed their attendance to the event). The second type is the declined user (users who have explicitly declined attendance to the event). The last type is the pending user (users who are still undecided, if they should attend or not).

Let's look at managing the events first. Managing events here refers to a user managing his own list of events that he has confirmed, is pending, or has declined to attend. The *manage events* route simply points the user to the *manage events* page.

```
get '/events' do
  haml :'/events/manage'
end
```

The *manage events* page shows the user a list of events that he has either created, is attending, or pending a confirmation.

```
=snippet :'/snippets/top'
.span-24
  .span-3
    %img.span-3{:src => "#{@user.photo_url}"}
    =snippet :'/snippets/links'
  .span-15
    %hr.space
    .span-3
      %div.icons.icons_event
      %strong{:style => 'vertical-align:bottom;font-size:18px;'}
Events
    .span-8  
    .span-4.last.right
      %a.button{:href =>"/event/add"} new event

    .span-15
      %hr.space
      - @user.all_events.each do |event|
        .span-11
          %strong #{event.name}
          .quiet #{event.description}
          .quiet Venue : #{event.venue}
          .quiet Date/time : #{event.time.strftime "%I:%M %p"},
#{event.date.strftime "%d %b %Y"}
        .span-4.last.right
```

```
            %form{:id => "form_event_#{event.id}", :method => 'post',
:action => "/event/#{event.id}"}
                %input{:type => 'hidden', :name => '_method', :value =>
'delete'}
                - if event.user == @user
                  %a.button{:href => '#', :onclick => '$("#form_event_' +
"#{event.id}" + '").submit();'} delete
                %a.button{:href => "/event/#{event.id}"}
                  - if @user.pending_events.include? event
                    pending
                  - else
                    view
        %hr.space
        %hr


  .span-6.last
    %h3  Suggestions
    - if @user.friend_events.empty?
      No suggested events
    - else
      Your friends are attending these events:
      %ul
        - @user.friend_events[0..9].each do |event|
          %li
            %a{:href => "/event/#{event.id}"} #{event.name}
```

From the User class you might remember that the all_events method returns all confirmed and pending events only, and these events should be later than or equal to today's date.

```
has n, :confirms
  has n, :confirmed_events, :through => :confirms, :class_name =>
'Event', :child_key => [:user_id], :date.gte => Date.today
  has n, :pendings
  has n, :pending_events, :through => :pendings, :class_name =>
'Event', :child_key => [:user_id], :date.gte => Date.today

def all_events
   confirmed_events + pending_events
end
```

For each event that is displayed, if the user is the creator of the event, we also allow him to delete it.

```
- @user.all_events.each do |event|
      .span-11
        %strong #{event.name}
        .quiet #{event.description}
        .quiet Venue : #{event.venue}
        .quiet Date/time : #{event.time.strftime "%I:%M %p"},
#{event.date.strftime "%d %b %Y"}
      .span-4.last.right
        %form{:id => "form_event_#{event.id}", :method => 'post',
:action => "/event/#{event.id}"}
          %input{:type => 'hidden', :name => '_method', :value =>
'delete'}
          - if event.user == @user
            %a.button{:href => '#', :onclick => '$("#form_event_' +
"#{event.id}" + '").submit();'} delete
          %a.button{:href => "/event/#{event.id}"}
            - if @user.pending_events.include? event
              pending
            - else
              view
```

Note if the user has not decided to attend the event yet, we indicate that he is pending in this list. To cater for that connection, we also display a list of suggested events, which are events that the user's friends are also attending.

```
%h3 Suggestions
   - if @user.friend_events.empty?
     No suggested events
```

```
        - else
          Your friends are attending these events:
          %ul
            - @user.friend_events[0..9].each do |event|
              %li
                %a{:href => "/event/#{event.id}"} #{event.name}
```

These friend's events goes through the user's friends list and retrieve all their
confirmed events, then sort them out by chronological order.

```
    def friend_events
        events = []
        friends.each do |friend|
            events += friend.confirmed_events
        end
        return events.sort {|x,y| y.time <=> x.time}
    end
```

We will now move on to create an event. As mentioned previously, the *add event*
route is very simple.

```
    get '/event/add' do
        haml :'/events/add'
    end
```

The *add event* page provides a form that sends the event creation data to the *create
event* route.

```
    =snippet :'/snippets/top'
    .span-24
      .span-3
        %img.span-3{:src => "#{@user.photo_url}"}
        =snippet :'/snippets/links'
      .span-20
        %h3 Create a new event
        Create a new event here. Add people you would like to invite.
        %form{:method => 'post', :action => '/event'}
          %input{:type => 'hidden', :name => '_method', :value => 'put'}
          %p Name
          %p
            %input.span-10{:type => 'text', :name => 'name'}
          %p Description
          %p
            %textarea.span-10{:name => 'description'}
          %p Venue
          %p
```

```
     %input.span-10{:type => 'text', :name => 'venue'}
   %p Date
   %p
     %input.span-4#date{:type => 'text', :name => 'date'}
     :javascript
       var opts = { formElements:{"date":"d-ds-m-ds-Y"} };
       datePickerController.createDatePicker(opts);
   %p Time
   %p
     %input.span-2#time{:type => 'text', :name => 'time'}
     :javascript
       $("#time").timePicker({
         startTime: "08:00",
         show24Hours: false,
         separator: ':',
         step: 15});
   %p People you want to invite
   %p
     %input.span-10{:type => 'text', :name => 'invites'}
   %p
     %input{:type => 'submit', :value => 'create this event'}
```

In the *add event* page, we allow users to set a list of users that they want to invite. This will effectively add the newly created event into each of the user's pending events list. In the mini requests snippet, this will be shown as a pending event.

Next, we look at viewing the event. As before, the *view event* route is simple.

```
get '/event/:id' do
  @event = Event.get params[:id]
  haml :'/events/event'
end
```

Viewing the event however is much more demanding.

```
=snippet :'/snippets/top'
.span-24
  .span-3
    %img.span-3{:src => "#{@user.photo_url}"}
    =snippet :'/snippets/links'
  .span-15

    %h3 #{@event.name}
    .span-14
      .span-3 Date
      .span-10 #{@event.date.strftime "%d %b %Y"}
    .span-14
      .span-3 Time
      .span-10 #{@event.time.strftime "%I:%M %p"}
    .span-14
      .span-3 Venue
      .span-10 #{@event.venue}

    %hr.space

    %h3 Description
    =@event.description

    %h3 Confirmed attendees
    - @event.confirmed_users.each do |user|
      .span-2
        %a{:href => "/user/#{user.nickname}"}
          %img.span-1{:src => "#{user.photo_url}", :alt => "#{user.
formatted_name}"}

  %hr.space

    %h3 Pages
    .span-3.push-12.right
      - if @event.user == @user
        %a.button{:href =>"/event/#{@event.id}/page/add"} new page
    - @event.pages.each do |page|
      .span-12
```

```
          %a{:href => "/event/page/#{page.id}" } #{page.title}
            .quiet Date created : #{page.created_at.strftime "%I:%M %p, %d
%b %Y"}
        .span-3.right.last
          %form{:id => "form_page_#{page.id}", :method => 'post',
:action => "/event/page/#{page.id}"}
            %input{:type => 'hidden', :name => '_method', :value =>
'delete'}
            - if @event.user == @user
              %a.button{:href => '#', :onclick => '$("#form_page_' +
"#{page.id}" + '").submit();'} del
            %a.button{:href => "/event/page/edit/#{page.id}"} edit
      %hr.space
      %hr
    %hr.space

    %h3 Wall
    =snippet :'/snippets/event_wall_box'

    %hr.space

    -@event.wall.posts.each do |post|
      .span-2
        %img.span-2{:src => "#{post.user.photo_url}"}
      .span-4
        #{post.user.formatted_name}
        %br
        #{post.created_at.strftime "%d %b %Y"}
        %br
        #{post.created_at.strftime "%I:%M %P"}
      .span-8
        #{post.text}
      %hr
    %hr.space

  .span-6.last
    %h3 Your RSVP
    =snippet :'/snippets/rsvp'

    %h3 Awaiting reply
    - @event.pending_users.each do |user|
      .span-2
        %a{:href => "/user/#{user.nickname}"}
          %img.span-1{:src => "#{user.photo_url}", :alt => "#{user.
formatted_name}"}
```

We will split the description of this page into several parts:

- Displaying information about the event
- Showing the list of confirmed attendees and the list of pending attendees
- Listing the pages created for this event
- Showing the event wall
- Showing the RSVP form

The uppermost part shows the event information. This is quite straightforward and the page just dumps whatever has been created.

```
%h3 #{@event.name}
    .span-14
      .span-3 Date
      .span-10 #{@event.date.strftime "%d %b %Y"}
    .span-14
      .span-3 Time
      .span-10 #{@event.time.strftime "%I:%M %p"}
    .span-14
      .span-3 Venue
      .span-10 #{@event.venue}

%hr.space

%h3 Description
=@event.description
```

Showing the list of confirmed attendees is also relatively straightforward, as with showing the list of pending attendees. We show the list of confirmed attendees on the middle column, while the list of pending attendees is on the right column.

```
%h3 Confirmed attendees
    - @event.confirmed_users.each do |user|
      .span-2
        %a{:href => "/user/#{user.nickname}"}
          %img.span-1{:src => "#{user.photo_url}", :alt => "#{user.
formatted_name}"}

%h3 Awaiting reply
    - @event.pending_users.each do |user|
      .span-2
        %a{:href => "/user/#{user.nickname}"}
          %img.span-1{:src => "#{user.photo_url}", :alt => "#{user.
formatted_name}"}
```

In both cases we show the profile picture of the user. Showing event pages is similarly straightforward. We only allow the event administrator to create or delete event pages. We will be looking at pages later in this chapter.

```
%h3 Pages
    .span-3.push-12.right
      - if @event.user == @user
        %a.button{:href =>"/event/#{@event.id}/page/add"} new page
    - @event.pages.each do |page|
```

```
    .span-12
      %a{:href => "/event/page/#{page.id}" } #{page.title}
        .quiet Date created : #{page.created_at.strftime "%I:%M %p, %d
%b %Y"}
      .span-3.right.last
        %form{:id => "form_page_#{page.id}", :method => 'post',
:action => "/event/page/#{page.id}"}
          %input{:type => 'hidden', :name => '_method', :value =>
'delete'}
          - if @event.user == @user
            %a.button{:href => '#', :onclick => '$("#form_page_' +
"#{page.id}" + '").submit();'} del
          %a.button{:href => "/event/page/edit/#{page.id}"} edit
```

As for the event wall, we include the *event wall box* snippet and show the list of posts just below the snippet.

```
%h3 Wall
  =snippet :'/snippets/event_wall_box'

%hr.space

-@event.wall.posts.each do |post|
  .span-2
    %img.span-2{:src => "#{post.user.photo_url}"}
  .span-4
    #{post.user.formatted_name}
    %br
    #{post.created_at.strftime "%d %b %Y"}
    %br
    #{post.created_at.strftime "%I:%M %P"}
  .span-8
    #{post.text}
```

The *event wall box* snippet was described earlier. Finally let's look at the RSVP form.

```
%form{:action => "/event/#{@event.id}", :method => 'post'}
  %p
    %input{:type => :radio, :name => 'attendance', :value => 'yes',
:checked => @event.confirmed_users.include?(@user) } Attending
  %p
    %input{:type => :radio, :name => 'attendance', :value => 'maybe',
:checked => @event.pending_users.include?(@user) } Maybe Attending
  %p
    %input{:type => :radio, :name => 'attendance', :value => 'no',
:checked => @event.declined_users.include?(@user) } Not Attending
%input{:type => 'submit', :value => 'send'}
```

The input is a radio button, which allows the user to indicate if he is attending, maybe attending, or not attending. Submitting this form goes to the *event rsvp* route.

```
post '/event/:id' do
  event = Event.get params[:id]
  case params[:attendance]
  when 'yes'
    Pending.first(:user_id => @user.id, :event_id => event.id).destroy
if event.pending_users.include? @user
    Decline.first(:user_id => @user.id, :event_id => event.id).destroy
if event.declined_users.include? @user
    Confirm.create(:confirmed_event => event, :confirmed_user => @
user)

  when 'no'
    Confirm.first(:user_id => @user.id, :event_id => event.id).destroy
if event.confirmed_users.include? @user
    Pending.first(:user_id => @user.id, :event_id => event.id).destroy
if event.pending_users.include? @user
    Decline.create(:declined_user => @user, :declined_event => event)

  when 'maybe'
    Confirm.first(:user_id => @user.id, :event_id => event.id).destroy
if event.confirmed_users.include? @user
    Decline.first(:user_id => @user.id, :event_id => event.id).destroy
if event.declined_users.include? @user
    Pending.create(:pending_user => @user, :pending_event => event)
  end

  redirect "/event/#{event.id}"
end
```

We need to switch between each type of attendance and add the event to the respective queues under the user.

Forming groups

Groups in Colony place groups of one or more users together and provide services for the group. Groups and events are very similar to each other, except that groups are not time-based (unlike events), and do no have a concept of attendance. Groups however have users who are called members of a group.

The implementation of groups is quite similar to that of events. Let's look at managing a group first. Managing groups in Colony as with managing events means providing a page for users to look and control groups that he is either an admin or a member of. The *manage groups* route is simple, similar to the *manage events* route.

```
get '/groups' do
  haml :'/groups/manage'
end
```

The *manage groups* page lists the groups a user belongs to.

```
=snippet :'/snippets/top'
.span-24
  .span-3
    %img.span-3{:src => "#{@user.photo_url}"}
    =snippet :'/snippets/links'
  .span-15
    %hr.space
    .span-3
      %div.icons.icons_group
      %strong{:style => 'vertical-align:bottom;font-size:18px;'}
Groups
    .span-8  
    .span-4.last.right
      %a.button{:href =>"/group/add"} new group

    .span-15
      %hr.space
      - @user.groups.each do |group|
        .span-11
          %strong #{group.name}
          .quiet #{group.description}
        .span-4.last{:style => 'text-align:right;'}
          %form{:id => "form_group_#{group.id}", :method => 'post',
:action => "/group/#{group.id}"}
            %input{:type => 'hidden', :name => '_method', :value =>
'delete'}
            - if group.user == @user
              %a.button{:href => '#', :onclick => '$("#form_group_' +
"#{group.id}" + '").submit();'} delete
            %a.button{:href => "/group/#{group.id}"} view
        %hr.space
        %hr

  .span-6.last
    %h3  Suggestions
    - if @user.friend_groups.empty?
      No suggested groups
    - else
```

```
Your friends have joined the following groups:
%ul
  - @user.friend_groups[0..9].each do |group|
    %li
      %a{:href => "/group/#{group.id}"} #{group.name}
```

Furthermore, the user can delete the group(s) in which the user is the administrator. Also as with events, there is a list of suggested groups. These are the groups that the user's friends belong to. The code to retrieve this list is in the User class. Note the last line where we remove the groups that the users already belong to.

```
def friend_groups
  groups = []
  friends.each do |friend|
    groups += friend.groups
  end
  groups - self.groups
end
```

The *add group* route redirects us to the *add group* page.

```
get '/group/add' do
  haml :'/groups/add'
end
```

The *add group* page is a simple one.

```
=snippet :'/snippets/top'

.span-24
  .span-3
    %img.span-3{:src => "#{@user.photo_url}"}
    =snippet :'/snippets/links'
  .span-20
```

```
%h3 Create a new group
Create a new group here, use it to share information!

%form{:method => 'post', :action => '/group'}
  %input{:type => 'hidden', :name => '_method', :value => 'put'}
  %p Name
  %p
    %input.span-10{:type => 'text', :name => 'name'}
  %p Description
  %p
    %textarea.span-10{:name => 'description'}
```

The *add group* form is submitted to the *create group* route.

```
put '/group' do
  g = Group.create(:name => params[:name], :description =>
params[:description],  :user => @user)
  g.members << @user
  g.save
  redirect "/group/#{g.id}"
end
```

This route creates a group and adds the user as both the administrator as well as a member of the group that redirects the user to the *view group* route.

Viewing a group is simpler than viewing events. The *view group* route again points us to the *view group* page.

```
get '/group/:id' do
  @group = Group.get params[:id]
  haml :'/groups/group'
end
```

The *view group* page is quite like the *view event* page. The only differences are that instead of an RSVP form, we display the group admin, and instead of displaying users who are undecided on attending the event, we have a form to allow the users to join or leave the group. We will skip most of the description of this page, and concentrate on the membership forms.

```
=snippet :'/snippets/top'
.span-24
  .span-3
    %img.span-3{:src => "#{@user.photo_url}"}
    =snippet :'/snippets/links'
  .span-15

    %h3 #{@group.name}
    =@group.description

    %h3 Members
    - @group.members.each do |user|
```

```
    .span-1
      %a{:href => "/user/#{user.nickname}"}
        %img.span-1{:src => "#{user.photo_url}", :alt => "#{user.
formatted_name}"}

  %hr.space

  %h3 Pages
  .span-3.push-12.right
    - if @group.user == @user
      %a.button{:href =>"/group/#{@group.id}/page/add"} new page
  - @group.pages.each do |page|
    .span-11
      %strong
        %a{:href => "/group/page/#{page.id}" } #{page.title}
      .quiet Date created : #{page.created_at.strftime "%I:%M %p, %d
%b %Y"}
    .span-4.last.right
      %form{:id => "form_page_#{page.id}", :method => 'post',
:action => "/group/page/#{page.id}"}
        %input{:type => 'hidden', :name => '_method', :value =>
'delete'}
        - if @group.user == @user
          %a.button{:href => '#', :onclick => '$("#form_page_' +
"#{page.id}" + '").submit();'} delete
          %a.button{:href => "/group/page/edit/#{page.id}"} edit
    %hr.space
    %hr
  %hr.space

  %h3 Wall
  =snippet :'/snippets/group_wall_box'

  %hr.space

  -@group.wall.posts.each do |post|
    .span-2
      %img.span-2{:src => "#{post.user.photo_url}"}
    .span-4
      #{post.user.formatted_name}
      %br
      #{post.created_at.strftime "%d %b %Y"}
      %br
      #{post.created_at.strftime "%I:%M %P"}
    .span-8
      #{post.text}
    %hr
  %hr.space

.span-6.last
  %h3 Group admin
```

```
  .span-3
    %img.span-3{:src => "#{@group.user.photo_url}"}
    %a{:href => "/user/#{@group.user.nickname}"} #{@group.user.
formatted_name}
  %hr.space
  %h3 Your membership
  - if @group.members.include? @user
    You are a member of this group.

  - unless @group.user == @user
    %form{:method => 'post', :action => "/group/leave/#{@group.id}"}
      %input{:type => 'submit', :value => 'leave this group'}

  - else
  You are not a member of this group yet.
    %form{:method => 'post', :action => "/group/join/#{@group.id}"}
    %input{:type => 'submit', :value => 'join this group'}
```

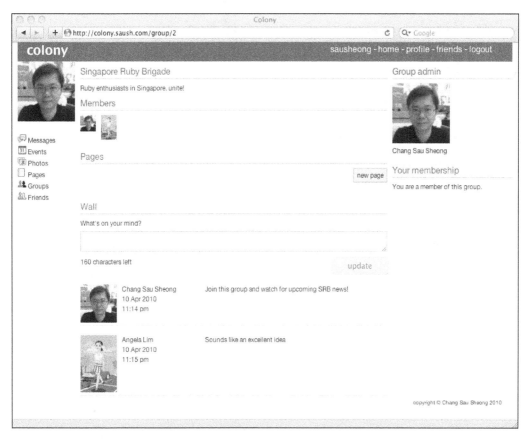

If the user is already a member in this group we display the leave group form, which is just a single button that posts to the *leave group* route. The group admin however is not allowed to leave the group.

```
%h3 Your membership
   - if @group.members.include? @user
     You are a member of this group.

     - unless @group.user == @user
       %form{:method => 'post', :action => "/group/leave/#{@group.
id}"}
       %input{:type => 'submit', :value => 'leave this group'}

  - else
    You are not a member of this group yet.
    %form{:method => 'post', :action => "/group/join/#{@group.id}"}
    %input{:type => 'submit', :value => 'join this group'}
```

The route removes the user from the list and redirects the user back to viewing the group.

```
post '/group/leave/:id' do
  group = Group.get params[:id]
  if group.members.include?(@user)
    group.members.delete(@user)
    group.save
  end
  redirect "/group/#{params[:id]}"
end
```

Similarly if the user is not yet a member, the page shows a join group form that submits to the *join group* route.

```
post '/group/join/:id' do
  group = Group.get params[:id]
  unless group.members.include? @user
    group.members << @user
    group.save
  end
  redirect "/group/#{params[:id]}"
end
```

This will add the user to the list of group members and redirect the user back to viewing the group.

Sharing content through pages

Colony's pages are a means of allowing users to create their own full-page content, attaching it to themselves, a page, or a group. The implementation of Colony's pages is distributed in the various objects that contain pages. Let's look at the user pages first.

Each user can have one or more pages. The implementation of user pages is in a file called `pages.rb`. We start off with managing pages. The *manage pages* route simply redirects to the *manage pages* page; pass in a local variable named `owner`, with the value of a string `user`.

```
get '/user/pages' do
  haml :'/pages/manage', {:locals => {:owner => 'user'}}
end
```

The *manage pages* page is quite small. It is essentially a list of pages belonging to the user, with the options to edit and delete the pages. Where is the local variable `owner` used? It is at the new page link. We share the *manage pages* page among the other owners of the page, such as group and event, so we need to tell this page who the owner is, in order to call the correct route. While it's possible to create a single route to manage different owners, it is deliberately separated into different routes. This is because we want each feature to be more modular and each page implementation to be customizable.

```
=snippet :'/snippets/top'
.span-24
  .span-3
    %img.span-3{:src => "#{@user.photo_url}"}
    =snippet :'/snippets/links'
  .span-21.last
    %hr.space
    .span-11
      %div.icons.icons_pages
      %strong{:style => 'vertical-align:bottom;font-size:18px;'} Pages
    .span-10.last.right
      %a.button{:href =>"/#{owner}/page/add"} new page

    .span-21.last
      %hr.space
      - if @user.pages.empty?
        You don't have any pages yet.

      - @user.pages.each do |page|
        .span-11
```

```
      %strong
        %a{:href => "/user/page/#{page.id}" } #{page.title}
        .quiet Date created : #{page.created_at.strftime "%I:%M %p,
%d %b %Y"}
      .span-10.last.right
        %form{:id => "form_page_#{page.id}", :method => 'post',
:action => "/user/page/#{page.id}"}
          %input{:type => 'hidden', :name => '_method', :value =>
'delete'}
          %a.button{:href => '#', :onclick => '$("#form_page_' +
"#{page.id}" + '").submit();'} delete
          %a.button{:href => "/user/page/edit/#{page.id}"} edit
```

Note that this list of pages can also be found on the user page, where the pages are listed at the right column. To create a page, the user will click on the **new page** link to the top right of the *manage user pages* page. This will go to the *add page* route.

```
get '/user/page/add' do
  @page = Page.new
  haml :'/pages/add', {:locals => {:owner => 'user'}}
end
```

The route sends the user to the *add page* page, with the local variable `owner` with a value of a string `user`. This again is used to tell the form to post to the correct route; in this case it is the *create user page* route.

```
=snippet :'/snippets/top'

.span-24
  .span-3
    %img.span-3{:src => "#{@user.photo_url}"}
    =snippet :'/snippets/links'
  .span-21.last
    %h3 Create a new page
    Create a new page here. Use
    %a{:href => 'http://daringfireball.net/projects/markdown/basics'}
markdown
      for the body text and copy this link to be used elsewhere!
    %hr.space
    %form{:method => 'post', :action => "/#{owner}/page"}
      - if @page.title.nil?
        %input{:type => 'hidden', :name => '_method', :value => 'put'}
      - else
        %input{:type => 'hidden', :name => 'id', :value => "#{@page.
id}"}
      - if owner == 'event'
        %input{:type => 'hidden', :name => 'eventid', :value => "#{@
event.id}"}
      - if owner == 'group'
        %input{:type => 'hidden', :name => 'groupid', :value => "#{@
group.id}"}
      %strong Title
      %p
        %input.span-10{:type => 'text', :name => 'title', :value =>
"#{@page.title}"}
      %strong Body
      %p
        %textarea.span-18{:name => 'body', :style => 'height: 350px;'}
#{@page.body}
      %p
        - if @page.title.nil?
          %input{:type => 'submit', :value => 'create this page'}
        - else
          %input{:type => 'submit', :value => 'modify this page'}
```

We use Markdown for markup text input for pages. Conveniently, Haml supports Markdown and as you would see later, it is displayed rather nicely. Why use Markdown instead of using a rich text editor, which can be more intuitive and user friendly to end-users? After some consideration, I took this design path because we want a consistent look and feel to the pages while retaining flexibility of content creation by the users. If we have used a rich text editor, it is inevitable that the look and feel of the pages would be radically different and this would have a downstream bad effect on the user experience with the application. With Markdown, the look and feel can be consistent with the rest of the site, and at the same time, the user doesn't need to worry about making it look good, they just need to enter the text content and link accordingly.

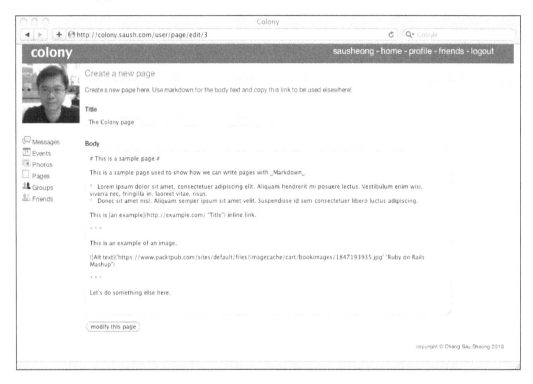

The *create page* form submits to the *create user page* route which redirects the user to the *view page* page after the `Page` object is created.

```
put '/user/page' do
  p = Page.create(:title => params[:title], :body => params[:body],
:user => @user)
  redirect "/user/page/#{p.id}"
end
```

Displaying the page is quite simple.

```
=snippet :'/snippets/top'
.span-24
  .span-3
    %img.span-3{:src => "#{@user.photo_url}"}
    =snippet :'/snippets/links'
  .span-15
    %h3 #{@page.title}
    :markdown
      #{@page.body}

    %hr.space

    =snippet :'/snippets/comment_and_like', {:locals => {:item => @
page}}

  .span-6.last
    %h3 Other pages
    =snippet :'/snippets/mini_pages', {:locals => {:owner => @user,
:owner_name => 'user'}}
```

As mentioned earlier, Haml conveniently provides Markdown support, so all the Markdown content the user created earlier will be parsed and converted into HTML for displaying in the page. Just under the page, we place the *comment and like* snippet, passing in the page as a local variable. We'll come back to this snippet in a later section.

We also place the *mini pages* snippet at the right column in order to display the list of pages that the user also owns.

```
- if owner.pages.empty?
  #{owner.formatted_name} has no pages.
%ul
  - owner.pages.each do |page|
    %li
      %a{:href => "/#{owner_name}/page/#{page.id}"}#{page.title}
      - if page.event
        %a{:href => "/event/#{page.event.id}"} (#{page.event.name})
```

This just lists all the user's pages. The final resulting page looks like this:

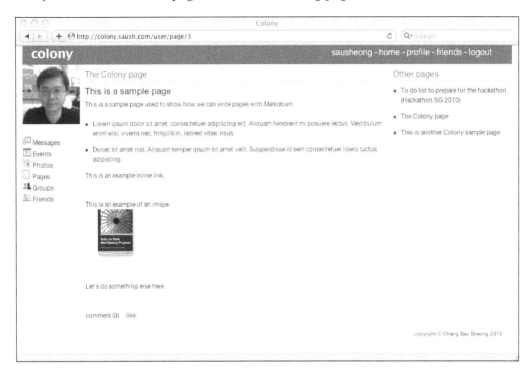

As mentioned earlier, pages belong to events, groups, and users. The implementation of the event pages and group pages are very similar to that of the user pages. The implementations are placed together with the features that own them, for example, the event page routes are all in the `pages.rb` file, but the views are shared amongst all owning features.

Let's look at some examples of these implementations. Take the *create event page* route — the only difference is that we set the event association in the `Page` object to the owning event.

```
put '/event/page' do
  event = Event.get params[:eventid]
  p = Page.create(:title => params[:title], :body => params[:body],
:user => @user, :event => event)
  redirect "/event/page/#{p.id}"
end
```

Notice that the page still has a user. This is because each page must have an owner, regardless of it being owned by a user, an event, or a group. The differences in the other routes as well as in the groups are similar to this.

Commenting and liking

The commenting and liking features are implemented together. Firstly all objects that can be liked or commented on, such as Status, Post, Photo, and Page include the `Commentable` module.

```
module Commentable
  def people_who_likes
    self.likes.collect { |l| "<a href='/user/#{l.user.nickname}'>#{l.
user.formatted_name}</a>"  }
  end
end
```

This allows us to retrieve all users who have liked this object. Also, all these classes have a *one-to-many* relationship with Like and Comment classes.

```
has n, :comments
has n, :likes
```

Commenting and liking, unlike other features, are not implemented through full standalone pages. The views are through a *comment and like* snippet in a file named `comment_and_like.haml` that is attached to the various places where commenting and liking are needed.

There are a few sections to this snippet:

- Links to commenting and liking
- The comment form
- A list of comments

The following is the `comment_and_like.haml` file:

```
.span-15.last
  .span-2
    %a{:href =>"#", :onclick => "$('#comment_box_#{item.class.
to_s}_#{item.id}').toggle();$('#comment_box_#{item.class.to_s}_#{item.
id}').focus();"} comment (#{item.comments.size})

  .span-13.last
    %form{:method => 'post', :action => "/like/#{item.class.
to_s.downcase}/#{item.id}", :id => "form_like_#{item.class.to_s.
downcase}_#{item.id}"}
      %input{:type => 'hidden', :name => 'return_url', :value =>
request.url.to_s}
      %input{:type => 'hidden', :name => '_method', :value => 'put'}
    %a{:href =>"#", :onclick => "$('#form_like_#{item.class.to_s.
downcase}_#{item.id}').submit();"} like
```

```
    - unless item.likes.empty?
      #{item.likes.size} people likes this.
#{item.people_who_likes.join(', ')} liked it.

  .span-13.hide.last{:id => "comment_box_#{item.class.to_s}_#{item.id}"}
    %form{:method => 'post', :action => "/comment/#{item.class.to_s.
downcase}/#{item.id}"}
      %textarea.span-10{:name => 'text', :style => 'height: 30px;'}
      %input{:type => 'hidden', :name => 'return_url', :value =>
request.url.to_s}
      %input{:type => 'hidden', :name => '_method', :value => 'put'}
      %br
      %input{:type => 'submit', :value => 'comment'}

  - unless item.comments.empty?
    .span-14.push-1.last
      - item.comments.each do |comment|
        .span-1
          %a{:href => "/user/#{comment.user.nickname}"}
            %img.span-1{:src => "#{comment.user.photo_url}"}
        .span-12.last.comment_box
          #{comment.text}
          %br
          %em.quiet
            =time_ago_in_words(comment.created_at.to_time)
```

The first few lines of code provide a link to toggle the comment field, allowing the user to enter his comments. It also provides some statistical information on the comments, such as the number of comments there are for the item.

```
%a{:href =>"#", :onclick => "$('#comment_box_#{item.class.
to_s}_#{item.id}').toggle();$('#comment_box_#{item.class.to_s}_#{item.
id}').focus();"} comment (#{item.comments.size})
```

Next, we have a form masquerading as a link that allows users to like the item.

```
%form{:method => 'post', :action => "/like/#{item.class.to_s.
downcase}/#{item.id}", :id => "form_like_#{item.class.to_s.
downcase}_#{item.id}"}
      %input{:type => 'hidden', :name => 'return_url', :value =>
request.url.to_s}
      %input{:type => 'hidden', :name => '_method', :value => 'put'}
    %a{:href =>"#", :onclick => "$('#form_like_#{item.class.to_s.
downcase}_#{item.id}').submit();"} like
      - unless item.likes.empty?
        #{item.likes.size} people likes this.
#{item.people_who_likes.join(', ')} liked it.
```

This also shows the number of people who liked the item, as well as showing the people who liked it (this is where we use the method from the `Commentable` module). The form submits to the *create like* route.

```
put "/like/:class/:id" do
    return unless %w(status activity post photo page).include?
params[:class]
    clazz = Kernel.const_get(params[:class].capitalize)
    item = clazz.get params[:id]
    if Like.first(:user_id => @user.id, "#{params[:class]}_id".to_sym =>
item.id).nil?
        Like.create(params[:class].to_sym => item, :user => @user)
    end
    redirect params[:return_url]
end
```

This route is more interesting to describe than the others as it uses some metaprogramming. Let's look at it in details. The URL route has two parameters— class and ID. The class is the class of the object that is likable while the ID is the ID of that object. The first line of the code rejects any other types of objects other than Status, Activity, Post, Photo, or Page.

Next, we get the Class object through `Kernel.const_get`, which returns an object's class (which is also an object, since everything in Ruby is an object!). We call the `get` method of this Class object, given the ID and this returns the actual object that we want. Once we have the object, we check if the user has already liked this object. If not, we create *add a like* to this object and go back to the calling URL.

The implementation of the commenting feature is in the *create comment* route in the `comments.rb` file, and is almost the same as the *create like* route.

```
put "/comment/:class/:id" do
    return unless %w(status activity post photo page).include?
params[:class]
    clazz = Kernel.const_get(params[:class].capitalize)
    item = clazz.get params[:id]
    Comment.create(:text => params[:text], params[:class].to_sym =>
item, :user => @user)
    redirect params[:return_url]
end
```

That's all for the application flow. It has been a lengthy discussion and we've covered a lot of ground. If there are any parts that are less understood you should go through the chapter again or read the code in full and run it carefully. However, most of the codes are straightforward enough.

Deploying the clone

As usual, I will deploy to the local machine (your desktop or laptop) and then to Heroku. The steps are quite similar except for one or two minor differences.

Deploying locally

For development purposes we would normally run it through the command line using the built-in web server. However before we do this, we need to set up the database. I assume that for this application you would have installed MySQL.

1. At the command line go into the MySQL interactive command console:

   ```
   $ mysql -u <username> -p <password>
   ```

   Then do the following:

   ```
   mysql> create database colony;
   ```

   This will create the database.

2. Next, go into IRB and run this command:

   ```
   > require 'models'
   ```

   This will require in the necessary classes for creating the database tables.

3. Run the following command:

   ```
   > DataMapper.auto_migrate!
   ```

   This will create the tables for the application.

4. To run the application, we need to run this at the command line:

   ```
   $ ruby colony.rb
   ```

   Then go to `http://localhost:4567/` to see the login page.

Try logging in. If you have added `localhost` to the list of applicable URLs in RPX you will be able to log.

Deploying to the cloud

As in the other clones, we will also show how the deployment can go to the Heroku cloud platform.

1. First, create a `config.ru` file. This is the Rack configuration file, which is actually just another Ruby script. All you need to have in this file is this:

```
%w(sinatra colony).each  { |lib| require lib}
run Sinatra::Application
```

2. Install the Heroku gem. Just do the following:

```
$ sudo gem install heroku
```

   Heroku provides us with a set of useful tools packaged in a gem, very much like Capistrano.

3. Initialize an empty Git repository in the Colony folder:

```
$ cd colony
colony $ git init
Initialized empty Git repository in .git/
colony $ git add .
colony $ git commit -m 'initial import'
```

4. Create the Heroku application

```
colony $ heroku create colony
Created http:// colony.heroku.com/ | git@heroku.com: colony.git
Git remote heroku added
```

   You will be prompted for your username and password the first time you run a Heroku command. Subsequently this will be saved in `~/.heroku/credentials` and you won't be prompted anymore. It will also upload your public key to allow you to push and pull code.

5. Push your code to Heroku:

```
colony $ git push heroku master
```

   This will push your code and load your application into deployment. The application is now deployed, but you'll need to create the database as before.

6. Log in to the Heroku console and create the database:

```
colony $ heroku console
Ruby console for colony.heroku.com
>> DataMapper.auto_migrate!
```

7. Heroku allows you access to a console similar to IRB but with the environment of your deployment loaded up, just like `script/console` in Ruby on Rails. To create the database, just run `DataMapper.auto_migrate!` and it will create the database accordingly.

8. You have just deployed Colony to the cloud! You can also change settings to point to a different domain. The final configuration of Colony is at `http://colony.saush.com`. Try it out!

Summary

This is the final chapter in the book and we have covered a lot of ground here. We talked about social networking services in the previous chapter and discussed the features and design of Colony, our Facebook clone. We also went through the data model of the clone. In this chapter we continued to describe the implementation of Colony.

We described the application flow of Colony in detail, feature-by-feature. We started by describing the overall structure of the application flow, followed by the user authentication and login mechanism. After that we described the landing page and the friends list feature as well as the user's activity feeds. We went on describing walls and wall posts followed by user photos and messages. Next were the events, groups, and pages features. We wrapped up the description of the Colony application flow with the comments and liking feature.

Finally we completed the chapter with our usual description of deploying the clone on both a cloud platform (Heroku) and on a standalone server.

Index

friend model 67
functional design 65
private directed message, sending 68
public directed message, sending 68
public timeline 69
re-tweeting 69
scalability 74
stability 74
statuses, posting 66
third party access control 71
third party authentication 71
user management 71, 72
users, following 66
Tweetclone, building
  APIs, implementing 111-115
  application flow, building 90
  data model 80
tweetclone.rb file 91
tweets route, Tweetclone application flow 105
Twitter
  about 60
  features 61, 65
Twitter, features
  easy access 64
  fan versus friend 62
  public conversations 62
  simple premise 62
  text messaging 64
  user behavior, understanding 63

U

update_box snippet 98
update route, Tweetclone application flow 104
Url object, Tinyclone data model 42
URLs 32
URL shortener
  about 31
  benefits 33
  bit.ly 31
  features 31, 35
  is.gd 31

limitations 34, 35
TinyURL 31
user authentication, Colony 230-233
user class, Colony data model 207-211
user class, Photoclone data model 135-137
user class, Tweetclone data model
  about 81, 83, 85
  properties 82
user features, Facebook 199
user management 71
user management, Colony 230-233
user management, Photoclone 125
user page, Colony
  about 253, 254
  activity feeds 253, 254
user timeline API route 114

V

views, Sinatra 14
Visit object, Tinyclone data model
  about 44
  set_country method 45

W

wall 202
wall class, Colony data model 223
wall, Colony
  implementing 255-258
  posting to 255-258
wall posts 202
Webshots 121
WELL 196

X

Xiaonei 197
XmlSimple 45

Y

Yahoo! 360 197
YouTube 197

Thank you for buying
Cloning Internet Applications with Ruby

About Packt Publishing

Packt, pronounced 'packed', published its first book "*Mastering phpMyAdmin for Effective MySQL Management*" in April 2004 and subsequently continued to specialize in publishing highly focused books on specific technologies and solutions.

Our books and publications share the experiences of your fellow IT professionals in adapting and customizing today's systems, applications, and frameworks. Our solution based books give you the knowledge and power to customize the software and technologies you're using to get the job done. Packt books are more specific and less general than the IT books you have seen in the past. Our unique business model allows us to bring you more focused information, giving you more of what you need to know, and less of what you don't.

Packt is a modern, yet unique publishing company, which focuses on producing quality, cutting-edge books for communities of developers, administrators, and newbies alike. For more information, please visit our website: www.packtpub.com.

About Packt Open Source

In 2010, Packt launched two new brands, Packt Open Source and Packt Enterprise, in order to continue its focus on specialization. This book is part of the Packt Open Source brand, home to books published on software built around Open Source licences, and offering information to anybody from advanced developers to budding web designers. The Open Source brand also runs Packt's Open Source Royalty Scheme, by which Packt gives a royalty to each Open Source project about whose software a book is sold.

Writing for Packt

We welcome all inquiries from people who are interested in authoring. Book proposals should be sent to author@packtpub.com. If your book idea is still at an early stage and you would like to discuss it first before writing a formal book proposal, contact us; one of our commissioning editors will get in touch with you.

We're not just looking for published authors; if you have strong technical skills but no writing experience, our experienced editors can help you develop a writing career, or simply get some additional reward for your expertise.

open source
community experience distilled

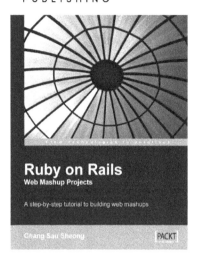

Ruby on Rails Web Mashup Projects

ISBN: 978-1-847193-93-3   Paperback: 272 pages

A step-by-step tutorial to building web mashups

1. Learn about web mashup applications and mashup plug-ins

2. Create practical real-life web mashup projects step by step

3. Access and mash up many different APIs with Ruby and Ruby on Rails

Learning jQuery 1.3

ISBN: 978-1-847196-70-5   Paperback: 444 pages

Better Interaction Design and Web Development with Simple JavaScript Techniques

1. An introduction to jQuery that requires minimal programming experience

2. Detailed solutions to specific client-side problems

3. For web designers to create interactive elements for their designs

4. For developers to create the best user interface for their web applications

Please check **www.PacktPub.com** for information on our titles

Learning Ext JS

ISBN: 978-1-847195-14-2   Paperback: 324 pages

Build dynamic, desktop-style user interfaces for your data-driven web applications

1. Learn to build consistent, attractive web interfaces with the framework components

2. Integrate your existing data and web services with Ext JS data support

3. Enhance your JavaScript skills by using Ext's DOM and AJAX helper

4. Extend Ext JS through custom components

jQuery 1.4 Reference Guide

ISBN: 9781849510042   Paperback: 336 pages

A comprehensive exploration of the popular JavaScript library

1. Quickly look up features of the jQuery library

2. Step through each function, method, and selector expression in the jQuery library with an easy-to-follow approach

3. Understand the anatomy of a jQuery script

4. Write your own plug-ins using jQuery's powerful plug-in architecture

Please check **www.PacktPub.com** for information on our titles